I0939024

Reshaping the Sexes in
Sense and Sensibility

MORELAND PERKINS

Reshaping the Sexes in
Sense and Sensibility

UNIVERSITY PRESS OF VIRGINIA ❧ *Charlottesville and London*

THE UNIVERSITY PRESS OF VIRGINIA
© 1998 by the Rector and Visitors of the University of Virginia
All rights reserved
Printed in the United States of America

First published 1998

∞ The paper used in this publication meets the minimum requirements of the American National Standard for Information Sciences—Permanence of Paper for Printed Library Materials, ANSI Z39.48-1984.

Library of Congress Cataloging-in-Publication Data

Perkins, Moreland, 1927–
Reshaping the sexes in Sense and Sensibility / Moreland Perkins.
p. cm.
Includes bibliographical references and index.
ISBN 0-8139-1800-6 (cloth : alk. paper)
1. Austen, Jane, 1775–1817. Sense and sensibility. 2. Women and literature—England—History—19th century. 3. Man-woman relationships in literature. 4. Women intellectuals in literature. 5. Sex role in literature. 6. Heroines in literature. I. Title.
PR4034.S43P47 1998
823'.7—dc21
97-34862
CIP

For my mother, Marion O'Sullivan Perkins
my alternative mother, Bessie Randolph Price
my father, E. M. Perkins, Sr.
and my sister, Nancy Perkins Kalina

Contents

Acknowledgments

Early and late, Josie Singer has critiqued with a fine ear multiple versions of this work. Reading with no tolerance for the obscure and the needlessly difficult, she has been responsible for multiple improvements. Evelyn Barker's enthusiasm gave encouragement when it helped, as did that of Bronia Wheeler. Jay Hullett kindly arranged for a deconstructionist critic to deplore my theoretical naiveté, which stimulated me to test that criticism elsewhere in the literary profession. In consequence, David F. Wheeler's hearty approval reassured me, Wayne Booth made an extremely helpful suggestion about the idea of a gender study, and Charles Barker supplemented that suggestion with expert information. The enthusiasm of University Press of Virginia Humanities Editor Cathie Brettschneider has provoked in me more effort to keep making this little book better. Two able readers for the Press agreed upon several needed improvements, to good effect.

I have read a number of Austen critics with profit, pleasure, and admiration, including but by no means limited to those cited, invoked, or attacked herein. They have all taught me to aspire to be one of their number.

I have found that for me the experience of living so long and closely with Austen has entailed that I dedicate this book to my original family. Although my mother died in 1951, I have been more than ever conscious during these Austen years of her presence within me.

To those I have acknowledged who are still in reading distance goes my heartfelt thank you, and to those who are not, my grateful tribute.

Note on the Texts

All quotations from *Sense and Sensibility* are from the Penguin English Library Edition (Harmondsworth, 1969), cited parenthetically in the text. Page numbers are supplemented with chapter numbers— e.g., ch. 31:212—to facilitate cross-reference to the edition of Austen's fiction edited by R. W. Chapman, which is used by most scholars. The following key will help:

Chapman	Penguin
Volume 1: chapters 1–22	Chapters 1–22
Volume 2: chapters 1–14	Chapters 23–36
Volume 3: chapters 1–14	Chapters 37–50

Within the text other Austen works are cited in the following editions, and with these abbreviations:

NA   *Northanger Abbey* (Harmondsworth: Penguin Books, 1972)
PP   *Pride and Prejudice* (Harmondsworth: Penguin Books, 1972)
E   *Emma* (Harmondsworth: Penguin Books, 1966)
L   *Jane Austen's Letters,* 3d ed., ed. Deirdre Le Faye (New York: Oxford Univ. Press, 1995)

Reshaping the Sexes in
Sense and Sensibility

It is frequently remarked that more than almost any other novelist Jane Austen can be read and reread with increasing delight. This quality comes from the sentence-to-sentence brilliance of the novels.

Julia Prewitt Brown, *Jane Austen's Novels*

Introduction

*D*ID JANE AUSTEN know how good her work was? My answer starts clearing the way for a preliminary argument about an aspect of her fiction.

Some critics who appreciate Austen's genius will not allow her to enjoy it herself. Below is a typical view of Austen's authorial self-knowledge. It is novelist Margaret Drabble's:

> She was a private and modest person, and even when fame and recognition came her way, she did not move a step to meet them, politely refusing invitations to meet other celebrities, and continuing in her own quiet domestic circle. Unlike Charlotte Brontë, who craved for recognition and excitement, and found herself temperamentally unable to cope with them when she got them, Jane Austen seems to have been secure and confident in her choice of privacy. Was she aware of the enduring quality of her own works, and of the reputation she would enjoy? It is impossible to say. She certainly cared deeply about her novels, was excited by their publication, and involved in their fate: she refers to them several times as her "children." But one suspects that she was

1

> morally incapable of the kind of arrogance that would have
> let her think of herself as a great or important writer. . . . Even
> her own nephew, in a highly laudatory account of her, refers
> to Walter Scott as "a greater genius than my aunt," a judg-
> ment which few would now condone.[1]

The drift is clear, although whether she would have thought of herself
"as a great or important writer" isn't my question. Without having to
indulge in exactly that vainglory, she could nonetheless know how
well she wrought and how extraordinary her own talent was.

Why are experts so unready to believe Jane Austen knew how
good she was? Because she was an unmarried woman living with her
original family on a small income who, when she wasn't writing novels—or writing to the Prince Regent's librarian about writing them—
lived her life as most unmarried gentlewomen of little means did, that
is, privately and modestly.

But whenever one is inclined to think her a privately modest *novelist*—an entirely other matter—one should read again her correspondence with that functionary of the Regency court who signaled to
her her fame in high places: neither a Byron nor a Scott could have
handled such fatuous attention from a royal household with more
confident and imperturbable irony and humor (*L,* 296–97, 305–7,
311–12). Furthermore, the genius of which I believe Austen was aware
was explicitly intellectual in a way not characteristic of most novelists
of equal talent. Her logicianlike economy, analytical wit, precise yet
fertile irony, dense satire, and reasoning heroines are experienced by
the reader as manifesting the spontaneous creativity of a more specifically intellectual form of energy than we can feel concentrated in
her mentor, Samuel Richardson (who of course is absent as narrator),
or in the powerfully expressive writing of, say, Dickens, Melville, or
Lawrence, to mention three more novelists of genius who wrote in
English.

The foregoing remarks are fragments of an argument aiming at
this conclusion: that Austen would have been so conscious of herself as
a living refutation of ruling ideas of genteel gender that, inescapably,

she would have taken many of these ideas to be artificial constructions of her patriarchal society. She would therefore have perceived the lived-in genders of her class as at least in part mere artifacts of these ideas.

So much for a priori reasoning about texts. Do Austen's novels in fact exhibit a belief by the author that received ideas of gender are social constructions designed to create what they describe? One way her novels could manifest this belief at work is through any efforts they make at fictional *re*constructions of patriarchal gender conceptions. A question suggests itself: do we find that Austen undertook to represent her fictional male and female protagonists as sharply deviating, in traits, powers, and habits, from the dominant, socially constructed concepts of genteel gender?—in all her novels?—in some?—in one only?—in none? Did she in fact fictionally reconstruct her protagonists' gender?

We need only consult our mental images of Anne Elliot and Frederick Wentworth to know that Austen did not use the profile of these protagonists to show the outline of a gender-reshaping project: each is easily read as conforming in too many notable features to a version of the era's gender stereotypes. This consideration alone makes it unlikely that Austen's last novel would show itself to be the climax of an early-to-late progression in explicitness as to gender reform.

The novel just preceding *Persuasion* also fails to suggest a late stage of such a progression. Compared to Wentworth, Mr. Knightley exemplifies a different version of nineteenth-century patriarchy's prototype of the ruling-class male, but emphatically a version. With him as hero, it will be difficult for his female complement to go sharply against the grain of her gender's standard. Yet some of that difficulty *is* accepted as a challenge by the author—and, as she anticipated, Emma, partly in consequence of some rather serious deviation from her gender's norm, has had her hostile readers. But we know there is no more central attribute of the era's socially constructed model of masculine gender than the male's dominion over the Realm of Truth: the man's intellectual constructions correspond with reality, the woman's do not. And the almost defining mark of Emma's depicted life, as of *Emma's* comedy, is how far her most earnestly held and enacted beliefs fall short of correspondence with reality. Mr. Knightley, on the other hand, though fallible, is steadily wiser than Emma.

What, then, of *Mansfield Park,* the first novel written wholly in Austen's second period of fictional creation? In the event that (possibly owing to old prejudices) we find the male protagonist, Edmund Bertram, no proper hero, we may here see a strong chance of a gender-reforming intention. But if we start from the other side of the eventual love story, Fanny Price is, among all her more interesting traits, so emphatically, so vulnerably, so almost intolerably early nineteenth-century-feminine in her passivity and fragility that no reconstructive project involving her eventual lover could make the novel appear aggressively reformist about gender. That, of course, will be true no matter how much success we may have at uncovering subtle gender subversion—for example, in the novel's eventual match-ups between gender and grasp of truth (female Fanny's insight versus patriarch Sir Thomas's blindness).

So, in the search for more open and thoroughgoing remodeling of gender, we are led back to the opening phase of Jane Austen's authorial life. However, in all I say, I shall not only ignore Austen's juvenilia (and *Lady Susan*). I shall even ignore *Northanger Abbey,* brilliant novel that it is, and this for a reason analogous to the one that might lead me to ignore *Sons and Lovers* in an analogous study of D. H. Lawrence: Austen's full moral powers are nowhere near fully brought to bear upon *the creation of her heroine* in *Northanger Abbey,* as they are in her other five novels. (In Lawrence, it is instinctual energy that had not yet been liberated—hence I intend no more than an analogy with Austen.) I shall abbreviate this difference between *Northanger Abbey* and Austen's other novels by speaking of the others as (in regard to creation of the heroine) her five "morally ambitious," "serious," or "earnest" novels, although in the ordinary sense of those words, *Northanger Abbey* can of course be described as all those things.[2]

We turn, then, to *Pride and Prejudice,* the second of the two morally ambitious novels whose early versions Austen wrote no later than in her early twenties. But we find that, on an imaginary scale that measures degrees of conformity to received gender concepts of the late-Georgian/Regency era, Darcy ranks with Knightley and Wentworth. And for all her free spirit and irony, Elizabeth Bennet could not be so many men's favorite fictional love object, then and now, without meeting gender requirements endowed with a very long life by an equally long-lived patriarchy. We had better take a quick look at *Sense and Sensibility*, to see if we even have a theme.

It may surprise us that we must regress in time, rather than progress, in order to find the fullest development of our theme: for it is in *Sense and Sensibility*, probably first drafted before *Pride and Prejudice*, that Jane Austen most aggressively undertakes to reconstruct dominant concepts of gender. As to open attack focused upon heroines and their heroes: in *Pride and Prejudice* she pulls back from *Sense and Sensibility* a full step for the man, half a step for the woman; compared to *Sense and Sensibility*, *Mansfield Park* is on balance also less explicitly gender reforming; *Emma* is of two minds on the subject; and of the five novels, *Persuasion* is perhaps the least aggressive about fictionally remodeling its protagonists' gender. All this says nothing of various subtler, subversive procedures (working in *Persuasion*, for example, through Mrs. Croft and Sir Walter Elliot); but these may not appear especially noteworthy to us unless we have already appreciated the more open revision of gender norms with which Austen began in *Sense and Sensibility*.

There is a strong tendency among critics to disparage Edward Ferrars as romantic hero. (A rare exception is Alison Sulloway. She remarks that he is the *only* Austen hero who does not condescend to women![3] I add that this is already a deviation from his gender's standard.) I suspect that Edward's gender dissonance has stymied even professional readers. According to patriarchy's concept of feminine gender, a woman is to lack irony; but if she *will* have it, let it be self-deprecating. Edward Ferrars' low-key irony is not always noticed. One reason: his irony is almost always self-deprecatory and therefore is so inconsistent with the prevailing idea of irony as a form of masculine aggression that even critics often pass it by unnoticed.

Edward is not only nonaggressive in his irony, he lacks aggression altogether: for the most part he is retiring, he is passive, and he is as backward a lover as *ladies* are enjoined to be. He is often silent in contexts where, according to the received view, it would become a genteel female to be inhibited, but not a man of his rank. Not only Marianne, even Elinor is provoked by Edward's reticence. Furthermore, Edward's familial situation offers a gender inversion of an already classical plot for fictional *heroines:* he is being bullied by the Ferrars matriarch to marry an heiress against his inclination. As to society, Edward lacks ambition and the desire to be somebody in the world: he has no interest in realizing the possibilities of eminence offered by his forthcoming wealth. Against the grain of the affluent gentry's model for men, but consonantly with the female model, he aspires to nothing higher than a happy domestic life. He is not an egotist, seems utterly unconscious of patriarchy's seductive powers for an elder son, and is even something of a democrat. Yet Edward is presented as the appropriate object of love for the chief heroine of the story, Elinor Dashwood. What is more, despite the author's deconstruction of Edward's gender, he is successfully rendered as an attractive man, as I shall argue in chapter 2.

But perhaps, as she will sometimes at least partly do in later books, Austen redresses the balance by matching one gender-remodeled protagonist with an *un*remodeled complement. How well do Elinor's salient attributes match up with the socially constructed concept of feminine gender? In chapters 1, 3, 5, and 6, among other matters of comparable interest, I offer evidence that the match is very weak indeed. If so, this will leave only the novel's secondary hero and heroine to save society's (gender) face, if it is to be saved. But first, and in bare outline, what are the reasons for holding that in constructing Elinor, Austen opposes the patriarchally imposed concept of genteel feminine gender?

However many private exceptions were acknowledged, the official conception of gender restricted intellectual power to the male. And professional intellectuals (under other labels) were limited to men not merely in concept but in fact; the few recognized exceptions, in the form of a historian or of a theorist of women's education or rights, merely proved the rule, by being so very few—and often by being editorially denied *any* gender! In chapter 1, I argue that Austen's Elinor Dashwood is one of the few intellectuals fully rendered in English-language fiction—though of course she can be only a "lay intellectual," not a pro, as I shall explain (and of course she antedates this use of the label). Never again in her fiction will Jane Austen flagrantly attack so strategically central an ingredient of the patriarchally sponsored conception of male and female difference.

Elinor's intellectuality colors all the elements of her portrait, not least the content of her emotional life: a second major affront to the social construction of feminine gender lies deeply embedded in the rationality of Elinor's passions. A rational passion is not a contradiction in terms. In chapters 1 and 3 I develop several ideas about Elinor's emotional life that integrate its intensity with its rationality.

When, in chapters 5 and 6, I try to understand the ethical content of Elinor's conduct, I appeal both to her intellectuality and to her particular form of passionate engagement. But I am also led to develop an analogy between aspects of her public persona and the vocation of politician-statesman—another domain forbidden to women by the official gender divisions enacted in England's patriarchal real world. Here, then, I find a third strand in Austen's reconstruction of gender in this novel probably first undertaken so early as age nineteen.

Does Austen restore some balance, does she make a partial peace with the received view of gender by means of her portrait of the secondary heroine, Marianne Dashwood, and of Marianne's lover? Here we need to remind ourselves that the secondary hero is not Willoughby—he is (on the whole) the villain; that hero is Colonel Brandon. To try to produce one's mental image of Brandon is to answer the question as to his gender type: never mind that he is a soldier—Brandon the soldier is entirely offstage. As rendered, secondary hero Brandon is but a pale shadow of even Edward Ferrars's self-effacing presence. In Brandon as he is presented to us, the patriarchally motivated, dominant idea of masculine gender has been deconstructed with a vengeance.

That leaves us with Marianne Dashwood, who will not engage our full attention until chapter 7. There can be little doubt that many critics perceive Marianne as quintessentially "feminine" because they perceive her as ruled by sentimental passion. In chapter 7 I take issue with several recent critics who, what's more, believe Marianne to be in principle committed to the moral authority of one's passions. Those critics, however, do not ask how Marianne fits into Austen's gender configurations. Answering this question is not easy.

As Colonel Brandon's soldiering is not only undepicted but leaves scarcely a discernible mark on the man we encounter, so too there is a Marianne who has no manifestation "before our eyes": she is spoken of but never rendered for us. This is the Marianne who marries Colonel Brandon. Of course, if one gives this absent personage equal weight with the person present and visible to us, she makes a great difference to how we fit the total Marianne into Austen's fictional construction of gender in this novel. Because of her weight in the novel's *plot,* the absent Marianne has to be taken seriously. However, just now I want for a few moments to put that invisible Marianne out of mind.

The Marianne who *is* rendered for us has some resemblance to an excessively liberated fictional woman, Elinor Joddrel, who, three years after Marianne Dashwood had appeared in print, figured in the then-famous Fanny Burney's last novel, *The Wanderer* (1814). In her introduction to *The Wanderer,* Margaret Drabble says of Fanny Burney's Elinor, "She is a character who could never have appeared in the pages of Jane Austen; she belongs to another world." In fact, as Drabble notes, Burney's Elinor Joddrel is partly modeled on Mary Wollstonecraft, in both her actions and her ideas. Margaret Drabble correctly describes Burney's Elinor Joddrel as a "New Woman of her time" who "is bold, emotional, reckless, capricious."[4] Burney's Elinor openly courts the man she loves; she attempts suicide when rejected; she espouses egalitarian ideas about the sexes. In all this she mimics Mary Wollstonecraft.

As a public figure, Wollstonecraft was very much a part of Jane Austen's world. She died at the age of thirty-eight when Austen was twenty-two years old. A year later her letters to her lover (the father of her out-of-wedlock daughter) were published by her famously "freethinking," theoretical-anarchist husband, William Godwin—with whose political ideas and fiction we can be sure Austen was acquainted—who also published that year a surprisingly uncensored memoir of his wife. Both the letters and the memoir attracted scandalized attention. Some feminist critics, Claudia L. Johnson, for example, believe, I think with good reason, that in her fiction Austen was subtly responsive to Mary Wollstonecraft's famous *Vindication of the Rights of Women,* published when Austen was seventeen. (That book is likely to have been infamous in Austen's Tory household, but this wouldn't mean unread.)

One of Wollstonecraft's biographers sees a resemblance between her and Marianne Dashwood. After noting that the son of a close friend of Wollstonecraft was a boarding pupil with Austen's father, Claire Tomalin calls attention to a resemblance between Wollstonecraft, Elinor Joddrel, and Marianne Dashwood which she finds suggested by Marianne's remark, made after her recovery from her self-induced illness: "Had I died—it would have been self-destruction" (ch. 46:337).[5]

Marianne most strikingly breaks the gender mold in her courtship behavior. Once Willoughby has shown sexual interest in her, his behavior and hers are pretty nearly indistinguishable—and he is a forward lover. She recognizes no need to wait until Willoughby has "declared himself" in order freely to produce unambiguous public displays and private expressions of her affection for him. She has no interest in perceptions by the rest of the world of their intimacy. She believes that authenticity in a woman entails showing her loving feelings for a man as freely as he shows his for her. When some misunderstanding seems to her to have arisen between them, she pursues and courts Willoughby, because that is the only honestly self-expressive thing to do. In almost all aspects of the conduct of courtship, and of its thorny complications, she considers men and women to be equals. Marianne rejects many of the rules prescribed by the socially constructed concept of the feminine in favor of what she believes to be within an individual woman's power: to define for herself the decorum suited to her gender.

Even if, as I doubt, those critics are right who see Marianne as captured by a romantic notion of gender no less conventional than the dominant conception—even then Marianne could still be said to exhibit a woman's right to make her own personal choice from among the known conventions. It strongly suggests itself, then, that at least in a central portion of the conceptual territory, Austen does mean in this novel to extend her reform of the patriarchal agenda for women even to her most passionately romantic heroine.

To be sure, given the fact of her lover's concealed faults, it is because Marianne has rejected the official decorum of the genteel female that she comes to grief and is thereby persuaded, at the very end of the novel (we are *told*), to come round to patriarchy's oppressive conception of a young woman's way. So it can plausibly be argued that, on balance, in presenting Marianne to us, Austen does not fictionally reshape gender.

I acknowledge the persuasiveness of this argument. In chapter 7 I shall give reasons for wanting to respond to it with both a no and a yes. That will require consideration of the invisible Marianne, the one who is *not* presented to us, who submits, offstage, to patriarchy's rule and, we are told, gladly marries Colonel Brandon. For the present, let me raise one question by comparing the Burney and Austen examples. Fanny Burney's creation, Elinor Joddrel, is made out to be outlandish if not actually grotesque; the case against her is intrinsic to her presentation, and independent of externally administered sanctions. This is not true of social rebel Marianne. On the basis of her rendered self—the self that is presented to us "in person"—right-minded readers, as I conceive them, are and I think are meant to be almost entirely on Marianne's side. It is the deficient world (defective Willoughby) that does her in. Which is the author faulting, then: Marianne or male honor? Female openness or patriarchy?

1

Elinor Dashwood: The Heroine as an Intellectual

ECAUSE MANY FIRST-TIME readers of *Sense and Sensibility* find Marianne the more appealing of the two elder Dashwood sisters, they may think of her as the primary heroine. For those readers, Marianne's early disappointment, long suffering, and ultimate fade-out can figure as a major disincentive for rereading the novel. However, once we start to understand how much there is in Austin's rendering of Elinor Dashwood that is not only appealing but politically significant, the realization that the novel is written as her story may awaken in us a desire to return to it and read her closely. No one has more cogently made the case for the novel's being Elinor's story than Stuart Tave:

> *Sense and Sensibility* is the story of Elinor Dashwood. . . . The whole of Marianne's story is included within Elinor's: Marianne's begins later and it ends earlier. . . . The whole of the story comes to us through Elinor. . . . There may be things that Elinor doesn't know [about Marianne] . . . but if Elinor doesn't know . . . we don't know. . . . Marianne's story could not be resolved except for what Elinor does, advising her, protecting her, providing her an example . . . ; even the two

men in Marianne's life are understood by the reader, and by
Marianne, as they speak to and are interpreted by Elinor.
There is no part of Marianne's story that is not a part of Elinor's, but there are large and important parts of Elinor's story
that are not part of Marianne's.[1]

Professor Tave's perception of Elinor's centrality perfectly coheres
with my own experience of the novel. However, neither he nor any
other critic I have read finds quite the elements of her characterization
that I believe account for her special interest. These features can all, I
think, be tied to Austen's intention to reshape gender in this early
novel. And the most fecund characteristic is the following. In depict-
ing Elinor Dashwood, Jane Austen achieved something uncommon in
our major fiction: the rendering of an intellectual. Even more un-
heard of, a female intellectual. In her first morally ambitious drafting
of a heroine, Jane Austen accorded herself the political freedom, not
to be indulged again, of creating one who is nearly as gender disso-
nant, because nearly as accomplished an intellectual, as Austen herself
would have been when precociously composing the first version of
this novel, probably in 1795 at about Elinor's age of nineteen.[2]

To judge from the absence of acknowledgment by critics, even today an intellectual is not easy to recognize if she is female, and both
her experience and her immediate subject matter are chiefly found in
domestic, personal, and small-scale social life, especially if it is known
that she was born and raised in the eighteenth century. This block has
somewhat blurred critical perception of both Elinor and Jane Austen.
Critics' resistance is not explained by the fact that our current understanding of the phrase "an intellectual" has come so much later
than those times. Austen's peers never spoke of the ruling class's ideology either, but that doesn't mean they didn't have one. Part of the
point of Julia Prewitt Brown's remark, that "Jane Austen was not an
intellectual in the sense in which George Eliot was" (try to picture
Austen translating Spinoza, as Eliot did), is that Austen *was* of course
an intellectual.[3]

My thesis about Elinor Dashwood is that Austen endowed her
with enough of the habits and powers of thought belonging to Austen

herself to qualify Elinor also as an intellectual, to wit: unrelenting, dispassionate, analytical inquiry into the causes, contents, contexts, and outcomes of individual persons' conduct and experience, all conceived as ineluctably social; and the habit of taking pleasure in the pure play of ideas over her subject matter. If we acknowledge, as we do, that today a rigorously thoughtful but nonpublishing psychoanalyst or art critic or urban anthropologist may be an intellectual, then we must allow the same stature to a talented analyst of human conduct, character, and convention who is equally dedicated to concretely applied reason—although we imagine her functioning this way long before the phrase "an intellectual" was put to its current use.

The (apparently unwitting) disciple of Austen whose moral sensibility was possibly closest to hers, Henry James, never, I think, created as protagonist that rare creature in major English fiction, a convincing intellectual; but James's own disciple Ford Madox Ford gave us, in Christopher Tietjens, an intellectual who makes in several respects an interesting contrast with Elinor Dashwood. Tietjens, younger son of an ancient Yorkshire landed family, is a brilliant mathematician working with precocious distinction in "the Imperial Department of Statistics." He is also endowed with an encyclopedic curiosity and memory. By quick brush strokes the first novel of Ford's four-volume work, *Parade's End*, succeeds, with Tietjens, in painting a charismatic portrait of an intellectual. Because Tietjens' intellectuality operates in his romantic life not discernibly at all or else in ways that are largely either irrelevant to important concerns or just plain eccentric, Ford is left free to make Tietjens sometimes impulsive or moody or irrational in personal action without ceasing to seem an intellectual.

Tietjens' versatility of temperament means that Ford's fabrication of this intellectual was in two respects less demanding than Austen's creation of *her* fictional intellectual. First, because Tietjens' intellectuality only occasionally manifests itself in his romantic life, he can be rendered as a man of dramatically opposing aspects, hence fascinating in his variety and unpredictability. Second, Tietjens' eccentricity and suppressed yet evident emotionality can quickly endear him to many readers. On the other hand, because Elinor is not, could not then be, a professional person and is the heroine of one troubled love story and the anxious monitor of another, the domain of application for her intellect is almost entirely the actions, circumstances, and feelings that figure in affairs of the heart. Because of this limitation, Elinor's intellect must be steadily—hence for some readers dauntingly—on display; and for the same reasons, her orientation to her own emotions will be more rational than many readers can find attractive. Permeating all this is Elinor's gender dissonance: many readers then and now will experience intellectual display in a *man's* informal conversation, and rational self-control in *his* conduct, as more natural and attractive than they find either in a woman. For immediate reader appeal, Ford's fictional intellectual has a head start over Austen's.

Austen spent the first twenty-five years of her life in the rectory of her Oxford-educated father, who was both a scholarly minister and a teacher. Two of her older brothers, also Oxford graduates, became ministers, and the eldest, ten years her senior, had strong literary interests and showed some poetic skill as a young man. Had she wished to, she could have created a scholar-clergyman whom we today would call (though she wouldn't) a professional intellectual. (To be sure, she would need to expend some ingenuity to conform to her self-injunction never to write of men talking only with men.)

In her next novel she will make a gesture toward a male intellectual, secular Mr. Bennet. But at the start, if she wanted an intellectual, she wanted a fictional translation of her own disproof of patriarchy's gender paradigm: it would be a woman. This could gratify her.

Elinor's being an intellectual but not a professional one has the effect that she will be "at work" full-time: there will be no holidays from intellectual work while away from office, lab, or study. No matter how strongly Elinor's own interest is affected or her desire engaged or her emotions aroused, in almost every emotionally potent situation her chief expense of energy will go first toward understanding and next to bringing her action and her feeling into accord with reason. No more for Elinor than for Jane Austen is the habit of dispassionate analysis a matter of choice: it composes the very texture of Elinor's temperament.

As narrator of her fictions, Jane Austen had an intimate relationship to her heroines. This intimacy has several interesting aspects. Just now I attend to only one of them: the harmony she creates between the habits of thought—especially the analytical wit and irony—of herself as narrator and Elinor. This is a two-way street: the narrator's thought patterns are as much colored by her heroine's as the latter's are borrowed from the author's.

For example, the narrator of *Sense and Sensibility* is more inclined to an abstruse, mock-metaphysical wit than is the narrator of *Pride and Prejudice*. The same contrast holds between Elinor Dashwood and Elizabeth Bennet. Although bright, Elizabeth is not an intellectual. She falls short of Elinor in this way despite the fact that she is witty in a way Elinor is not; for Elinor's wit is scarcely social and never sociable, whereas Elizabeth's is always part of her gaiety and sometimes part of her sexuality. The mock-metaphysical wit of Elinor and her narrator reinforce each other in helping render Elinor's portrait as an intellectual; the narrator's higher flights raise the altitude of her heroine's by a kind of attraction or osmosis.

Consider the private meditation below in which Austen shares with Elinor the narrator's disposition to a witty abstruseness in condemning Edward's disagreeable mother: they (she) imagine(s), as (a) mock-philosopher(s), a uselessly *hypothetical* because utterly imaginary *duty* of Elinor's to *rejoice!* Elinor has at last met Mrs. Ferrars, but only after her love for Edward has been thwarted by her learning of his secret engagement to Lucy Steele:

> Elinor's curiosity to see Mrs Ferrars was satisfied.—she had found in her every thing that could tend to make a farther connection between the families, undesirable.—She had seen enough of her pride, her meanness, and her determined prejudice against herself, to comprehend all the difficulties that must have perplexed the engagement, and retarded the marriage, of Edward and herself, had he been otherwise free;—and she had seen almost enough to be thankful for her *own* sake, that one greater obstacle preserved her from suffering under any other of Mrs Ferrars's creation, preserved her from all dependence upon her caprice, or any solicitude for her good opinion. Or at least, if she did not bring herself quite to rejoice in Edward's being fettered to Lucy, she deter-

mined, that had Lucy been more amiable, she *ought* to have
rejoiced. (ch. 41:293)

With the climactic "she determined," the narrator makes conclusive
the transfer to Elinor of the most abstruse element in this reflection.
Jane Austen does not assign to Elizabeth Bennet such an intricate
mental construction by displaying, for example, Elizabeth's dismay
over an encounter with Lady Catherine de Bourgh. What pleases us in
Elizabeth is a very different sort of wit. Lady Catherine pays her med-
dling visit to Elizabeth and asks her whether she knows that a report
is being spread with the news she will marry Lady Catherine's nephew,
Mr. Darcy:

> "I never heard that it was."
> "And can you likewise declare, that there is no *founda-*
> *tion* for it?"
> "I do not pretend to possess equal frankness with your
> ladyship. *You* may ask questions which *I* shall not choose to
> answer."
> ". . . Has he, has my nephew, made you an offer of
> marriage?"
> "Your ladyship has declared it to be impossible."
> ". . . You may have drawn him in."
> "If I had, I shall be the last person to confess it."
> ". . . Your alliance will be a disgrace; your name will never
> even be mentioned by any of us."
> "These are heavy misfortunes. . . . But the wife of
> Mr. Darcy must have such extraordinary sources of hap-
> piness necessarily attached to her situation, that she could,
> upon the whole, have no cause to repine." (*PP,* ch. 56:
> 363–65)

Elizabeth does here display an exceptionally nimble wit. In its context,
"I do not pretend to possess equal frankness with your ladyship" is an
almost-polite parry that turns her opponent's blow against herself.
And "Your ladyship has declared it to be impossible"—also fired off

fast—is enough, one would think, to make Lady Catherine feel she is defeating herself. Amazingly, "If I have, I shall be the last person to confess it" maintains the wickedly creative trick of making Lady de Bourgh's words come back at her like boomerangs. Elizabeth Bennet's intellect here functions like that of a nimble defense attorney. Elinor Dashwood's works more like a philosopher's.

In a moment we'll contemplate Elinor being openly aggressive, though at second-hand, toward Mrs. Ferrars, but first let us enjoy an example of the author-narrator's aggression toward the same woman, so that we may notice the kinship between the narrator's attack and Elinor's. One way that Edward Ferrars's mother is depicted as something of a monster is through Austen's ironically mock-metaphysical account of Mrs. Ferrars's habit of disowning a son from time to time. In the last chapter of the book, Austen goes after this favorite target in a way that, when we reread the book, affects our experience of an earlier attack on the same woman by Elinor. (Remember, Edward is the eldest son.) Thus the narrator on Mrs. Ferrars:

> Her family had of late been exceedingly fluctuating. For many years of her life she had had two sons; but the crime and annihilation of Edward a few weeks ago, had robbed her of one; the similar annihilation of Robert had left her for a fortnight without any; and now, by the resuscitation of Edward, she had one again.
>
> In spite of his being allowed once more to live, however, he did not feel the continuance of his existence secure, till he had revealed his present engagement; for the publication of that circumstance, he feared, might give a sudden turn to his constitution, and carry him off as rapidly as before. With apprehensive caution therefore it was revealed, and he was listened to with unexpected calmness. . . .
>
> What she would engage to do towards augmenting their income, was next to be considered; and here it plainly appeared, that though Edward was now her only son, he was by no means her eldest; for while Robert was inevitably endowed with a thousand pounds a-year, not the smallest ob-

jection was made against Edward's taking orders for the sake
of two hundred and fifty at the utmost. (ch. 50:362–63)

Now look at Elinor's way of openly deriding Mrs. Ferrars to her
brother, John Dashwood, the older woman's son-in-law. John has just
queried his sister about Colonel Brandon's motive in bestowing a rector's living upon Edward Ferrars. Edward had been disowned by his
mother for refusing to break his engagement to Lucy Steele. Now
John assumes the living from Brandon will enable Edward and Lucy
to marry. Rereading this exchange from chapter 41, one remembers
the just quoted, more brilliant development in chapter 50 of the same
theme by the narrator, and Elinor as intellectual benefits by a kind of
fusion of the narrator's developed metaphor with Elinor's embryonic
one. John is speaking of Brandon's gift of a living to Edward:

> "Mrs Ferrars," added he, lowering his voice to the tone
> becoming so important a subject, "knows nothing about it at
> present, and I believe it will be best to keep it entirely con-
> cealed from her as long as may be.—When the marriage
> takes place, I fear she must hear of it all."
> "But why should such precaution be used?—Though it
> is not to be supposed that Mrs Ferrars can have the smallest
> satisfaction in knowing that her son has money enough to
> live upon,—for *that* must be quite out of the question; yet
> why, after her late behaviour, is she supposed to feel at all?—
> she has done with her son, she has cast him off for ever, and
> has made all those over whom she had any influence, cast him
> off likewise. Surely, after doing so, she cannot be imagined li-
> able to any impression of sorrow or of joy on his account—
> she cannot be interested in any thing that befalls him.—She
> would not be so weak as to throw away the comfort of a child,
> and yet retain the anxiety of a parent!" (ch. 41:293)

One has to do no more than compare this attack with any to be found
in another Austen heroine to realize that nowhere else will so much
intellectual energy be given over to the meticulous development of an

ironic metaphor in order merely to register contempt. Only an intellectual would spontaneously express her abhorrence of such conduct by presenting it as a mock-logical scandal created by the mock-
paradox of Mrs. Ferrars's expected maternal distress from the news of
good fortune befalling a son who is no longer a son. It is as if Elinor
can enjoy her personal aggression only if she can embed it within—
and offer to her proxy target, John Dashwood—the purer pleasure of
the play of ideas.

When Elizabeth Bennet tells her sister Jane the story from Wickham that alleges dastardly behavior on the part of Bingley's best friend,
Darcy, Jane—who habitually thinks the best of everyone—seeks a
way to believe neither man dishonorable:

> "They have both," she said, "been deceived, I dare say, in
> some way or other, of which we can form no idea. Interested
> people have perhaps misrepresented each to the other. . . ."
>
> "Very true, indeed; and now, my dear Jane, what have
> you got to say in behalf of the interested people who have
> probably been concerned in the business? Do clear *them*
> too, or we shall be obliged to think ill of somebody." (*PP*, ch.
> 17:128)

Here as always Elizabeth's repartee adds a small piece to the picture of
a very bright person. But neither here nor elsewhere does it suggest
that Elizabeth takes the kind of pleasure Elinor does in the play of
ideas for its own sake. And yet it is not that Elinor ever ascends into
the realm of pure theory. On the contrary, she indulges in her intellectual pleasures only when the play of ideas is embedded within pursuit of a practical end she deems worthy, or anyhow necessary.

Examples of Elinor's (and her narrator's) mock-metaphysical wit
add color, scope, and a larger coherence to the central element in
Austen's portrait of Elinor as intellectual, that is, to Elinor's analyses of
character, conduct, and human causality. Surely exemplary here and
proving the value, for appreciating Elinor, of having read to the end of
the novel in reading its beginning, are Elinor's explanations of Willoughby, late in the story, after his visit with her when Marianne is ill.

I pick three passages, in order of ascending level of abstraction. First, Elinor to Marianne on how a marriage to Willoughby would have faltered:

> "Your marriage must have involved you in many certain troubles and disappointments, in which you would have been poorly supported by an affection, on his side, much less certain. Had you married, you must have been always poor. His expensiveness is acknowledged even by himself, and his whole conduct declares that self-denial is a word hardly understood by him. His demands and your inexperience together on a small, very small income, must have brought on distresses which would not be the *less* grievous to you, from having been entirely unknown and unthought of before. *Your* sense of honour and honesty would have led you, I know, when aware of your situation, to attempt all the economy that would appear to you possible; and perhaps, as long as your frugality retrenched only on your own comfort, you might have been suffered to practise it, but beyond that—and how little could the utmost of your single management do to stop the ruin which had begun before your marriage?—Beyond *that*, had you endeavoured, however reasonably, to abridge *his* enjoyments, is it not to be feared, that instead of prevailing on feelings so selfish to consent to it, you would have lessened your own influence on his heart, and made him regret the connection which had involved him in such difficulties?" (ch. 47:341–42)

This is dense causal reasoning that packs into a very short passage a multitude of factors figuring in several different causal chains that convincingly converge on a single result, the alienation of Willoughby's affections from Marianne. I have made no survey to warrant saying that the single sentence beginning "*Your* sense of honour," which makes up the entire second half of this passage, is the longest assigned to an Austen heroine, but I suspect it is the most complex bit of causal reasoning to be found in a single sentence so assigned. Compare the whole passage with a rejoinder in *Emma* by Emma Woodhouse to Mr. Knightley, who has been arguing that Harriet Smith can do no better than to marry Robert Martin, farmer, because of the limits set by Harriet's origins, upbringing, present circumstances, and abilities:

> "You are a very warm friend to Mr Martin; but, as I said be-fore, are unjust to Harriet. Harriet's claims to marry well are not so contemptible as you represent them. She is not a clever girl, but she has better sense than you are aware of, and does not deserve to have her understanding spoken of so slight-ingly. Waving that point, however, and supposing her to be, as you describe her, only pretty and good-natured, let me tell you, that in the degree she possesses them, they are not triv-ial recommendations to the world in general, for she is, in fact, a beautiful girl, and must be thought so by ninety-nine people out of an hundred; and till it appears that men are much more philosophic on the subject of beauty than they are generally supposed, till they do fall in love with well-informed minds instead of handsome faces, a girl, with such loveliness as Harriet, has a certainty of being admired and sought after, of having the power of choosing from among many, consequently a claim to be nice. Her good-nature, too, is not so very slight a claim, comprehending as it does, real, thorough sweetness of temper and manner, a very humble opinion of herself, and a great readiness to be pleased with other people. I am very much mistaken if your sex in general would not think such beauty, and such temper, the highest claims a woman could possess." (*E*, ch. 8:89–90)

If in comparison with Elinor's temperament of an intellectual Eliza-beth Bennet appears no more than bright, it may be fair to say Emma, with respect to analytical and argumentative bent, seems merely clever.

Like a true intellectual, Elinor can go over much the same ground a second time and give an explanation that coheres with the first yet is fresh:

"At present," continued Elinor, "he regrets what he has done. And why does he regret it?—Because he finds it has not answered towards himself. It has not made him happy. His circumstances are now unembarrassed—he suffers from no evil of that kind; and he thinks only that he has married a woman of a less amiable temper than yourself. But does it thence follow that had he married you, he would have been happy?—The inconveniences would have been different. He would then have suffered under the pecuniary distresses which, because they are removed he now reckons as nothing. He would have had a wife of whose temper he could make no complaint, but he would have been always necessitous—always poor; and probably would soon have learnt to rank the innumerable comforts of a clear estate and good income as of far more importance, even to domestic happiness, than the mere temper of a wife." (ch. 47:342)

By now a student of the eighteenth century may be perceiving—or recalling—that Elinor Dashwood's modes of thought resemble, possibly more than those of any other of her author's creations do, those of Samuel Johnson, one of the intellectuals of that century most admired by Jane Austen. Not only the lucidity, the balanced symmetry in explanatory structure, but also the fluid movement of the argument, the centrality of familiar abstractions, and the extended reach of a single sentence's thought remind us of Elinor's affinity to the great Johnson. Moreover, a similarity of moral sensibility emerges when we consider, on the one hand, the dispassionate objectivity with which, near the end of the novel, Elinor appraises Willoughby's character, given her sympathy for him after their dramatic late interview, and on the other, that sympathy itself, given the horrors in her family life for which she justly blames Willoughby. All this shows most vividly in the analysis Elinor meditates within herself when Willoughby has concluded his explanation of his behavior toward Marianne with, "Now you know all."

Elinor made no answer. Her thoughts were silently fixed on the irreparable injury which too early an independence and its consequent habits of idleness, dissipation, and luxury, had made in the mind, the character, the happiness, of a man who, to every advantage of person and talents, united a disposition naturally open and honest, and a feeling, affectionate temper. The world had made him extravagant and vain— Extravagance and vanity had made him cold-hearted and selfish. Vanity, while seeking its own guilty triumph at the expense of another, had involved him in a real attachment, which extravagance, or at least its offspring, necessity, had required to be sacrificed. Each faulty propensity in leading him to evil, had led him likewise to punishment. The attachment, from which against honour, against feeling, against every better interest he had outwardly torn himself, now, when no longer allowable, governed every thought; and the connection, for the sake of which he had, with little scruple, left her sister to misery, was likely to prove a source of unhappiness to himself of a far more incurable nature. (ch. 44:324)

In somewhat the way Elinor needed to filter her hostility toward Mrs. Ferrars through the metaphor of a mock-paradox, here her charity for Willoughby reaches him from almost the height of a Platonic Realm of Universals to which the misfortune of his depravity is ascribed: independence generated in him idleness, dissipation, and luxury; the world introduced into his disposition extravagance and vanity, which in turn brought on coldheartedness and selfishness; for vanity (personified) sought its triumph, accidentally leading him—because of his openness and affectionate temper—into an attachment which . . . and so on and so on. Both Willoughby and his environment have been analyzed into causally determining "propensities." Under the explanatory projects of the theorizing intellect, all individuals tend to become, for the moment, intersections of causally effective abstractions. In this abstractionism Elinor surpasses Samuel Johnson.

Reading the following representative passage of similar analysis by Johnson, one perceives the affinity but also notes that Johnson makes less frequent use of abstractions as the subjects of verbs than Elinor did. The passage is taken from the last six or seven paragraphs of Johnson's life of Richard Savage, in his *Lives of the English Poets:*

It cannot be said that he made use of his abilities for the direction of his own conduct: an irregular and dissipated manner of life had made him the slave of every passion that happened to be excited by the presence of its object, and that slavery to his passions reciprocally produced a life irregular and dissipated. He was not master of his own motions, nor could promise anything for the next day. . . .

His friendship was . . . of little value; for . . . it was always dangerous to trust him, because he considered himself as discharged by the first quarrel from all ties of honour or gratitude . . . he could not bear to conceive himself in a state of dependence, his pride being equally powerful with his other passions, and appearing in the form of insolence at one time, and of vanity at another.

Quite possibly Elinor's revaluation of Willoughby on the occasion of his late visit to her reminds a reader of Elizabeth Bennet's revaluation of Wickham, in *Pride and Prejudice,* when she read the explanatory letter Darcy wrote her after she refused him in marriage. Of course there are similarities. But to return to Elizabeth's mind at work on a project that is somewhat similar to the one we just examined is to become convinced that Austen had no intention of making Elizabeth an intellectual, and to be made more sure of one's impression of Elinor as just that. Elizabeth is passionate, variable, swiftly moving in both thought and feeling, the two always interlocked. Sustained independent analysis is not her way. From Elinor's analysis of a complex personality and its rich societal context we feel we receive illumination; by contrast, Elizabeth merely absorbs an explicitly told story we already know, and connects it with her experience.

She read, with an eagerness which hardly left her power of comprehension, and from impatience of knowing what the next sentence might bring, was incapable of attending to the sense of the one before her eyes. His belief of her sister's insensibility, she instantly resolved to be false, and his account of the real, the worst objections to the match, made her too angry to have any wish of doing him justice. He expressed no regret for what he had done which satisfied her; his style was not penitent, but haughty. It was all pride and insolence.

But when this subject was succeeded by his account of Mr Wickham, when she read with somewhat clearer attention, a relation of events, which, if true, must overthrow every cherished opinion of his worth, and which bore so alarming an affinity to his own history of himself, her feelings were yet more acutely painful and more difficult of definition. Astonishment, apprehension, and even horror, oppressed her. She wished to discredit it entirely, repeatedly exclaiming, "This must be false! This cannot be! This must be the grossest falsehood!"—and when she had gone through the whole letter, though scarcely knowing any thing of the last page or two, put it hastily away, protesting that she would not regard it, that she would never look in it again.

In this perturbed state of mind, with thoughts that could rest on nothing, she walked on; but it would not do; in half a minute the letter was unfolded again, and collecting herself as well as she could, she again began the mortifying perusal of all that related to Wickham, and commanded herself so far as to examine the meaning of every sentence. . . . She put down the letter, weighed every circumstance with what she meant to be impartiality—deliberated on the probability of each statement—but with little success. On both sides it was only assertion. Again she read on. But every line proved more clearly that the affair, which she had believed it impossible that any contrivance could so represent, as to render Mr Darcy's conduct it less than infamous, was capable of a turn which must make him entirely blameless throughout the whole. (*PP*, ch. 36:233–34)

Against my use of this contrast between Elinor and Elizabeth it might be objected that Willoughby is merely the lover of Elinor's sister whereas Darcy and Wickham belong to Elizabeth's own amorous adventures; so Elinor *should* be more dispassionate than Elizabeth. But this is the closest Elizabeth comes to the kind of analysis Austen assigns to Elinor. If for Elizabeth personal engagement alone will generate even this much mental work, this too contributes to the difference in nature that Austen has rendered in her two portraits.

However, we do have presented to us Elinor's mind in play when her own romantic life is smashed by Lucy Steele's revelation of her engagement to Edward Ferrars. It is, I think, only if we conceive Elinor as uniquely invested by Austen with the private vocation of the lay intellectual that her response in this crisis can seem credible, natural, true. Here it is:

> However small Elinor's general dependance on Lucy's veracity might be, it was impossible for her on serious reflection to suspect it in the present case, where no temptation could be answerable to the folly of inventing a falsehood of such a description. What Lucy had asserted to be true, therefore, Elinor could not, dared not longer doubt; supported as it was too on every side by such probabilities and proofs, and contradicted by nothing but her own wishes. Their opportunity of acquaintance in the house of Mr Pratt was a foundation for the rest, at once indisputable and alarming; and Edward's visit near Plymouth, his melancholy state of mind, his dissatisfaction at his own prospects, his uncertain behaviour towards herself, the intimate knowledge of the Miss Steeles as to Norland and their family connections, which had often surprised her, the picture, the letter, the ring, formed altogether such a body of evidence, as overcame every fear of condemning him unfairly, and established as a fact, which no partiality could set aside, his ill-treatment of herself.—Her resentment of such behaviour, her indignation at having been its dupe, for a short time made her feel only for herself; but other ideas, other considerations soon arose. Had Edward been intentionally deceiving her? Had he feigned a regard for her which he did not feel? Was his engagement to Lucy, an engagement of the heart? No; whatever it might

once have been, she could not believe it such at present. His
affection was all her own. She could not be deceived in that.
Her mother, sisters, Fanny, all had been conscious of his regard for her at Norland; it was not an illusion of her own vanity. He certainly loved her. What a softener of the heart was
this persuasion! How much could it not tempt her to forgive!
He had been blameable, highly blameable, in remaining at
Norland after he first felt her influence over him to be more
than it ought to be. In that, he could not be defended; but if
he had injured her, how much more had he injured himself;
if her case were pitiable, his was hopeless. His imprudence
had made her miserable for a while; but it seemed to have de-
prived himself of all chance of ever being otherwise. She
might in time regain tranquillity, but *he,* what had he to
look forward to? Could he ever be tolerably happy with
Lucy Steele; could he, were his affection for herself out of the
question, with his integrity, his delicacy, and well-informed
mind, be satisfied with a wife like her—illiterate, artful, and
selfish?

The youthful infatuation of nineteen would naturally
blind him to every thing but her beauty and good nature; but
the four succeeding years—years, which if rationally spent,
give such improvement to the understanding, must have
opened his eyes to her defects of education, while the same
period of time, spent on her side in inferior society and more
frivolous pursuits, had perhaps robbed her of that simplicity,
which might once have given an interesting character to her
beauty.

If in the supposition of his seeking to marry herself, his
difficulties from his mother had seemed great, how much
greater were they now likely to be, when the object of his
engagement was undoubtedly inferior in connections, and
probably inferior in fortune to herself. These difficulties, indeed, with an heart so alienated from Lucy, might not press
very hard upon his patience; but melancholy was the state of

the person, by whom the expectation of family opposition and unkindness, could be felt as a relief!

As these considerations occurred to her in painful succession, she wept for him, more than for herself. Supported by the conviction of having done nothing to merit her present unhappiness, and consoled by the belief that Edward had done nothing to forfeit her esteem, she thought she could even now, under the first smart of the heavy blow, command herself enough to guard every suspicion of the truth from her mother and sisters. . . .

The necessity of concealing from her mother and Marianne, what had been entrusted in confidence to herself, though it obliged her to unceasing exertion, was no aggravation of Elinor's distress. . . .

From their counsel, or their conversation she knew she could receive no assistance, their tenderness and sorrow must add to her distress, while her self-command would neither receive encouragement from their example nor from their praise. She was stronger alone, and her own good sense so well supported her, that her firmness was as unshaken, her appearance of cheerfulness as invariable, as with regrets so poignant and so fresh, it was possible for them to be. (ch. 23:157–59)

If we have read the whole novel—especially through to the end of chapter 48, when Elinor learns Edward is unmarried, unengaged, and free to marry her—we now read this passage believing Elinor does love Edward because we have "seen" that she does. However, we also believe that for months before this revelation she had, from prudence based on Edward's inconsistent behavior toward her, suppressed the feeling of love. Her mental control had showed itself clearly in an early exchange with Marianne, who complained because Elinor refused to acknowledge her feelings of love for Edward, referring to them instead as (mere) "esteem" and "liking." Provoked by this evasion, Marianne says, "Use those words again and I will leave the room this moment." Elinor replies, "Till his sentiments are fully known, you cannot won-

der at my wishing to avoid any encouragement of my own partiality
by believing or calling it more than it is" (ch. 4:55). Surely this was
reasonable—and even more provident than she knew.

But now, with Lucy's news of her engagement to Edward, something is needed other than prudence, which has little application to
this sudden "extinction of all her dearest hopes" (ch. 23:158). Intel-
lectually and morally—here these two are one—her response is imaginative and creative. It is guided in part by a conservative principle of
moral appraisal, that is, a principle that says: in any trying situation,
conserve the highest goods that *can* be conserved consistent with the
truth. She finds that Edward loves her, a conclusion needing a clear
head and some courage in these unfavoring circumstances. She finds
that Edward's injury to her is redeemed by its source in love of her.
She concludes Edward "had done nothing to forfeit her esteem." And
that she herself has "done nothing to merit her present unhappiness":
the only part of the world she *can* control she has managed responsi-
bly. Also she helps herself conserve, in her appraisal, not only justice
but her own feeling for Edward by finding that his conduct of his affairs of the heart has far more seriously injured himself than her. This
judgment is just, but it causes her to weep for him more than for herself—thus it helps conserve her feeling of love for him. Along the way
she explains Edward's early infatuation with Lucy and subsequent dis-
affection in a manner both insightful and conservative of Edward's
character and his mature taste and judgment. It is a tribute to Austen's
own imagination that she invented for Elinor, in a situation so poignant with loss, an analysis that is so creatively useful to Elinor's emotional equilibrium yet does not depart from the truth. For a woman
to be moved to forgive an offense because the offender has softened
her heart by loving her is to abandon neither the truth nor high moral
ground, although in itself it appeals to neither of these: it is simply an
impeccable movement of the heart. The head has not surrendered to
the heart, nothing is more evident; but neither has it suppressed the
heart, which in Elinor is not something readers may feel they can always count on.

The integration in Elinor of analytical intellect, affective imagination, a disciplined will governed by a sensitive conscience, and a habit

of conserving the good is in these circumstances so exceptional that we may now for the first time recognize Austen's intention to achieve in Elinor this difficult outcome: a credible idealization. (I say much more about this aim in chapters 5 and 6). Perhaps in order quickly to improve the balance in Elinor's portrait by bringing into our view baser elements of her temperament, in the very next chapter of the novel Austen lowers Elinor into her nasty battle with Lucy Steele.

The next occasion of Elinor's analyzing the unhappy triangle comes four months later, when she has to tell Marianne of its existence because Edward's engagement to Lucy is about to become public knowledge. At this point the reader may feel Elinor does fall into distortion of the truth:

> "Now, I can think and speak of it with little emotion. I would not have you suffer on my account; for I assure you I no longer suffer materially myself. I have many things to support me. I am not conscious of having provoked the disappointment by any imprudence of my own, and I have borne it as much as possible without spreading it farther. I acquit Edward of all essential misconduct. I wish him very happy; and I am so sure of his always doing his duty, that though now he may harbour some regret, in the end he must become so. Lucy does not want sense, and that is the foundation on which every thing good may be built.—And after all, Marianne, after all that is bewitching in the idea of a single and constant attachment, and all that can be said of one's happiness depending entirely on any particular person, it is not meant—it is not fit—it is not possible that it should be so.— Edward will marry Lucy; he will marry a woman superior in person and understanding to half her sex; and time and habit will teach him to forget that he ever thought another superior to *her*." (ch. 37:264)

Does Elinor by now believe Edward and Lucy will somehow marry? Possibly, for when, a short time later, Edward leaves her after she has extended to him Colonel Brandon's offer of a living, we have this: "'When I see him again,' said Elinor to herself, as the door shut him out, 'I shall see him the husband of Lucy'" (ch. 40:289). On the other hand, not quite; for when she is (mis)informed that Edward and Lucy have married, near the end of the book, we read this:

> Elinor now found the difference between the expectation of an unpleasant event, however certain the mind may be told to consider it, and certainty itself. She now found, that in spite of herself, she had always admitted a hope, while Edward remained single, that something would occur to prevent his marrying Lucy; that some resolution of his own, some mediation of friends, or some more eligible opportunity of establishment for the lady, would arise to assist the happiness of all. But he was now married, and she condemned her heart for the lurking flattery, which so much heightened the pain of the intelligence. (ch. 48:347)

To complete this picture of Elinor's frail normality under the utter certainty of her loss, the passage continues, a little further on:

> She saw them in an instant in their parsonage-house; saw in Lucy, the active, contriving manager, uniting at once a desire of smart appearance, with the utmost frugality, and ashamed to be suspected of half her economical practices;—pursuing her own interest in every thought, courting the favour of Colonel Brandon, of Mrs. Jennings, and of every wealthy friend. In Edward—she knew not what she saw, nor what she wished to see;—happy or unhappy,—nothing pleased her; she turned away her head from every sketch of him. (ch. 48:347)

We may believe, then, that when Elinor expounded the Edward-Lucy-Elinor situation for her sister, her spirits were still being severely tried by it.

I think we must admit the intellectual in Elinor somewhat flounders here. We remember that at the end of her constrained battle with Lucy, an ending "to which both of them submitted without any reluctance," Elinor had "sat down to the card table with the melancholy persuasion that Edward . . . had not even the chance of being tolerably happy in marriage, which sincere affection on [Lucy's] side would have given" (ch. 24:168). Elinor is nonetheless entitled upon cooler reflection to revise an opinion formed immediately after an unpleasant verbal duel, without being read as dishonest with Marianne. The two grounds on which she founds her belief in Edward's prospective happiness with Lucy may manifest more the rationalist in Elinor than the rationalizer. First is the view, of ancient and respectable lineage, that a man who always does his duty must in the long run be happy. Second, and perhaps more surprising in Elinor, is the view that "sense . . . is the foundation upon which every thing good may be built." (She puts sense before character?) Nevertheless, if we allow "sense" to mean here being thoroughly sensible in the ordinary affairs of life, this is, though somewhat pagan, surely a respectable view. Did she believe Lucy had this sort of intelligence? Yes. That is how one reads Elinor's early observation that "Lucy was naturally clever; her remarks were often just and amusing . . . but her powers had received no aid from education. . . . Elinor saw, and pitied her for, the neglect of abilities which education might have rendered respectable" (ch. 22:149). However, Elinor is now simply discounting, without justification offered, what she is also reported as seeing in Lucy: her "thorough want of delicacy, of rectitude, and integrity of mind," not to mention her being "illiterate, artful, and selfish," while Edward is so much the opposite (ch. 22:149, 23:158). Of course the fact that Elinor picks out only sense in Lucy as the basis for being hopeful shows that she has not forgotten Lucy's failings. But in reassuring Marianne she discounts these failings, without offering an explanation for doing so.

As to the antiromantic arrow she lets loose at Marianne in favor of the possible ending of one love and growth of another, there is no doubt Elinor does believe in this, for it came up in an earlier discussion with Colonel Brandon, who remarked:

"Your sister, I understand, does not approve of second attachments."

"No," replied Elinor, "her opinions are all romantic."

"Or rather, as I believe, she considers them impossible to exist."

"I believe she does. But how she contrives it without reflecting on the character of her own father, who had himself two wives, I know not." (ch. 12:86)

This is eminently reasonable. Its application to Edward and his two loves, however, is less so. In short, Elinor as intellectual is human enough: I cannot make out her hopeful prognosis for Edward as a calculated effort merely to mislead Marianne; rather, in her own interest Elinor seems to succumb to some contortion of her thought—at least for the moment.

Having read Elinor's explanation with Marianne that way, I have to admit that an alternative interpretation is not implausible: this reading takes Elinor's contortional moves to be more strongly motivated by her desire to keep Marianne's emotional temperature down than I find them to be, so that Elinor is not deceiving herself, only Marianne. My own belief is that Austen would have given us some explicit sign if she had meant Elinor to be here disingenuous with Marianne; but I find none.

I end my focus on Elinor Dashwood as an intellectual with a rather striking instance of what Alison Sulloway calls Austen's "techniques of simultaneous revelation and concealment" of her feminist sorties.[4] The "concealment" on this occasion consists in a largely indirect manifestation of Elinor's life as an intellectual; the "revelation" occurs through her mother's mimicking the logician's skeptical questioning she anticipates from conversation with Elinor when matters of moment are in hand. In this camouflaged maneuver, the gender reform embodied in Elinor is nonetheless revealed by the paradigmatically patriarchal role the mother assigns to her daughter: Elinor is enacted by her mother as an analytical intellect dashing with cold logic the romantic hope dear to a more "feminine" heart.

Indeed by returning all the way to the first chapter, we find Elinor there portrayed in a role clearly far more "standard" for the husband of a mother of marriageable daughters than for either a daughter or even the mother herself. There Elinor is said to have the "strength of understanding, and coolness of judgment . . . to be the counselor of her mother and . . . frequently to counteract . . . that eagerness of mind in Mrs. Dashwood which must generally have led to imprudence" (ch. 1:42)

Much later, in chapter 15, Elinor and her mother try to understand the shocking manner of Willoughby's departure from their neighborhood. The "simultaneous revelation and concealment" of Austen's gender reform works here in this way: the style of skeptical logician shows itself not directly in Elinor's conversation but in emotionally romantic Mrs. Dashwood, who is presented as shaping at least the rhetorical form of her reasoning discourse with Elinor into a structure not natural to her but learned by her from long experience of Elinor's critical, even skeptical habits of thought. Mrs. Dashwood begins a reassuring explanation of Willoughby's behavior with unnatural awareness of her own fallibility: "You, Elinor, who love to doubt where you can—it will not satisfy you, I know." She ends her hopeful interpretation of Willoughby's conduct with an equally uncharacteristic acknowledgment of alternative explanations:

> "You will tell me, I know, that this may, or may *not* have happened; but I will listen to no cavil, unless you can point out any other method of understanding the affair as satisfactory as this. And now, Elinor, what have you to say?"
>
> "Nothing, for you have anticipated my answer."
>
> "Then you would have told me that it might or might not have happened. Oh! Elinor, how incomprehensible are your feelings! You had rather take evil upon credit than good. You had rather look out for misery for Marianne and guilt for poor Willoughby, than an apology for the latter. . . . Are no probabilities to be accepted, merely because they are not certainties? Is nothing due to the man whom we have all so much reason to love, and no reason in the world to think ill of?"
> (ch. 15:105–6)

Of course clearheaded Elinor's problem with this last remark is that they now have one reason to think ill of Willoughby, his sudden, strange departure. Of the role of another piece of disconfirming evidence, Elinor has this to say: "I confess . . . that every circumstance except *one* is in favour of their engagement; but that *one* is the total silence of both on the subject, and with me it almost outweighs every other" (ch. 15:107). Mrs. Dashwood exemplifies a common confusion of skepticism with both cynicism and pessimism when she upbraids Elinor with "You had rather take evil upon credit than good." The outlook of the cynic is itself a failing considered so stereotypically masculine that it is more or less tolerated in men but abhorred in women. In fact, Elinor has no inclination toward either cynicism or pessimism; her principled skepticism is nonetheless both a common mark of the intellectual, hence of the male in her era, and an excluded ingredient of the socially constructed concept of genteel feminine gender.

Austen has been careful, however, to make Elinor's skepticism subject to lapses where love enters. When Edward sprang on them his own milder version of an unexpected and incomprehensibly early departure from them,

> Elinor placed all that was astonishing in this way of acting to his mother's account; and it was happy for her that he had a mother whose character was so imperfectly known to her, as to be the general excuse for everything strange on the part of her son. . . . She was very well disposed . . . to regard his actions with all the . . . generous qualifications, which had been rather more painfully extorted from her, for Willoughby's service, by her mother. (ch. 19:126)

This is all very well, but the cases of Edward and Willoughby are so different that Austen's conflating them must be taken as only half serious. Perhaps, too, on behalf of Elinor's larger generosity, we should not let pass unnoticed how tender her earliest response to Willoughby had been. When Elinor's mother rhetorically asked about Willoughby, "Can he be deceitful?" Elinor replied: "I hope not, I believe not. . . . I love Willoughby, sincerely love him; and suspicion of his integrity cannot be more painful to yourself than to me" (ch. 15:108). The novel as a whole confirms as truthful this spontaneous expression of her early—and renewable—affection for Willoughby. We shall find occasion, two chapters further on, to take a closer look at Elinor's emotional life. She *is* an intellectual. She is *not* a cold one.

2

Edward Ferrars and Jane Austen's Democracy

MONG AUSTEN'S MALE lovers Edward Ferrars is said to make a poor showing when measured against Knightley, Darcy, or Wentworth. Whatever failure Edward might have deserved with the heroine of another Austen fiction, in his own novel he is a more interesting success than most critics have noticed.

It may help us see Edward as Austen meant we should if at first we connect him, not with other male lovers, but with an early Austen heroine: with Catherine Morland of *Northanger Abbey*.

Critics do not complain of Catherine's mediocrity, in part because Austen makes evident from page one of *Northanger Abbey* that Catherine's excessive normality is part of the point of this parody of both the Gothic and the sentimental novel. In *Northanger Abbey* it is explicit at the start that fun is being made of the sentimental novel:

No one who had ever seen Catherine Morland in her infancy, would have supposed her born to be an heroine. Her situation in life, the character of her father and mother, her own person and disposition, were all equally against her. Her father was a clergyman, without being neglected, or poor, and a very respectable man . . . and he had never been hand-

some. . . . He was not in the least addicted to locking up his
daughters. Her mother was a woman of useful plain sense,
with a good temper, and, what is more remarkable, with a
good constitution. . . . A family of ten children will be always
called a fine family, where there are heads and arms and legs
enough for the number; but the Morlands had little other
right to the word, for they were in general very plain, and
Catherine, for many years of her life, as plain as any. She had
a thin awkward figure, a sallow skin without colour, dark
lank hair, and strong features;—so much for her person;—
and not less unpropitious for heroism seemed her mind. She
was fond of all boys' plays, and greatly preferred cricket not
merely to dolls, but to the more heroic enjoyments of infancy, nursing a dormouse, feeding a canary-bird, or water-
ing a rose-bush. Indeed she had no taste for a garden; and if
she gathered flowers at all, it was chiefly for the pleasure of
mischief—at least so it was conjectured from her always pre-
ferring those which she was forbidden to take.—Such were
her propensities—her abilities were quite as extraordinary.
She never could learn or understand any thing before she was
taught; and sometimes not even then, for she was often inat-
tentive, and occasionally stupid. (*NA*, ch. 1:37)

In short, Catherine Morland is to be an antiheroine. Part of the pleasure intended to be found in her by the original readers is in the way
her example points up the unreality of many heroines of then-current
fiction. And part of the unreality of those heroines is their cohering so
neatly, even as children, with their gender's official paradigm.

When Austen introduces Edward Ferrars in chapter 3 of *Sense and
Sensibility,* she executes a similar deflation of a central character, but
now with no suggestion that parody is afoot. So it will be right to ask
for the ulterior motives of the deflation.

Edward Ferrars was not recommended to [the Dashwood
women's] good opinion by any peculiar graces of person or
address. He was not handsome, and his manners required intimacy to make them pleasing. He was too diffident to do jus-

tice to himself; but when his natural shyness was overcome, his behaviour gave every indication of an open affectionate heart. His understanding was good, and his education had given it solid improvement. But he was neither fitted by abilities nor disposition to answer the wishes of his mother and sister, who longed to see him distinguished—as—they hardly knew what. They wanted him to make a fine figure in the world in some manner or other. His mother wished to interest him in political concerns, to get him into parliament, or to see him connected with some of the great men of the day. Mrs John Dashwood wished it likewise; but in the mean while, till one of these superior blessings could be attained, it would have quieted her ambition to see him driving a barouche. But Edward had no turn for great men or barouches. All his wishes centered in domestic comfort and the quiet of private life. (ch. 3:49)

As we shall see, subsequent characterizations by the elder Mrs. Dashwood, and by Edward himself, are similarly deflationary. But unlike *Northanger Abbey,* here no parody is under way. Why is it, then, that Elinor's story—that this novel—should have so deflated a hero?

Several connected reasons suggest themselves. The most general one, with fewest implications specifically for Edward, is an impulse in Austen that works at a morally deeper level than her search for truths about sense and sensibility. She wants to exhibit the ordinary experiences of ordinary people in a way that shows them to be not only as important in the true ordering of things but also as interesting as the unusual experiences of exceptional people. The upshot is a fictional democracy not only of persons but of lives, situations, and events. This democracy is as much an expression of her special literary genius as of her humanity, for it characterizes all her fiction and looms large among her discoveries about the power of the novel. Her much more famous contemporary, Walter Scott, recognized her achievement both in a published review of her work and in this remark in his *Journal:* "That young lady had a talent for describing the involvements and feelings and characters of ordinary life which is to me the most wonderful I ever met with. The Big Bow-wow strain I can do myself like any now going, but the exquisite touch which renders ordinary commonplace things and characters interesting from the truth of the description and the sentiment is denied to me."[1] Edward Ferrars is an emblem in this novel for that Austenian egalitarianism. For Austen this democratic project is not sharply distinguishable from her concern for realism: realistic heroes are more like everybody else than fictional heroes have usually been. And both her democratic and her realistic projects overlap with her undertaking to reconstruct gender: a democratic hero, Austen believes, will not only be closer to everyday reality, he will share more features with women than the official version of his gender ever authorizes. This last equation has already begun to emerge: what marks Edward as a kind of Everyman who is unrecognized in the ruling class's patriarchal ideology is his modesty, his quiet reticence, his "open, affectionate heart," the fact that "all his wishes centered in domestic comfort and the quiet of private life." All these qualities figure centrally in patriarchy's paradigm for the *feminine* gender.

A reason for *this* novel's hero to deviate from patriarchy's preferred male—from a masculine model Austen finds congenial in *Emma, Persuasion,* and *Pride and Prejudice*—is that Elinor Dashwood is Austen's most flagrantly gender-dissonant heroine. Although she is in her own way quite as susceptible as Marianne to both the "person" and the personality of Willoughby, the mate suited to Elinor's personality as a committed intellectual is the modest and (after adolescence) clear-eyed Edward Ferrars. As the attractive force of the good fit between these gender-reforming lovers works upon us, and as Elinor's distinctive appeal reveals itself, the appealing man that Edward is becomes more accessible to us. His portrayal works for Austen's egalitarianism, it works for her realism, it works for her reshaping of genders—and it works for the love story she has to tell.

Here is a related reason for deflating Edward as hero: Mrs. Dashwood's experience of Edward—an evolving appreciation that works against the grain of her spontaneous taste—is meant to function as a model, even as a guide, for the readers who may find their own discriminations improved by this instance of Austen's project of almost concealed, gender-reforming work. For this work to be effective, both Mrs. Dashwood and the reader need to be surprised by finding Ed-

ward attractive despite his unprepossessing presence. In finding him
attractive, we readers, perhaps unwittingly, are being converted to
Austen's democracy, her realism, and her reconstruction of gender—
but not only of masculine gender: for our progress in appreciating Edward is inseparable from our developing appreciation of Elinor. And
Austen uses Elinor variously in remodeling feminine gender: Elinor
belongs not only to the officially male class of intellectuals; we shall
later notice in her other like blurrings of boundaries.

When Mrs. Dashwood's husband is barely in his grave, Edward's
sister Fanny unconscionably descends upon the Dashwood household in the role of new mistress of the estate. Edward visits too, and
Mrs. Dashwood's role as our model for reading Edward begins, with
counterpoint from the narrator's amused irony about Mrs. Dashwood's will to suffer in peace: "Edward had been staying several weeks
in the house before he engaged much of Mrs Dashwood's attention. . . . She saw only that he was quiet and unobtrusive, and she liked
him for it. He did not disturb the wretchedness of her mind by ill-
timed conversation" (ch. 3:50).

When Elinor suggested to her mother that she probably would
like Edward when she knew more of him, Mrs. Dashwood "now took
pains to get acquainted with him" and found that "even that quietness
of manner which militated against all her established ideas of what a
young man's address ought to be, was no longer uninteresting when
she knew his heart to be warm and his temper affectionate" (ch. 3:50).
Here and elsewhere we are invited to approach Edward through the
mediation of Mrs. Dashwood's warm discrimination of merit in him.
For us to take an interest in a young man who is not distinguished in
looks, address, grace, ambition, talent, confidence, conversation, or
achievement, for us to care about him because he has an affectionate
heart, is honest in his modesty, and, among other attractions, because
he falls in love with—and enlists the love of—a woman whom it is
hard, though just, to perceive as admirable and lovable, this is for us
to become a little better than we were. So too it is enlarging for us to
loyally sustain our interest in Edward with close reading throughout
the novel, and to rejoice (a little more with each reading) in the discrimination and good luck of two gender-dissonant protagonists for
being in love with each other.

Austen has taken care to draw a portrait of Edward that is designed to grow in its appeal to us as we reread earlier portions of the book with full knowledge of Edward's circumstances and of both his moral fiber when severely tested and his transforming joy when freed from a disastrous engagement. One portion of this portrait that is visible from a first reading, though probably not in its full colors, is Edward's more than modesty: his self-deprecation. However, let me step back—or down—for a moment from Edward to his shadow that Austen has painted onto the wall (and floor) behind Edward's figure: I mean to Colonel Brandon. For Brandon helps us get a just perspective on Edward's self-diminishing tendencies.

In the next to last chapter of the novel we are told (in case we had missed it) of Brandon's and Edward's "resemblance in good principles and good sense, in disposition and manner of thinking" (Ch. 49:359). One reason we ought not to have missed it is that Elinor so often responds to Brandon in a way like her response to Edward, indeed sufficiently so to help "fix that suspicion" in Edward's mind that Brandon is a rival (ch. 41:288). When, very late in the novel, Mrs. Dashwood replaces Willoughby with Brandon in her romantic hopes for Marianne and says to Elinor that, since only one of her eligible daughters can marry Brandon, "I believe Marianne will be the most happy with him of the two," Elinor "was half inclined to ask her reason for thinking so, because satisfied that none founded on an impartial consideration of their age, characters or feelings, could be given" (ch. 45:328). Elinor finds Brandon an attractive person.

Because of the way Austen offers testimony to Brandon's solid qualities through Elinor's private thoughts and her conversations with Marianne, we believe in them. But mostly we do not experience them. They are not rendered for us. Brandon does not come to life. Time and again we are told of his grave silence and sober demeanor, and more than once of his despair of personal happiness. A reader can take little interest in a ghostly presence who is self-condemned by such remarks as these: "My affection for her . . . was such, as perhaps, judging from my present forlorn and cheerless gravity, you might think me incapable of having ever felt" (ch. 31:215).

Yet on rereading the novel we realize that Colonel Brandon's ghostly presence as an alternative, paler Edward makes more vivid for us—by contrast—the bright colors of Edward's self-deprecating wit. This contrast holds even when, as we understand in rereading, Edward has come to the Dashwoods directly from a disheartening two-week visit with Lucy Steele, and is doubtless in a state of unhappy conflict apt to make him seem "forlorn and cheerless." Here again it is from within the ambience of Mrs. Dashwood's value-enhancing feeling for Edward that we readers experience the hero's deflation:

> Mrs Dashwood was surprised only for a moment at seeing him; for his coming to Barton was, in her opinion, of all things the most natural. Her joy and expressions of regard long outlived her wonder. He received the kindest welcome from her; and shyness, coldness, reserve could not stand against such a reception. They had begun to fail him before he entered the house, and they were quite overcome by the captivating manners of Mrs Dashwood. Indeed a man could not very well be in love with either of her daughters, without extending the passion to her; and Elinor had the satisfaction of seeing him soon become more like himself. His affections seemed to reanimate towards them all, and his interest in their welfare again became perceptible. He was not in spirits however; he praised their house, admired its prospects, was attentive, and kind; but still he was not in spirits. The whole family perceived it, and Mrs Dashwood, attributing it to some want of liberality in his mother, sat down to table indignant against all selfish parents.
>
> "What are Mrs Ferrars's views for you at present, Edward?" said she, when dinner was over and they had drawn round the fire; "are you still to be a great orator in spite of yourself?"
>
> "No. I hope my mother is now convinced that I have no more talents than inclination for a public life!"
>
> "But how is your fame to be established? for famous you must be to satisfy all your family; and with no inclination for expense, no affection for strangers, no profession, and no assurance, you may find it a difficult matter."
>
> "I shall not attempt it. I have no wish to be distinguished;

and I have every reason to hope I never shall. Thank Heaven!
I cannot be forced into genius and eloquence."

"You have no ambition, I well know. Your wishes are all
moderate."

"As moderate as those of the rest of the world, I believe.
I wish as well as every body else to be perfectly happy; but like
every body else it must be in my own way. Greatness will not
make me so." (ch. 17:116–17)

A second reading of the novel does not help Colonel Brandon—he
remains ghostly. But after a first reading we now know Edward's
troubles justify his low spirits: he appears to be doomed by his sense
of honor to life imprisonment with Lucy Steele, and he is in love with
Elinor, whom he has no right to court. Were Edward less scrupulous
he would either break his engagement or proceed with Elinor as if he
had done so. If he had less life, less hope of happiness, less "sensibility," he would not see Elinor. His conflict is genuine, and not discred-
itable. Because of it the inconsistency of his behavior toward Elinor
and her family is inevitable. So far as we know, the full strength of
Edward's tendency to self-deprecation that we observe may have its
source in this unhappy situation of his own making. In any event, his
self-deflation strikes me as both admirably honest and in its wit surprisingly spirited. His "I have no wish to be distinguished; and I have
every reason to hope I never shall" is a bit of dramatic irony. It figures
too as the author's shortest proof of Edward's intellectual and moral
distinction: he displays the wit of a cultural elite when he affirms the
modesty of the morally select.

An interesting—I think important—transition occurs at the last
paragraph of Edward's just-quoted remarks to Mrs. Dashwood. She
characterized him by his lacks: of assurance, ambition, expansiveness,
immoderate wishes, a profession, and the amusing (but accurate)
qualification she picked out for a successful politician: "affection for
strangers." Edward does not dissent from these negatives, but he rejects the suggestion of singularity, and he makes an emphatic statement of solidarity with the world at large. In three sentences out of the
four that form his response, he makes a repeating identification of

himself with "the rest of the world," with "everybody else." Here he explicitly takes upon himself the role of emblem for his author's subtle and several-sided egalitarianism. I shall return to this point. Apart from the emblematic role, this is a self-expression of some strength and originality, and of high professional promise for a man who, as we rereaders know, will shortly become a minister credited with "the ready discharge of his duties in every particular"—high praise from this narrator (ch. 50:366).

Although there are passages in this novel as fine as any in her fiction, on the whole the prose style of *Sense and Sensibility* is somewhat inferior to that of Austen's later works. Common here, however, is evidence of Austen's sensitivity to prose rhythm. This, for example, accounts in part for the third of Edward's three affirmations of solidarity with "everyone else" that I cited just above. Remember that Mrs. Dashwood had said to him, "Your wishes are all moderate": "As moderate of those of the rest of the world, I believe. I wish as well as every body else to be perfectly happy; but like every body else it must be in my own way." The two sentences balanced on the semicolon gain a kind of equality of emphasis by the repetition of a shortened variation of the "everybody else" phrase ("like" replacing "as well as"). Austen's rhythmic sense works to emphasize the moral force of the *number* of Edward's declarations of solidarity: the rhythmic impetus gives expressive power to this democratic affirmation (whose democracy the author enhances with the questionable grammar of Edward's last clause).

Another passage shows Austen using prose rhythm to capture an aspect of Edward's emotional life, his ambivalence about staying on at the Dashwoods' cottage. He suffers from a conflict between his desire for Elinor and his duty to Lucy Steele. He had arrived to visit the woman he wishes to spend his life with fresh from a visit of two weeks to Lucy, the woman he *must* spend it with. Unaccountably to the Dashwoods but understandably to rereaders, he begins his visit in very bad spirits. There is improvement in his mood, but this yields still more bafflement for his hosts from his determination, after a short visit, to leave them without apparent reason. We hear the rhythmic pounding of "to be gone," "going away," "go he must," "he should go," "to be gone," "he must go," "he must leave," developing into two series of abrupt, agitated sentences and at last lengthening into grim reconciliation, as if following a painful sigh.

> Edward remained a week at the cottage; he was earnestly pressed by Mrs Dashwood to stay longer; but as if he were bent only on self-mortification, he seemed resolved to be gone when his enjoyment among his friends was at the height. His spirits, during the last two or three days, though still very unequal, were greatly improved—he grew more and more partial to the house and environs—never spoke of going away without a sigh—declared his time to be wholly disengaged—even doubted to what place he should go when he left them—but still, go he must. Never had any week passed so quickly—he could hardly believe it to be gone. He said so repeatedly; other things he said too, which marked the turn of his feelings and gave the lie to his actions. He had no pleasure at Norland; he detested being in town; but either to Norland or London, he must go. He valued their kindness beyond any thing, and his greatest happiness was in being with them. Yet he must leave them at the end of a week, in spite of their wishes and his own, and without any restraint on his time. (ch. 19:126)

There is a strong rhythm here in which desire accumulates in waves and then breaks with a kind of thud against a resistant will. The insistent rhythm of conflict develops, to my ear—and with my understanding of the truth of his situation—an experience of strong desire overmastered, unhappily, by a strong will: a creditable conflict resolutely suppressed.

That Edward is near despair by the end of his visit to the Dashwoods is proved by his response to Mrs. Dashwood's effort to cheer him up the last morning before his departure from Barton:

> "You are in a melancholy humour . . . But remember that the pain of parting from friends will be felt by every body at

times. . . . You want nothing but patience—or give it a more fascinating name, call it hope. . . . How much may not a few months do?"

"I think," replied Edward, "that I may defy many months to produce any good to me." (ch. 19:128)

Earlier in this conversation, Mrs. Dashwood says to him, "I think, Edward, you would be a happier man if you had any profession to engage your time and give an interest to your plans and actions" (ch. 19:127). Not only does Edward now wholeheartedly agree and show he thinks his "want of employment" evil in itself; much later, when he and Elinor are united, he explains his early and nearly disastrous attachment to Lucy Steele as "the consequence of ignorance of the world—and want of employment," both of which he believes arose from his mother's not having "given me some active profession when I was removed at eighteen from the care of Mr. Pratt" (ch. 49:352). It is the conflict between his own and his family's tastes in professions that has made him an idle and useless being, he explains to Mrs. Dashwood. It is clear that both the narrator and Edward believe that Mrs. Ferrars (assisted by her daughter Fanny) failed Edward in ways nearly as serious as those guardians who accounted for Willoughby's early habits of "idleness, dissipation, and luxury" failed that young man (ch. 44:324). Edward's good humor, his telling yet unmalicious wit in explaining to Mrs. Dashwood the joint effects of his own and his family's "nicety" is exceptional:

"We never could agree in our choice of profession. I always preferred the church, as I still do. But that was not smart enough for my family. They recommended the army. That was a great deal too smart for me. The law was allowed to be genteel enough; many young men, who had chambers in the Temple, made a very good appearance in the first circles, and drove about town in very knowing gigs. But I had no inclination for the law, even in this less abstruse study of it, which my family approved. As for the navy, it had fashion of its side, but I was too old when the subject was first started to enter

> it—and, at length, as there was no necessity for my having
> any profession at all, as I might be as dashing and expensive
> without a red coat on my back as with one, idleness was pro-
> nounced on the whole to be the most advantageous and hon-
> ourable, and a young man of eighteen is not in general so
> earnestly bent on being busy as to resist the solicitations of
> his friends to do nothing." (ch. 19:127–28)

It is easy to forget that Edward is the eldest son of a wealthy family and
hence to overlook that Austen thought this sufficient reason for this
family to stop him from entering the clergy. It is worth our notice that
Edward is here given an avowal—subdued indeed—of a longstand-
ing belief in the church as his vocation. It was, simply, "not smart
enough for my family." The rhetorical balance he establishes between
church and army is nice. The ironically amusing image of law stu-
dents who "drove about town in very knowing gigs" is extended with
gently mocking wit by labeling this and other ways of making "a very
good appearance in the first circles" as "this less abstruse study" of the
law to which his family urged him. Finally, he uses his sometimes
commendable sense of solidarity with "every body else" vaguely to
pardon his own part in embracing idleness, by appealing to the inclinations "in general" of a young man of eighteen. On the one hand,
Austen here endows Edward with good humor in misfortune, displayed in creative, precise irony and wit, and, on the other hand, she
lets him use these powers to produce a self-deprecating self-portrait
that shows him to have been almost passive in the face of major obstacles to self-fulfilment, and to be now idle and aimless. These quiescent aspects of himself that Edward paints with his utterance are in
fact not admirable, but they are partly offset and contradicted by the
superbly expressive power with which he paints them. Austen is
showing us that, "like everyone else," Edward is uniquely interesting.
What is more, once we attend to him with something like Mrs. Dashwood's "acquired taste" for his oblique distinction, his gender dissonance augments rather than diminishes his appeal—especially on
rereading, when we have also had space and time to notice his robust
side, of which we had better now take some notice.

Edward's expressive powers show themselves only in situations that naturally bring them into play among persons with whom he is comfortable. Marianne's distress over his inexpressive reading of the poet Cowper tells us only that he is not a performer. Elinor assures Marianne that Edward's taste in both literature and visual art is "delicate and pure"; she even believes that had he had instruction, "he would have drawn very well," an opinion so amiably baseless for Elinor it must be weightless for the reader (ch. 4:54, 53).

However, Edward is no aesthete, and Austen gives us (easy to overlook) evidence of a hardiness and practical outlook that is quite the equal not only of a Knightley but—remembering his helplessness on the cobb at Lyme Regis—even of a Captain Wentworth.

As soon as he is liberated from Lucy Steele, Edward begins a ride on horseback from Oxford to near Exeter that is a more athletic performance than any Austen ascribes to any other male character in her fiction. Perhaps Willoughby's almost nonstop ride from London to near Bristol, when he thinks Marianne dying, would match Edward's longer but slower ride, if Willoughby were not traveling by carriage. Knightley is often on horseback, but we are told of no rides even as long as Frank Churchill's eighteen-mile jaunt to London avowedly for a haircut.

From letters of Jane Austen and her parents we know that her rector father—like the holders of many moderate-income livings—took seriously the working of the farm that belonged to the rectory, the "glebe farm," as did her mother the dairy and garden portion of it. In American though not in English English, it would be accurate to call Jane Austen a farmer's daughter. So we can imagine the author identifying with Elinor when she writes of Edward that soon after Elinor accepted his proposal he "owed all his knowledge of the house, garden, and glebe, extent of the parish, condition of the land, and rate of the tythes, to Elinor herself, who had heard so much of it . . . with so much attention, as to be entirely mistress of the subject" (ch. 49:358). If I may exaggerate, we know that Edward and Elinor became serious farmers because when at last they have occupied the parsonage at Delaford, where Mrs. Jennings finds them "one of the happiest couples in the world," they "had in fact nothing to wish for, but the marriage of Colonel Brandon and Marianne, and rather better pasturage for their cows" (ch. 50:363).

That a farmerly relationship to the countryside is natural to Edward is shown in exchanges with Marianne on "the picturesque." These conversations show us a lively, forthright, and engaging Edward Ferrars.

> "Now, Edward," said she, calling his attention to the prospect, "here is Barton valley. Look up to it, and be tranquil if you can. Look at those hills! Did you ever see their equals? To the left is Barton park, amongst those woods and plantations. You may see one end of the house. And there, beneath that farthest hill, which rises with such grandeur, is our cottage."
>
> "It is a beautiful country," he replied; "but these bottoms must be dirty in winter."
>
> "How can you think of dirt, with such objects before you?"
>
> "Because," replied he, smiling, "among the rest of the objects before me, I see a very dirty lane." (ch. 16:114)

The subject is resumed two chapters later. And I include prefatory material showing Edward's way of trying to minimize his bad faith in visiting Elinor's family while engaged to Lucy; this will become relevant for us later, in chapter 4.

> He joined her and Marianne in the breakfast-room the next morning before the others were down; and Marianne, who was always eager to promote their happiness as far as she could, soon left them to themselves. But before she was half way upstairs she heard the parlour door open, and, turning round, was astonished to see Edward himself come out.
>
> "I am going into the village to see my horses," said he, "as you are not yet ready for breakfast; I shall be back again presently."
>
> Edward returned to them with fresh admiration of the

surrounding country; in his walk to the village, he had seen
many parts of the valley to advantage; and the village itself, in
a much higher situation than the cottage, afforded a general
view of the whole, which had exceedingly pleased him. This
was a subject which ensured Marianne's attention, and she
was beginning to describe her own admiration of these
scenes, and to question him more minutely on the objects
that had particularly struck him, when Edward interrupted
her by saying, "You must not inquire too far, Marianne—remember I have no knowledge in the picturesque, and I shall
offend you by my ignorance and want of taste if we come to
particulars. I shall call hills steep, which ought to be bold;
surfaces strange and uncouth, which ought to be irregular
and rugged; and distant objects out of sight, which ought
only to be indistinct through the soft medium of a hazy at-
mosphere. You must be satisfied with such admiration as I
can honestly give. I call it a very fine country—the hills are
steep, the woods seem full of fine timber, and the valley looks
comfortable and snug—with rich meadows and several neat
farm houses scattered here and there. It exactly answers my
idea of a fine country, because it unites beauty with utility—
and I dare say it is a picturesque one too, because you admire
it; I can easily believe it to be full of rocks and promontories,
grey moss and brush wood, but these are all lost on me. I
know nothing of the picturesque."

"I am afraid it is but too true," said Marianne; "but why
should you boast of it?"

"I suspect," said Elinor, "that to avoid one kind of affectation, Edward here falls into another. Because he believes
many people pretend to more admiration of the beauties of
nature than they really feel, and is disgusted with such pre-
tensions, he affects greater indifference and less discrimination in viewing them himself than he possesses. He is fastidious and will have an affectation of his own."

"It is very true," said Marianne, "that admiration of
landscape scenery is become a mere jargon. Every body pre-

tends to feel and tries to describe with the taste and elegance of him who first defined what picturesque beauty was. I detest jargon of every kind, and sometimes I have kept my feelings to myself, because I could find no language to describe them in but what was worn and hackneyed out of all sense and meaning."

"I am convinced," said Edward, "that you really feel all the delight in a fine prospect which you profess to feel. But, in return, your sister must allow me to feel no more than I profess. I like a fine prospect, but not on picturesque principles. I do not like crooked, twisted, blasted trees. I admire them much more if they are tall, straight and flourishing. I do not like ruined, tattered cottages. I am not fond of nettles, or thistles, or heath blossoms. I have more pleasure in a snug farm-house than a watch-tower—and a troop of tidy, happy villagers please me better than the finest banditti in the world." (ch. 18:121–22)

(The early nineteenth-century reader would understand that for William Gilpin, to whom Marianne alludes as "him who first defined what picturesque beauty was," Italian banditti in a landscape painting contribute a picturesque element.)

Austen has here given Edward a gently ironic, tactful, and discriminating response to the two women's speech. His irony lies in his three times declaring to Marianne his ignorance of the picturesque, on the one hand, and, on the other, showing himself to be acquainted with its vocabulary; one could believe he knew how to apply it and that he understood the principles of this branch of aesthetics. It is true there is an interpretation of his "ignorance" under which he might rightly make his claim to it: to be ignorant of the picturesque is to be incapable of responding to it as moving or fine—in other words, as he puts it, for it to be "all lost on me." Yet one can understand why Elinor suspects him of affectation—it is more than just her belief in his taste, which we know she has: he *does* show familiarity with "picturesque principles." And his reply to the woman he not only loves

but also, no doubt, admires for her analytical and even—as now—
her sometimes aggressive intellect—his reply is, let us say "assertive,"
to be sure, but more important, he expresses himself in a way that
makes it rather unnatural to think of his unresponsiveness to the picturesque as "ignorance" of it. He delivers a rapid succession of short,
strong assertions of the form, "I do not like, I am not fond of, I have
more pleasure in, I admire," and concludes with a long sentence that
rhetorically functions as a reductio ad absurdum of picturesque principles: a snug farmhouse and happy villagers are more pleasant than a
watchtower and banditti!

Is Elinor miffed by her put-down? "Marianne looked with amazement at Edward, with compassion at her sister. Elinor only laughed"
(ch. 18:123).

Is there another Austenian marriage that pleases its fabricator
more than this one between the two lovers whose genders she has
most radically reconstructed? I share the admiration so many feel for
the scene of reconciliation in *Persuasion* between Anne Elliot and
Captain Wentworth on the "quiet and retired gravel-walk" in Bath.
Yet I think Austen never seems quite so intensely to participate in the
achievement of successful lovers as she does in modest Edward's winning masterful Elinor—and Elinor's winning Edward. Here we are, at
the joyful climax of the novel:

> His errand at Barton, in fact, was a simple one. It was
> only to ask Elinor to marry him;—and considering that he
> was not altogether inexperienced in such a question, it might
> be strange that he should feel so uncomfortable in the present
> case as he really did, so much in need of encouragement and
> fresh air.
>
> How soon he had walked himself into the proper resolu-
> tion, however, how soon an opportunity of exercising it oc-
> curred, in what manner he expressed himself, and how he
> was received, need not be particularly told. This only need be
> said;—that when they all sat down to table at four o'clock,
> about three hours after his arrival, he had secured his lady,

engaged her mother's consent, and was not only in the rapturous profession of the lover, but in the reality of reason and
truth, one of the happiest of men. His situation indeed was
more than commonly joyful. He had more than the ordinary
triumph of accepted love to swell his heart, and raise his spirits. He was released without any reproach to himself, from an
entanglement which had long formed his misery, from a
woman whom he had long ceased to love;—and elevated
at once to that security with another, which he must have
thought of almost with despair, as soon as he had learnt to
consider it with desire. He was brought, not from doubt or
suspense, but from misery to happiness;—and the change
was openly spoken in such a genuine, flowing, grateful cheerfulness, as his friends had never witnessed in him before.
(ch. 49:351)

Austen's "in the reality of reason and truth" is exactly the right tribute
to Elinor—and through Elinor to Edward—if my reading of both is
sound. Elinor's intellectual energy and Edward's reticent domesticity
go against the grain of the socially constructed conception of each's
gender. That we still live with at least elements of the same conception
suggests itself from the effort we must make to discover the appeal of
each of these protagonists; whereas our reward for renouncing this
conception comes in the surprised exhilaration that our effort enables
us to share with the author, when Edward's confident journey brings
Elinor's passionate response.

I turn away now from Edward considered in himself to Austen's
democratic project in this novel, for which he serves as emblem.
    Recall one more time Edward's response to Mrs. Dashwood's re-
sistance to his family's unkind expectations. She remarks:

"You have no ambition, I well know. Your wishes are all
moderate."
"As moderate as those of the rest of the world, I believe.
I wish as well as every body else to be perfectly happy; but like

every body else it must be in my own way. Greatness will not
make me so." (ch. 17:116–17)

Earlier I remarked that when Edward in his second short utterance
three times affirms his equality with "every body else"—with "the rest
of the world"—he has been made to take upon himself a declaration
of the author's egalitarian literary project.

However, readers may be more easily persuaded that Edward is a
suitable emblem for a democratic vision than that Austen's novel embodies one. Her status bias has often been remarked: she is believed to
identify exclusively with that part of the British ruling class—the gentry—to which she and her family belonged. Suppose we ignore the
conversation of Elizabeth Bennet and her relatives with Mr. Darcy's
Pemberley housekeeper, Mrs. Reynolds, who is almost above servant
rank. Then I think the questioning in chapter 48 of Thomas, a "manservant" of the Dashwoods, when he mistakenly reports that Lucy
Steele has married Edward Ferrars, elicits from him the longest speech
in all of Austen's mature fiction by someone of servant rank. If the otherwise total absence of anyone from the "lower orders" in a speaking
part in this novel is not quite enough to convince us that here "every
body" is not everybody, perhaps the manner of Thomas's departure
from his moment on stage will clinch it. "Mrs Dashwood could think
of no other question [for Thomas, about the presumed marriage],
and Thomas and the table-cloth, now alike needless, were soon afterwards dismissed" (ch. 47:345). A servant and a tablecloth are alike.
The downward distance to Thomas's grammar from that of either
"illiterate" Steele sister is at least as great as the upward distance from
their vulgar speech to the Dashwoods' "elegant" discourse. It is hard
to resist acknowledging that for the narrator of the novel, relative to
any one of her protagonists "the rest of the world" includes neither
servants nor the "laboring poor"—for example, the workmen whose
"usual" yet "unaccountable dilatoriness" delays completion of Delaford Parsonage (ch. 50:363).

Having conceded so much "classism" to the narrator's outlook,
have I said *Edward's* "every body" is less than everybody? No—his
viewpoint need not coincide with the narrator's. Indeed, it cannot

generally do so if his modest outlook is to be as different as it manifestly is from the narrator's confident presence; and a novel's emblem can signify within the depicted world a progressive movement that the novel does not mean to hasten.

Although it *need* not, does Edward's view here in fact coincide with the narrator's? When he says his wishes are "as moderate as those of the rest of the world," one could suspect that "the world" is the one that, "by mixing more with" it (in pursuit of a profession) he might years ago have avoided entanglement with Lucy—and this world is surely formed entirely from members of the middle and upper ranks (ch. 49:352). However, the world with which Edward would have mixed in pursuing a profession would have been largely the "worldly" world, which is only part of the world composed of all those, even in only the middle and upper ranks, who wish happiness for themselves. So Edward's later remarks about "mixing with the world" surely do not reach back to fix his earlier reference to "the rest of the world." I see no way to be sure he sets social rank as a test for membership in "the rest of the world," unless the wish he names as the one he shares with everyone in it is a wish he would believe absent in the "lower orders." It is not. It is the wish long famous for being believed to move all humans: the wish to be happy. (At some risk I ignore Edward's "*perfectly* happy" as no more than stylistically elite.) For this reason, and because it coheres with the rest of this young man's portrait, I find Jane Austen's Edward Ferrars to be affirming solidarity with humans generally.

Always qualifying the implicit elitism of Austen's fictional world is an egalitarian tendency in the novel as a whole that is not to be limited to anyone's uplifting utterance. A massive, upward social migration is tangibly afoot in the novel's society, from comparative bondage to at least potential freedom: from the bondage of what Austen calls, in speaking of Lucy Steele, "narrow views" and "illiberal" attitudes, of relative discomfort or inconvenience or overwork, of little education and impoverished personal relationships, to the opposite of these, or at least to a position from which the opposite is possible. Austen's novel accepts this upward migration. There is no question of an alternative vision, another preferred social order where stasis between the ranks is the rule. It is not because she wishes to stanch it but because she accepts it that Austen, in this work, manifests a strong interest in rendering ugly aspects of this social and economic climbing. The rich but vulgar are not always pretty when moved by the desire to be not only rich but smart, nor are the merely smart always a happy sight meeting the genteel; and even the genteel but inelegant envying the elegant may not edify. That listing leaves out—as Austen does not—images of the poor but genteel seeking security, of the comfortable reaching for wealth, and of the rich trying to be richer. However, one reassuring aspect of this steady movement upward that those enumerations omit is the fact that each "superior" group for the most part—some more reluctantly and slowly than others—accepts the upward thrust from "below" as fitting. Once an occupant of a lower rung of the status ladder has raised himself or herself a rung, or is seen to be rising, he or she is accepted as (regrettable but) legitimate. Even when it is felt to be obnoxious, the energy of ambition is treated with at least tolerance and sometimes with respect. The novel seems to accept as some part of its own ambition at least the posing of one of the supreme social questions of its (and our) time, to wit: can the unrelenting enlargement of the social aggregate that constitutes "every body" be so achieved that the quantity and quality of pleasure, virtue, and culture in a society also increase?

It cannot surprise us that the most telling embodiment in this novel of the author's literary commitment to social democracy should be found in so warmhearted a vulgar woman as Mrs. Jennings—of whom I shall say more presently. It *is* a surprise to find something similar, though less pure, introduce itself into our experience of so morally deficient a vulgar young person as Lucy Steele.

First let us absorb the fact that nowhere else in her fiction has Jane Austen given nearly so large and strategic a role to someone whose social credentials are as weak as Lucy's. First as to her importance: for the heroine of no other novel has Austen created so serious a competitor for the man the heroine desires. Mary Crawford and Edmund Bertram never achieve engagement, and even on first reading their affair does not seem promising. Neither Elizabeth Bennet nor Emma has a "fair rival." When Admiral Croft cannot tell apart the two Musgrove sisters, it is hard to take seriously Louisa Musgrove's chances with Captain Wentworth. Furthermore, Lucy is very much a personal presence for Elinor—and even for Marianne. Several aspects of Lucy's presence force upon Elinor a tough test of temperament and character; and Lucy provokes bouts of disgust for Marianne. Finally, Lucy's actions, or their retrospective explanations, as early as chapter 22 and as late as the concluding chapter 50, determine or illuminate major movements of the plot.

Yet consider Lucy's social rank. Since she is poor and lacks elevated connections, her unassisted social rank is settled by her culture. Here is how Elinor perceives this culture—or rather, its absence: because Lucy Steele is "ignorant and illiterate," because her mental powers have "received no aid from education," because she is therefore suffering from a "deficiency of all mental improvement" and from a "want of information in the most common particulars," according to Elinor she and Lucy are "prevented [from] meeting in conversation on terms of equality" (ch. 22:149). That is a strong statement of social distance. How, for example, is Elinor to receive this sentence of Lucy's that explains how she came to know Edward: "It was there our acquaintance begun, for my sister and me was often staying with my uncle" (ch. 22:152).

No one else so socially disadvantaged has so much importance in an Austen novel. Emma's protégée, Harriet Smith, may be of comparable if ambiguous social position, but she is surely more a plaything than ever a "fair rival" of Emma's. Fanny Price's father stands as low in social rank as Lucy, but he is more a part of the background than the foreground of Fanny Price's life. Whatever her origins, Fanny's placement as a young woman at Mansfield Park—and her education there—entails for her a higher social rank than Lucy's. Mrs. Clay of *Persuasion* is doubtless lowly enough, but she is less important even than Robert Ferrars, since the potential lover she whisks off stage (the younger Mr. Elliot) poses not a fraction of the threat to Anne Elliot's happiness that Lucy Steele is to Elinor's. Like Mrs. Jennings's daughters, the new young wife of Mr. Elton in *Emma* has at least wealth and the consequent habit of confidence behind her.

To Lucy's material and social privation, and her cultural illiteracy,

Austen has added moral disability. Elinor perceives—and Austen has provided us with some of the data for the perception—that Lucy displays a "thorough want of delicacy, of rectitude, and integrity of mind," is insincere, "artful and selfish." Elinor also presumes that Lucy has spent the last four years (since age nineteen) in "inferior society and . . . frivolous pursuits."

Whenever the novel represents Lucy without mediation through Elinor, or displays the narrator's direct appraisal of Lucy, it confirms those harsh judgments by Elinor. My readers may therefore feel that Lucy's case contributes nothing to Austen's status as literary democrat and provides none of the novel's evidence that the author *accepts* the upward social mobility she depicts. This objection has merit.

Yet it seems to me that I find in the very moments of the narrator's rendering for us the reprehensible Lucy, or summing up Lucy's predatory career, a note, a tone, a nuance of appreciation that no rereading ever quite dissolves away for me. I am much inclined, therefore, to think the author found something to enjoy in the very perfection and energy of Lucy's scruple-free aggression. And I suspect Jane Austen of being moved, too, by sisterly sympathy for Lucy's hard lot as a young woman with a way to make in the world and no education or fortune to help.

The handicap of bad grammar that Lucy labors under is a badge of dishonor for the status-conscious Dashwood sisters. However, we are able to experience this flaw in her culture not merely as the blemish we know it is but also as grounds for sympathy with the odds she struggles against. Here Elinor has led the way: she "pitied her for . . . the neglect of abilities which education might have rendered so respectable" (ch. 22:149). We can follow Elinor's lead when we perceive the abysmal failure of taste and discernment in Lucy's way of trying to land conversational blows on Elinor. These efforts do not merely show Lucy's mean spirit; almost painfully they display her habituation to "inferior society"—as the example below illustrates. For me something else also shows through here.

When Lucy arrives in London and finds that Elinor has stayed there longer than Elinor had earlier predicted, long enough indeed for Edward's relatives and therefore Edward himself to arrive in London, Lucy launches her assault the moment she meets Elinor. Elinor "hardly knew how to make a very gracious return to the overpowering delight of Lucy in finding her *still* in town":

> "I should have been quite disappointed if I had not found you here *still*," said she repeatedly, with a strong emphasis on the word. "But I always thought I *should.* I was almost sure you would not leave London yet awhile; though you *told* me, you know, at Barton, that you should not stay above a *month.* But I thought, at the time, that you would most likely change your mind when it came to the point. It would have been such a great pity to have went away before your brother and sister came. And now to be sure you will be in no hurry to be gone. I am amazingly glad you did not keep to *your word.*" (ch. 32:225–26)

The something else I find sharply present is poignancy—from the justified desperation that fuels Lucy's defensive attack; and from this attack's being mounted with so much energy but with such palpably self-wounding weapons. These sources of pathos are so vivid I have to think Austen intended them to be taken as I have found them.

When Lucy seems to have success in her grasp, after Colonel Brandon has offered the Delaford living to Edward, her spirit, at once triumphant, manipulative, and provident, is rendered for us with such éclat that it can be exhilarating for this reader not merely in spite of but also because of Lucy's exuberantly manifest insincerity. Here is the report of her conversation with Mrs. Jennings just after getting the news of Colonel Brandon's presentation of a living to her fiancé, Edward:

> Her own happiness, and her own spirits, were . . . very certain; and she joined Mrs Jennings most heartily in her expectation of their being all comfortably together in Delaford Parsonage before Michaelmas. So far was she, at the same time, from any backwardness to give Elinor that credit which Edward *would* give her, that she spoke of her friendship for

them both with the most grateful warmth, was ready to own all their obligation to her, and openly declared that no exertion for their good on Miss Dashwood's part, either present or future, would ever surprise her, for she believed her capable of doing anything in the world for those she really valued. As for Colonel Brandon, she was not only ready to worship him as a saint, but was moreover truly anxious . . . that his tythes should be raised to the utmost; and secretly resolved to avail herself, at Delaford, as far as she possibly could, of his servants, his carriage, his cows, and his poultry. (ch. 41:291)

Right through to its very end, when Austen surprises us by blending uncommunicated private thoughts of Lucy's with the letter's content, this spirited meditation has a verve I never fail to enjoy. I ascribe a connected pleasure to the author.

We are told that the consistent motivation of both Elinor's nemesis, Lucy, and Marianne's unfaithful Willoughby is pretty nearly pure selfishness. But there is a difference in the spirit of Austen's summing up of Lucy's conduct from the accounting that begins in almost the same words for Willoughby's: "The whole of Lucy's behavior in the affair"—"The whole of [Willoughby's] behavior . . . from the beginning to the end of the affair." Elinor's sentence about Willoughby concludes: "has been grounded in selfishness," and the summary proceeds, as we have earlier observed, to accumulate instances, and then to discuss his unhappiness as inevitable, given his character and propensities (ch. 47:342). Even in the last words on Willoughby at the very end of the book, we are told that "his punishment was soon afterwards complete" in his discovery that if he had done the right thing and married Marianne, he almost certainly would have been restored to comfort by his cousin, Mrs. Smith (ch. 50:367). The partially quoted author's sentence on Lucy, however, which sums up Lucy's dealings with both Ferrars brothers and their mother, reads in full thus: "The whole of Lucy's behavior in the affair, and the prosperity which crowned it, therefore, may be held forth as a most encouraging instance of what an earnest, an unceasing attention to self-interest, however its progress may apparently be obstructed, will do in securing every advantage of fortune, with no other sacrifice than that of time and conscience" (ch. 50:364). Despite its condemning judgment, there is gaiety in Austen's irony. Of course in part this merely evinces the author's resolve to treat Lucy less seriously than Willoughby. Nevertheless, she immediately moves on to an explanation of Lucy's marrying Edward's brother instead of Edward that is so flowing and sparkling as to be a pleasing and thus seem a *pleased* accounting for Lucy's improbable—but suddenly credible—seduction of Robert Ferrars, who after all deserved no better, and for Lucy's abandonment of Edward, whom Lucy knew to wish just that, and for her conquest of Mrs. Ferrars, who deserved even worse. Lucy's manner of abandoning Edward and mastering Robert Ferrars and his mother is dishonest but in the circumstances not unfitting.

The truth is, we—I—experience a certain satisfaction in Lucy's success in part because it seems to us—to me—the author does the same. Of course we realize that part of the pleasure in both author and reader comes from the bad guys being done in by one of their own. Nevertheless, the gay fluency with which, in the final pages of the novel, Austen sweeps us through the string of Lucy's ignoble successes—that effectively mete out justice all round to those she touches—counterbalances, somewhat, the rich, ironic contempt for Lucy's being that permeates the same pages.

There is, too, a motive for Austen's almost secret pleasure in Lucy's success that one can glean from the case Claudia Johnson makes for Austen's animus in this novel against predatory males. I shall discuss Johnson's ideas in chapter 4, and strongly disagree with some of them. However, I think there is enough truth in her thesis that this motive can partly account for my sense that Austen finds satisfaction in Lucy's run of successes at *female* predation.

Further evidence for my reading of Lucy Steele shows itself to my eye in a document that I think manifests a subtle respect for Lucy: Lucy's letter to Edward announcing her marriage to his brother Robert. It is an impressive letter. In fact we can get a kind of gauge of the immediate effect upon Lucy of her wildly improbable success in marrying Robert by comparing this letter with the much longer, earlier one, to Elinor, at the end of chapter 38. Lucy's letter to Elinor (ch. 38:276) is slack, wordy, dishonest—although since it is filled with fiction about Edward's love, it is in that sense certainly more imaginative than the later letter, to Edward, which is honest and crisp yet comprehensive.

Without its postscript, here is the late letter from Lucy Steele to Edward Ferrars, written after Lucy has married his brother:

> Dear Sir
> Being very sure I have long lost your affections, I have thought myself at liberty to bestow my own on another, and have no doubt of being as happy with him as I once used to think I might be with you; but I scorn to accept a hand while the heart was another's. Sincerely wish you happy in your choice, and it shall not be my fault if we are not always good friends, as our near relationship now makes proper. I can safely say I owe you no ill-will, and am sure you will be too generous to do us any ill offices. Your brother has gained my affections entirely, and as we could not live without one another, we are just returned from the altar, and are now on our way to Dawlish for a few weeks, which place your dear brother has great curiosity to see, but thought I would first trouble you with these few lines, and shall always remain,
> Your sincere well-wisher, friend, and sister,
> Lucy Ferrars
> (ch. 49:354–55)

This letter strikes me as a surprisingly truthful notice of the end of an affair. She *has* long lost Edward's affection, and she has the distinction of being the first in the triangle to speak that truth within it. Surely this loss does free her to replace him without fault. Her belief in "being as happy with him as I once used to think I might be with you" is expressed with flawless precision—even the apparent redundance of "used to," added to "once," in fact lightly strikes a poignant note of reproof in recall of a habitual outlook Edward once encouraged in her, before his own emotional infidelity. (For all we know,

Lucy may really have cared for him years earlier.) As soon as she can afford to do so, because she has a replacement husband, who can question that she does indeed "scorn to accept a hand while the heart was another's"? Nor should we doubt that, in her new security, she does wish Edward well—certainly it is creditable that she expresses good wishes for him in his choice of the woman who replaced her in his affection and invites him to a friendship for which she scarcely has now a prudential need. She knows he has courted Elinor while engaged to her, so I find her being able to "safely say I owe you no ill-will" a generous expression which there is no reason to think dishonest; even if it is insincere, it is commendable civility. It may be that her use of the plural "my affections" is one of the faults of composition that embarrass Edward before Elinor; yet it is correctly applied to herself, in view of the multiplicity of objects of desire comprehended within "the establishment" Robert constitutes for her. Nor have we reason to doubt that Robert has, for the nonce, his own reasons, as Lucy has her different ones, for being unable to live without the new partner.

I am led to conclude that Austen's treatment of Lucy does illustrate her acceptance of the general effect of an upward social mobility she also found often unfortunate and unpleasant in its concrete details. Insofar as this acceptance is subtly signaled by Austen's not quite suppressed pleasure in Lucy's success, Lucy's place in the novel does contribute to the work's democratic thrust.

Although Edward Ferrars provides the emblem of an egalitarian ideal to which *Sense and Sensibility* largely only aspires, the novel's effort to embody somewhere within itself this ideal is most explicit neither in him nor in Lucy Steele but in Mrs. Jennings.

Of course the reader can discern directly from her speech the vulgarity of Mrs. Jennings. No doubt some genteel readers are put off by this. It is not, however, the readers' but the fictional protagonists' response to Mrs. Jennings that now interests me.

The two Dashwood sisters have no choice but to accept Mrs. Jennings as a social companion, despite her coarse style, because she is the guest of their sociable and kindly neighbor, landlord, and relation, Sir John Middleton. Moreover, she is his guest because she is the mother of his wife, Lady Middleton. Although no mention is ever made of the fact, it is evident upon young Lady Middleton's entrance that this daughter of Mrs. Jennings has raised her rank more than one level from the vulgarity of her mother and the "low way" in which her father had "got all his money." She is not only the wife of a baronet: her appearance and her manners show such "elegance" that the Dash-woods quickly perceive her as "well-bred" (ch. 6:63). Mrs. Jennings's second daughter, Charlotte Palmer, is the wife of a young landowner who is running for Parliament. Mrs. Jennings is, therefore, socially accepted by the Dashwoods not only from neighborliness but also from their respect for how far her daughters, by marriage and in Lady Middleton's case by the personal discipline sustaining her elegance, have improved their position in the world.

But to accept Mrs. Jennings during superficial meetings at the Middletons does not commit one to respecting her as an equal or admitting her to the intimacy of friendship. At the start of their acquaintance those further steps in acceptance would be unimaginable to the two sisters. Marianne, because of her fastidious elitism and impatient openness, was invariably disgusted by Mrs. Jennings's manners and often found it hard, even when urged by Elinor, "to behave with tolerable politeness" toward her (ch. 25:173). Nevertheless, anxious to be in London where she can see Willoughby, Marianne is eager to discount her own contempt for Mrs. Jennings and accept the older woman's invitation to visit her in London. Although the language of Elinor's early dismay with Mrs. Jennings is more restrained than Marianne's and her conduct more considerate, Elinor's early attitude is congruent with Marianne's. Here is Elinor's reason for opposing a stay with Mrs. Jennings in London: "My objection is this; though I think very well of Mrs. Jennings' heart, she is not a woman whose society can afford us pleasure, or whose protection will give us consequence" (ch. 25:172–73).

Even after the sisters have stayed for some time with Mrs. Jennings in London, and the latter has (ineptly) responded with sympathy to Marianne's distress over Willoughby's betrayal, the class barrier (effectively a difference of culture) renders Marianne incapable of perceiving Mrs. Jennings's kindness as genuine: "No, no, no, it cannot be," she cried: "she cannot feel. Her kindness is not sympathy; her good nature is not tenderness. All that she wants is gossip, and she only likes me now because I supply it" (ch. 31:211). Would Marianne have felt quite so sure of this if she had heard Mrs. Jennings speaking the following to Elinor about Willoughby, after his ugly rebuff to Marianne? "Aye, it is but too true. He is to be married very soon—a good-for-nothing fellow! I have no patience with him. . . . and I wish with all my soul his wife may plague his heart out. And so I shall always say, my dear, you may depend on it. I have no notion of men's going on in this way: and if ever I meet him again, I will give him such a dressing as he has not had this many a day" (ch. 30:203). This is— or should be—refreshing talk for the reader; but the sympathy with Marianne it shows is too coarse to be welcomed by Marianne.

When Marianne surprises Elinor and decides, despite her grief over Willoughby's brutality, to come downstairs and eat with the others, Jane Austen produces one of her rare metaphors—or is it only a near metaphor?—to describe Mrs. Jennings's comical efforts to make Marianne feel better, efforts Marianne can only find irresponsibly insensitive: "She treated her . . . with all the indulgent fondness of a parent towards a favorite child on the last day of its holidays. Marianne was to have the best place by the fire, was to be tempted to eat by every delicacy in the house, and to be amused by the relation of all the news of the day" (ch. 30:204).

Speaking to Elinor of Willoughby's money troubles—"they say he is all to pieces"—which explained his marrying a rich woman, Mrs. Jennings sees a simple answer that could only have exasperated Marianne if she had heard it, yet it manages to endear the older woman to the reader: "Why don't he, in such a case, sell his horses, let his house, turn off his servants, and make a thorough reform at once? I warrant you, Miss Marianne would have been ready to wait till matters came round" (ch. 30:205).

Sometimes Mrs. Jennings realizes her gaucherie, but too late to improve Marianne's attitude toward her. To Elinor she remarks: "And so the letter that came today finished it! Poor soul! I am sure if I had had a notion of it, I would not have joked about it for all my money" (ch. 30:206). I know of no use by Austen of the vulgar vernacular quite so startling and expressive as Mrs. Jennings' "for all my money."

Although the reader's detachment is of course unavailable to the sisters, Elinor as a guest of Mrs. Jennings nonetheless could wish Marianne had more tolerance for the older woman's deficiencies. She recognizes the injustice of Marianne's charges against Mrs. Jennings, and she ascribes it to "the too great importance placed by her on the delicacies of a strong sensibility, and the graces of a polished manner" (ch. 31:211).

But we do not yet know how much Elinor herself is willing to subtract (if anything) from *her* earlier valuation of a polished manner, when she opposed the sisters' visit to Mrs. Jennings. Some dozen chapters and almost a hundred pages after that demurer, we discover Elinor's change of heart toward Mrs. Jennings—and perhaps it is only then that some of us readers are ready to join Elinor in relinquishing our own snobbery. The decisive moment occurs when it becomes evident Marianne is seriously ill, and the attendant apothecary

> by pronouncing her disorder to have a putrid tendency, and allowing the word "infection" to pass his lips, gave instant alarm to Mrs Palmer, on her baby's account. . . . She set off, with her little boy and his nurse, for the house of a near relation of Mr Palmer's. . . . Mrs Jennings, however, with a kindness which made Elinor really love her, declared her resolution of not stirring from Cleveland as long as Marianne remained ill, and of endeavoring, by her own attentive care, to supply to her the place of the mother she had taken her from; and Elinor found her, on every occasion, a most willing and active helpmate, desirous to share in all her fatigues, and often by her better experience in nursing, of material use. (ch. 43:303–4)

Lest there be any doubt of Austen's point, we find that Marianne's moral reform, after her health has improved and as she is leaving Mrs. Jennings, manifests itself by her now fully acknowledging Mrs. Jennings's equality with herself:

and Marianne, after taking so particular and lengthened a
leave of Mrs Jennings, one so earnestly grateful, so full of respect and kind wishes as seemed due to her own heart from
a secret acknowledgment of past inattention . . . was carefully
assisted . . . into the carriage . . . and the others were left by
themselves . . . till Mrs Jennings was summoned to her chaise
to take comfort in the gossip of her maid for the loss of her
two young companions. (ch. 46:333)

Although for the genteel Mrs. Dashwood the servant Thomas is like a
tablecloth, the ungenteel Mrs. Jennings is the social equal of her maid,
at least for the moment; yet Mrs. Jennings becomes the respected and
loved, intimate friend of the elegant sisters. Given Jane Austen's concern for her own public status as a lady *even though* an author—an au-
thorship first identified, on this her first published novel's title-page,
merely as "BY A LADY"—she could not make a stronger affirmation
than this that honest warmth of feeling and unselfish kindliness deserve a more cordial respect than the diction and decorum that entitle
a woman to be called a lady.

3

Elinor's Emotions

I N AN INTRODUCTION to *Sense and Sensibility*, the novelist Stella Gibbons expresses a reaction to Elinor Dashwood that some readers have shared: "Elinor, not to mince words, is what some have forthrightly called a stick, and she bears those faint traces of having been worked *at* and *over* which . . . make a character unsympathetic to the general reader."[1] Although I probably had a similar impression of Elinor's personality in my earliest reading of the book—I was in high school—my readers will by now know I sharply disagree with Gibbons. Even as to Elinor's creation, I suspect she flowed as freely from Austen's pen as any heroine ever did. About this we can't know the truth, but about Elinor herself we can hope the truth is accessible.

The masculine shape of the stick image Gibbons uses for Elinor cannot but strike a reader interested in Austen's fictional reconstruction of gender. Alleged "stick-ness" in a fictional life pertains especially to the emotional quality of that life. One supposes that the emotional life of Elinor is perceived to be somehow masculine—or at the least, is felt to be inappropriate for the heroine of a romantic comedy. We have had occasion already, in considering Elinor's habits as an intellectual, to notice some sources—and some correctives—for this view. It will nonetheless be worthwhile to make a more focused inspection of Austen's ways of rendering her heroine's emotional life. It may be that her intention to make of Elinor an argument against patriarchy's agenda for women helped form the conception of emotion that Austen deployed in creating Elinor.

Although in the novel's first chapter we are told that "her feelings were strong" (ch. 1:42), the first full rendering of intense feeling in Elinor does not occur until chapter 29, when she responds to Marianne's shock from Willoughby's brutal letter. Moreover, whatever we are merely *told* about Elinor's feelings in the first half of the novel, it may seem to us that when her situation warrants strong emotion, Elinor is not *shown* to us feeling it. Hence our idea of Elinor as emotionally cool may have become so fixed by the midpoint of the novel that a single rendered instance of her sisterly empathy does not convert us. In our reading experience, Elinor's hearing from Lucy of her engagement to Edward may be a critical moment. With abstract language Austen writes that on this occasion Elinor "concealed [from Lucy] an emotion and distress beyond any thing she had ever felt before" (ch. 22:156). Reporting it both abstractly ("an emotion"), and *as* concealed from Lucy, tends also to keep from readers' view the emotion as *felt*. Even when Elinor finds herself alone, and pride before Lucy imposes no constraint, the author does not render for us an intense emotion in Elinor: rather, paragraph after paragraph describes the interior life of Elinor as occupied at this moment with analyzing the situation. Embedded in Austen's extended rendering of Elinor's analytical thinking, and therefore overshadowed by all this thinking, is, to be sure, the narrator's statement that Elinor "wept for him, more than for herself." This simple assertion has the look of a conventional but nonliteral remark—does the narrator *quite* mean to say Elinor really *wept?* Moreover, the statement loses force from its lack of plausibility: we do not, at the behest of a mere declaration from the author, fully believe in so much selflessness of feeling just after Elinor has suffered so lethal a blow to her hopes.

Something interior *is* rendered here by the author. Austen depicts in full for us Elinor's inwardly working out her analysis of the Lucy-Edward-Elinor triangle. As we shall see, thoughts appear as important elements in Elinor's emotions when the latter are rendered by Austen. But here she gives us not emotionally expressive thoughts suited to provide content for an emotion and thus to render it for readers but merely discursive thought. The emotion itself is not shown; its existence is simply declared.

A few pages later Austen does nonetheless go to much trouble to put in front of us a complex but indirect manifestation of that emotion. This takes the form of the closest thing to misconduct by Elinor we are ever shown. And I think we have evidence, again from the novelist Stella Gibbons, that it is easy for a reader to fail to understand that Elinor's ugly behavior here evinces her emotional shock from Lucy's revelation.

In chapter 24—devoted to a "dueling scene" between Elinor and Lucy—we see an indirect manifestation of Elinor's distress from the discovery of her loss of Edward. But *as* manifestation of painful emotion, Elinor's action is indirect indeed: Elinor's suffering, as underlying her conduct, is for readers an abstraction they must posit in order to explain Elinor's dishonesty and nastiness with Lucy. However, not every reader makes the needed postulation. Stella Gibbons expresses *her* sense of the failure of Austen's handling of Elinor in chapter 24:

> When we read how anxious [Elinor] is to learn all that she can about this engagement [between Lucy and Edward], we are shocked: at least, I am. Her attitude seems vulgar as Lucy's own. . . . In the passages describing Elinor's motives there is an elaboration and a *fine-spunness* which may convince the intellect but does not convince the feelings, and I believe the fact is that in the scene between the two girls Jane Austen's sense of comedy for once got a little out of hand. . . . For once the vulgarity, and the pain given to the finer spirit even while it contrived and planned, did not strike her as did the tart, lemony flavour of the situation.[2]

I need not share Gibbons's other impressions to agree that it is something of a shock to observe Elinor in this chapter: it is her sharpest moral descent. However, from the point of view of Austen's artistic concern for a realistic portrait of a subject who tends toward idealization, this descent is well motivated.

What bothers Gibbons is not so much Austen's as Elinor's motivation. I think there too Austen is on solid ground. But it will take some analytical effort to satisfy ourselves that "the passages describing Elinor's motives" do not succumb to "an elaboration and a *finespunness*" that show Austen losing control of her material. As always with Austen, and I shall say more of this presently, it is essential in reading her exposition of a character's emotion on an occasion to be fully conscious of how the particular occasion has gained its meaning for the character.

It is in the preceding chapter 23 that Elinor's motivation—a complex desire—for seeking out Lucy is put before us. The explanation of why she has this desire to seek out Lucy is provided by the shock Elinor gets a little earlier, in chapter 22: she discovers that a woman whom she has observed to be not only "ignorant and illiterate" but lacking in "delicacy . . . rectitude, and integrity of mind" has *for four years* been engaged to marry Edward Ferrars! (ch. 22:149).

For months Elinor has been and now remains confident that it is herself Edward loves: "Had Edward been intentionally deceiving her? . . . No. . . . His affection was all her own. She could not be deceived in that" (ch. 23:157). And of course, rereading, we know from Edward's behavior the moment he is released from his engagement, near the end of the novel, that Elinor is right.

We shall therefore accept as intense the emotional shock Elinor suffers from Lucy's revelation, *provided,* first, that we believe Elinor is equally attached to Edward, and, second, if Austen, by *some* means, *shows* us Elinor deeply affected by Lucy's revelation. The author is quite precise in *telling* how serious the loss is: "When she joined them at dinner only two hours after she had first suffered the extinction of all her dearest hopes . . . Elinor was mourning in secret over obstacles which must divide her for ever from the object of her love" (ch. 23:158). Obviously this also tells us she loves Edward. And two pages earlier, volume 1 (as the book was originally printed) ended with Elinor concealing her shocked mortification at learning from Lucy that the ring Edward wore contained Lucy's hair rather than her own. Lucy asks:

> "Perhaps you might notice the ring when you saw him?"
> "I did," said Elinor, with a composure of voice, under which was concealed an emotion and distress beyond any thing she had ever felt before. She was mortified, shocked, confounded. . . .
> The Miss Steeles returned to the Park, and Elinor was then at liberty to think and be wretched. (ch. 22:156)

Careful readers, motivated to look, will have satisfied themselves that cumulatively through the entire novel Austen does *show* us that Elinor loves Edward. (I offer more evidence later in this chapter.) Our concern at the moment is with how Austen at this point in the novel undertakes to exhibit for us—without ever *directly* showing us—what she explicitly has merely told us: that Elinor is deeply affected by discovering that (apparently) she has lost Edward.

For the most part, the passages following her shock impress us more with Elinor's power to rebound than with the depth of her emotion. Yet the author has insisted upon that depth; so she has a literary duty to show it. But in making manifest the intensity of Elinor's emotional shock Austen has a right to expect us to accept what she has insisted upon—the intense emotional shock—as *behind* the manifestation, thus as explaining the latter. We must be prepared to see the manifestation of Elinor's shock *as* that, prepared, in short, to see Elinor's desire for revenge as an upshot of her emotional hurt. The first such manifestation is that very motivation in Elinor to speak again with Lucy that Stella Gibbons found too "fine-spun": it is not so, if we understand that it arises from the blow Elinor's passionate being has suffered. Here we encounter a technique Austen uses again and again with the consummately controlled Elinor—but also often with the heroines of her other novels: she demonstrates an emotion through its indirect effects. The hurt from Lucy's revelation shows itself in Elinor's desire to do battle with Lucy; this desire shows itself tentatively by Elinor's first engaging Lucy for conversation, and then decisively in Elinor's conversational assaults upon Lucy.

Several elements in Elinor's makeup limit the *direct* manifestation of her emotional shock immediately upon hearing of Edward's engagement. Both her intellectual and her moral disposition as well as her love for Edward and her observations of Lucy—and her personal pride—ensure that she shall quickly attempt to conceal from Lucy her own pain, turn to analysis, clear Edward of blame, condemn Lucy yet affirm Lucy's right to Edward, set herself upon a course of honorable withdrawal from romantic connection with Edward, and hide from her family both the new facts and her distress. If despite so much self-constraint, arising mostly from her best self, Elinor is nonetheless deeply distressed and powerfully disturbed by Lucy's revelation, what way is open for this distress and disturbance to express itself? Its sources are disappointment of affection, crushing of hopes, frustration of desire, death of joy. Rereading the novel one remembers a moment from three chapters further on. Leaving for London, Elinor "could not witness the rapture of delightful expectation which filled the whole soul and beamed in the eyes of Marianne, without feeling how blank was her own prospect, how cheerless her own state of mind in the comparison" (ch. 26:175). There is also hurt pride. Upon rereading the Elinor-Lucy encounter, one is reminded of Elinor's later appeal to Marianne at *her* moment of deepest suffering from Willoughby's rejection: "It is reasonable and laudable pride which resists such malevolence" (ch. 29:201). It is not in Elinor's nature to feel, on her own behalf, what Marianne expresses in her reply: "No, no . . . misery such as mine has no pride." In Elinor, pride, like the sense of honor, works as strongly as it does in Fitzwilliam Darcy.

Suffering from such sources of distress at Lucy's hands yet working under morally compelling constraints, Elinor can find vent for her pain only by seeking to reengage Lucy, but now in a verbal battle. It is entirely plausible that she does, as the narrator explains, need to make quite sure "whether there were any sincerity in [Lucy's] declarations of tender regard for" Edward. Equally intelligible is her desire to convince Lucy of the truth of these lies: that "she was no otherwise interested in [Lucy's engagement to Edward] than as a friend" and "that her heart was unwounded" (ch. 23:159–60). One effective contribution to the realism in this novel's portrait of Elinor is Austen's thrusting her into a battle to which Elinor comes with so much contempt for her opponent, so much suppressed passion, and so much determination to lie about important matters that an able reader cannot fail to be struck by the degrading effect upon Elinor of the shock she has suffered from Lucy's revelation.

Of course the blackness of the comedy here comes from Lucy as well as from Elinor. Every rereader of the novel, at least, will easily observe that Lucy is not only dishonest; in this encounter she is bent on causing as much pain to Elinor as is consistent with keeping her words polite.

No less obvious, though startling, is the fact that not only is Elinor every bit as dishonest and aggressive as Lucy in aiming her own share of blows with the intention of hurting her "fair rival" (ch. 23:162); Elinor also deceives herself about the extent and character of her own falsehood. I count six blatant lies by Elinor. The last two of these are packed into a single sentence of Elinor's and are directly preceded by the narrator's comment that "Elinor blushed for the insincerity of Edward's future wife." So much for Elinor's self-honesty on this occasion! These two lies are so evidently insincere that she knows Lucy will recognize them as such and find them offensive. She refuses Lucy's invitation to detach her from Edward thus: "The power of dividing two people so tenderly attached is too much for an indifferent person" (ch. 24:167). We know from her thoughts eight paragraphs later that by the time she says this she knows not only that Lucy does not love Edward but also that Lucy believes Edward does not love her. Elinor's reflections on Lucy's jealousy of her, in the previous chapter, show us that Elinor is sure Lucy knows Elinor is *not* "an indifferent person" (ch. 23:159–60). Although Lucy, by baiting Elinor, provoked Elinor to land her blow, it is Elinor who has twice before baited Lucy with ironic references to Edward's and Lucy's "mutual affection" or "reciprocal attachment" (ch. 24:164, 165).

Because the hostile intent of Elinor's last, double-barreled blast is so obvious, Lucy comes close to disrupting the phony peace between them, when, "with some pique" and "laying a particular stress on" Elinor's self-description as "an indifferent person," Lucy replies that "if you could be supposed to be biased in any respect by your own feelings, your opinion would not be worth having" (ch. 24:167–68). Indeed, Elinor's private acknowledgment of her part in this battle is made explicit by the author, who, directly after Lucy's "pique," brings the battle scene to a close thus: "Elinor thought it wisest to make no answer to this, lest they might provoke each other to an unsuitable increase of ease and unreserve" (ch. 24:168). Austen has Elinor acknowledge her own aggression, but not her own "insincerity." And the narrator virtually affirms a surprising moral equivalence between the two rivals, so far as *this* nasty encounter goes, when she declares that "nothing had been said on either side, to make them dislike each other less than they had done before" (ch. 24:168).

The meaning of our experience as readers of this battle transcends our discerning the depth of Elinor's emotion, perceiving her moral weakness, and recognizing both of these as reactions to a personal loss. Much mental energy and more than the usual concentration of mind is needed by both duelists in order to give and to receive so much verbal attack without provoking or suffering "an unsuitable increase of ease and unreserve." Behind the intensity of energy in both is their shared awareness that their livelihoods are at stake. Their situation is for these two young women not unlike a young man's who is seeking an opening in a profession: he may care for the profession he has chosen to pursue; but often he cares even more that he should find a place and a means of supporting himself in *a* profession. For both Lucy and Elinor the only vocation, livelihood, and position in the world that is both available and acceptable to them is marriage. Neither can be sure how many chances she will have. One has Edward's pledge, the other his love. Both cannot win. And the loser may lose all. They are rivals indeed, competitors for an establishment in the world, but linked by the chains of female indenture. In the reader there may be evoked from this combat the surprised emotion of emergent compassion for two strong women of opposed moral quality who are yet joined in a common pathos. A darkness of the era is intensely present in the scene.

As I began by remarking, Elinor's emotions are never directly rendered for us in any part of this extended yet oblique manifestation of the distress she suffers from Lucy's revelations. Where *do* we find Elinor's emotions made directly present to us?

A fictional person's emotion can be made vividly present for readers by direct description of her conscious experience, or by describing her bodily disturbances, or her overt reactions and expressive behavior, or by describing disruptions of her behavior, or by giving us utterances that are either specific to that emotion or in the situation precisely expressive of it. Or an author may use all these and still other devices.

I find that in *Sense and Sensibility* the direct presentation to the reader of intensely felt emotion in Elinor Dashwood does not begin until Elinor's love for her sister confronts a crisis of devastating pain for Marianne.

In recounting to Elinor how she condemned herself during and after her serious illness, Marianne's most pointed self-accusation reads thus: "Had I died,—it would have been self destruction. . . . Had I died,—in what peculiar misery should I have left you, my nurse, my friend, my sister!" (ch. 46:337). At the thought of her own possible death from a kind of self-indulgence, nothing gives Marianne more pain than the thought of the injury it would have inflicted upon Elinor, her sister, her friend, her nurse. No reader could miss the fact that not only is Elinor a caring sister, she is a devoted one. It is also manifest that Marianne loves Elinor. If something less than manifest, it is nonetheless true that, within the limits set by opposed temperaments, the two sisters are in fact the sort of dear friends who are also intellectual comrades.

In the light of Jane Austen's biography, the salience of sisterly attachment in this her first morally ambitious novel, as also in her second (Jane and Elizabeth Bennet in *Pride and Prejudice*), should not surprise us. At her birth Jane's father wrote to a relative, "We have now another girl, a present plaything for her sister Cassy and a future companion." The companionship of the only two girls among eight siblings would be deeper and its future longer than the father could have imagined. Jane, three years younger than her sister, was sent off to boarding school at the early age of six because, according to her mother, "if Cassandra was going to have her head cut off, Jane would insist on sharing her fate." Even the extant letters Jane Austen wrote to her older sister—those that Cassandra felt comfortable preserving—suggest the depth of the sisters' friendship. Throughout Jane's forty-one and a half years of life, whenever she and Cassandra were at home in either Steventon or Chawton, they shared the same bedroom. Jane died with her head resting on a pillow in Cassandra's lap. Writing to Jane's favorite niece immediately after her sister's death, Cassandra Austen expressed her loss in this way: "Tho' I was then hopeless of a recovery I had no suspicion how rapidly my loss was approaching.—I *have* lost a treasure, such a sister, such a friend as never can have been surpassed,—She was the sun of my life, the gilder of every pleasure, the soother of every sorrow, I had not a thought concealed from her, & it is as if I had lost a part of myself" (*L,* 344). One cannot doubt that this lifelong sisterly bond served as a model for aspects of the tie between Elinor and Marianne.

That Austen can make vivid for us the immediate presence on a specific occasion of not merely the interior quality of thought but the content of an emotion, as well, is demonstrated in all of her novels and, closer to hand, in Elinor's feeling response to occasions of *Marianne's* suffering. In turning to Elinor suffering from Marianne's distress, we need to remark another reason, besides an Elinor-distorting habit we readers may have developed by chapter 29, for our failing to feel the full force of Elinor's intense emotion when at last it is directly presented to us. We fail in our reading because in the foreground of this portrait of pain Marianne looms so large: Marianne's situation here naturally preempts our empathic attention. Austen has made Elinor's emotion the figure we need to search out in the carpet. Let us trace its shape on Marianne's morning of despair.

It is the day after Willoughby at a London party has rebuffed Marianne with lacerating cruelty. The site is Mrs. Jennings's house.

"Before the house-maid had lit their fire the next day, or the sun gained any power over a cold gloomy morning in January," Elinor has been awakened in the sisters' bedroom by Marianne's sobs as she writes to Willoughby, "kneeling against one of the window-seats for the sake of all the little light she could command from it" (ch. 29:193). From what Elinor had witnessed at the party the night before, when she had been "robbed of all presence of mind . . . and [made] unable to say a word" by Willoughby's astonishing behavior to Marianne, she knew that any response Marianne might get from her letter to Willoughby would mean "an immediate and irreconcilable rupture with him" (ch. 28: 190, 192). So Elinor knows Willoughby has replied when, later that morning, as she, Marianne, and Mrs. Jennings are "just setting themselves . . . round the common working table," a servant brings to Marianne a letter the handwriting on which causes Marianne's complexion to turn to "a death-like paleness," and Marianne then runs from the room. Consistently with the proportions Austen is allotting to the figures of the two sisters in this portrait of suffering, on the first reading we experience Elinor's immediate reaction as a mere sign of what to expect for Marianne. But we can also appreciate Elinor's emotion as a matter of interest to the reader seeking to understand Austen's intention for her: "Elinor . . . felt immediately such a sickness at heart as made her hardly able to hold up her head, and sat in such a general tremor as made her fear it impossible to escape Mrs Jennings's notice" (ch. 29:194). Although what follows about Mrs. Jennings quickly diverts our attention, it contains nothing that negates this statement about Elinor, which, therefore, when isolated for attention, vividly expresses an important emotional truth about her: Elinor is deeply moved by the anticipation of Marianne's acute, justified distress. For a few minutes Elinor keeps up appearances by conversing with Mrs. Jennings. Then Elinor, "eager, at all events, to know what Willoughby had written, hurried away to their room."

Before recalling Elinor's next moments, let us refresh our memory of the letter from Willoughby that Marianne has just read—surely as brutal as any in English fiction, "a letter of which every line was an insult," as Elinor will quickly find:

Bond Street, January.
My Dear Madam,
    I have just had the honour of receiving your letter, for
which I beg to return my sincere acknowledgments. I am
much concerned to find there was anything in my behaviour
last night that did not meet your approbation; and though I
am quite at a loss to discover in what point I could be so unfortunate as to offend you, I entreat your forgiveness of what
I can assure you to have been perfectly unintentional. I shall
never reflect on my former acquaintance with your family in
Devonshire without the most grateful pleasure, and flatter
myself it will not be broken by any mistake or misapprehen-
sion of my actions. My esteem for your whole family is very
sincere; but if I have been so unfortunate as to give rise to a
belief of more than I felt, or meant to express, I shall reproach
myself for not having been more guarded in my professions
of that esteem. That I should ever have meant more, you will
allow to be impossible, when you understand that my affections have been long engaged elsewhere, and it will not be
many weeks, I believe, before this engagement is fulfilled. It
is with great regret that I obey your commands of returning
the letters, with which I have been honoured from you, and
the lock of hair, which you so obligingly bestowed upon me.
I am, dear Madam,
    your most obedient
        humble Servant,
            John Willoughby
(ch. 29:195–96)

It is in order to read this letter in private that Marianne has just returned to her room, where, on opening the door, Elinor

> saw Marianne stretched on the bed, almost choked by grief,
> one letter in her hand, and two or three others lying by her.
> Elinor drew near, but without saying a word; and seating
> herself on the bed, took her hand, kissed her affectionately

several times, and then gave way to a burst of tears, which at first was scarcely less violent than Marianne's. The latter, though unable to speak, seemed to feel all the tenderness of this behavior; and after some time thus spent in joint affliction, she put all the letters into Elinor's hands; and then covering her face with her handkerchief, almost screamed with agony. (ch. 29:195)

Before fully attending to every emotion that is rendered for them at this midpoint of the novel, readers might well have believed, like Marianne when lamenting Elinor's self-control in the face of some inexplicable behavior of Edward's, that her sister's affections were "calm" (ch. 19:129). After this moment neither Marianne nor the careful reader can sustain this errant belief. It may, however, occur to us, upon reflection on this moment, that Elinor will intensely feel an emotion only when doing so is the *only* way she can love someone she dearly loves. Her tender gestures—sitting down on the bed, taking Marianne's hand, "kissing her affectionately several times"—all are, in this awful moment, useless. Elinor feels this, and she feels that now, for this moment, her sister is not overreacting: it is the world in all its brutality (embodied in Willoughby) that has turned on her beloved sister and struck her down. Under this pressure Elinor does the only thing that can matter to Marianne: she takes upon herself Marianne's own grief and bursts into the same tears. Only then can Marianne "feel all the tenderness" in Elinor's response to her agony.

It takes nothing away from the spontaneity of Elinor's emotion to say that she felt exactly what it was necessary to feel exactly when it was necessary to feel it if she was to love Marianne as wholeheartedly as she knew she did. Nevertheless, what I have here made explicit for myself, in a way it was not when I was merely reading these pages, does, I think, show how deeply Elinor's *rationality* is imprinted in the mind of her author. For Elinor, the possibility of intensely felt—and expressed—emotion depends upon her reason having worked, quickly, and as if by reflex and without conscious effort, to appraise Marianne's young-womanly situation as objectively desperate and Elinor's customary motions of concern as useless. Although this aspect of the moment does not explicitly present itself to us when reading through it, our own subconscious reception of Elinor's full portrait registers for us how so rarely rendered, intensely felt an emotional expression of Elinor coheres, in its peculiar conditions, with her rationality.

This precisely constructed coherence in emotional rationality for Elinor is, I think, yet another bit of Austen's almost-concealed reforming work. It is the masculine gender that is authorized to embody such perfect rationality in its emotional life: even the manliest of men and most self-possessed of gentlemen is allowed tears, but only, as it were, when he bends over some mere youth of a comrade-in-arms struck down on a battlefield.

I will go a step farther. One reason Elinor's emotion in response to Marianne is overlooked—is indeed relatively invisible—is an effect of this rationality in Elinor's emotional life. It is partly because her emotion is in such exact correspondence with a reality outside of her, Marianne's anguish, that Elinor's pain is lost to sight for the reader by the more compelling quality of Marianne's despair. This somewhat resembles the situation of one of the most "masculine" of vocations: the scientist is conceived to be masked from our sight by the reality his thought is merely reflecting, so that his readers are expected to perceive only the external reality he reflects, not the physically imaginative intellect of the scientist who reflects it.

Through twelve more chapters and until 80 percent of the story is behind us, this depiction of Elinor's sympathetic suffering in chapter 29 stands alone in the book as truly rendering for us a strong emotion in Elinor. Chapter 43, in which Marianne's illness becomes serious and appears life-threatening, begins a sequence of eight concluding chapters that move forward with as much intensity, suspense, swiftness, and emotional power as any segment of similar length does anywhere in Austen's fiction. For the present our concern will be with chapter 43 itself, in which Elinor confronts Marianne's apparent brush with death. No more concretely and vividly rendered passion is to be found in Austen's fiction than Elinor's fearing for Marianne's death and wanting her survival. Nowhere in Austen's fiction is an emotion presented as more intensely felt than this one of Elinor's, directed toward her endangered sister. And—despite the exceptional moment in chapter 29—it is perhaps not until this very late chapter's presentation of Elinor that we are entitled to be convinced she is a passionate woman.

Two questions press themselves upon us: first, why is it that in fact—as Stella Gibbons's calling Elinor "a stick" proves—when Elinor's passionate side becomes manifest, even attentive readers can fail to discover it? I'll return to this question after looking more closely at some peculiarities in Elinor's way of feeling intense emotion. The answer to a second question will help us think about the first one: why is conclusive proof of Elinor's passionate nature withheld by the author until a mere 20 percent of the story remains to be told?

The deeply felt emotions of a normally socialized human being are, in general, richly imbued with thought that figures as a defining ingredient of the emotions. For example, consider how much thought must be ingredient in the indignation Elizabeth Bennet feels toward Darcy on account of his insulting mode of address in proposing marriage to her (*PP*, ch. 34: 220–25). Both ethical principle—present as sophisticated thought—and rules of decorum—also present as ideas—must be present to her mind, as partly *constituting* her indignation at their violation: without those ideas present to her, it could not *be* indignation she *feels*. Those ideas, together with many memory-ideas about details of the intersections of hers and Darcy's lives, provide much of her emotion's very content. They determine *what* it is she feels (though not *how* or how *much* she feels what she does feel). No one who is unaware, first of the customs of the embedding society, and second of the history of interactions and interconnection between Darcy and Elizabeth, could grasp the thoughts that constitute so much of the inner content of Elizabeth's feeling of indignation over Darcy's manner of proposing to her. Nor, of course—and decisive in narrative strategy for developing the kind of emotion that interests Jane Austen—nor could the rich content itself of that emotion even exist without that history. Since it took half the book to develop a history this rich, it took this long for all the ideas ingredient in Elizabeth's uniquely constituted, indignant emotion to become present within her, hence for precisely *this* emotion to be possible for her. Therefore,

the literary matter needed to render Elizabeth's complex emotion required half a novel to develop. Arguably, this moment of Darcy's marriage proposal halfway through *Pride and Prejudice* is the first occasion of Austen's truly rendering an intensely felt emotion of Elizabeth
Bennet.

So much delay of intense emotion is not unusual in Austen's
fiction. The first occasion of Elizabeth Bennet's being rendered as feeling the beginnings of love for Darcy—and, I will add, the first time I
personally am moved by Elizabeth's being moved—comes in chapters 43 and 44, when she and the Gardiners unexpectedly encounter
Darcy at his estate, Pemberley. And Emma in the novel named for her
is notorious for the late occurrence of her first feeling romantic love—
page 398 in a 465-page novel, with only 14 percent of the story left to
be told. *Mansfield Park* is a more complex case, but I think something
similar could be argued for it. If we put Marianne Dashwood aside as
a special case of a secondary heroine serving as foil to the primary one,
then only *Persuasion* among Austen's morally ambitious novels is a
clear exception to the rule of late introduction of fully rendered, intense emotion in an adult heroine.

A skeptically inclined reader may insist that all we learn for sure
about her emotions from Elizabeth Bennet's trip to Pemberley and its
neighborhood is that (besides embarrassment) she feels gratitude—
for Darcy's still loving her in spite of all. Let it be so. Then consider
how much *thought,* how much recalled history, goes into *this* emotion
fitted to *that* occasion! Two thirds of the book is needed to make it
possible. (And of course it is the beginning of love.)

I think what is involved here is important for understanding the
place of emotion, even of passion, in Austen's fiction, an understanding not perhaps figuring as one of the notable achievements in Austen
criticism. More than that, its mastery is needed for exactly appreciating the way reason invests the emotional life of Austenian heroines,
and through that insight, understanding a subtly hidden aspect of her
work at re-forming our ideas of the feminine. For perspective we need
at hand an opposing tendency. It will help if the reader will indulge me
by remarking a brief contrast I want to make with the fiction of D. H.
Lawrence. For that purpose nothing works better than the first novel
in which Lawrence's peculiar achievement is fully realized, *The Rain-*

bow, which may, as to first full flowering of genius, fairly be compared to Austen's *Pride And Prejudice.*

With 96 percent of the story yet to be told—after only twenty-one pages—one of the novel's protagonists, Tom Brangwen, encounters for the first time the Polish woman he will soon marry. He merely passes her on a road in the English countryside, he walking beside his horse and wagon, she walking alone in the opposite direction. Each is unknown to the other. Yet for Brangwen the powerful emotional connection that will last his lifetime is formed at this moment. All readers of both novelists will, upon reflection, understand why this can happen in Lawrence but not in Austen: in brief, it is because Austen requires of true lovers—and Lawrence does not require—that they shall have gained through their acquaintance with each other rather difficult knowledge of both their own and the other's *character,* knowledge that is attainable only over time and within complexly structured social networks of relationship and interaction. Because some implications of this understanding we all have of a difference between Austen and Lawrence are not so widely understood, it will be useful to look at the passage in *The Rainbow* I have in mind:

> When he was twenty-eight, a thick-limbed, stiff, fair man with fresh complexion, and blue eyes staring very straight ahead, he was coming one day down from Cossethay with a load of seed out of Nottingham. . . . He stared fixedly before him, watchful yet absorbed, seeing everything and aware of nothing, coiled in himself. . . .
>
> He walked steadily beside the horse, the load clanked behind as the hill descended steeper. . . .
>
> Slowly turning the curve at the steepest part of the slope, his horse britching between the shafts, he saw a woman approaching. . . .
>
> Then he turned to look at her. She was dressed in black, was apparently rather small and slight, beneath her long black cloak, and she wore a black bonnet. She walked hastily, as if unseeing, her head rather forward. It was her curious, absorbed, flitting motion, as if she were passing unseen by everybody, that first arrested him.

She had heard the cart, and looked up. Her face was pale and clear, she had thick dark eyebrows and a wide mouth, curiously held. He saw her face clearly, as if by a light in the air. He saw her face so distinctly, that he ceased to coil on himself, and was suspended.

"That's her," he said involuntarily. As the cart passed by, splashing through the thin mud, she stood back against the bank. Then, as he walked still beside his britching horse, his eyes met hers. He looked quickly away, pressing back his head, a pain of joy running through him. He could not bear to think of anything.

He turned around at the last moment. He saw her bonnet, her shape in the black cloak, the movement as she walked. Then she was gone round the bend.

She had passed by. He felt as if he were walking again in a far world, not Cossethay, a far world, the fragile reality. He went on, quiet, suspended, rarefied. He could not bear to think or to speak, nor make any sound or sign, nor change his fixed motion. He could scarcely bear to think of her face. He moved within the knowledge of her, in the world that was beyond reality.[3]

This passage renders for us, as exactly as such phenomena ever are rendered in words, the content of Tom Brangwen's intense emotion. It is noteworthy that the emotion is nearly devoid of thought. Its mental content, if you will, is a sensory object (the woman) and an experientially transformed ambient world, a changed sense of reality, of the substantial and the fragile, of the merely actual and the more than real. In experiencing a strong emotion directed toward her, Brangwen's mind provides for the passing woman almost no *conceptual* context beyond "woman"—except the momentous but, as instantaneous, the vaguely empty notion, "the one for me." Although there may be in her bearing and walk some subliminal cue for him of her (former) social rank (she is an immigrant, reduced from Polish aristocrat to English servant), she is for him essentially unsituated socially, without history or character; and he and she are without relationship. His emotion is virtually unviolated by thought, her impact on him unsponsored by accumulated meanings accruing to her presence from acquaintance or even hearsay knowledge. "He could not bear to think of anything. . . . He could scarcely bear to think of her face." The intelligibility and power of this rendering of an emotion could have been roughly the same had it occurred even on pages 3 and 4 of a novel: it needed very few pages of textual preparation.

Now compare the content of Tom Brangwen's emotion with that of Elizabeth Bennet's in chapter 43 of *Pride and Prejudice*. She is visiting Pemberley in the belief Darcy is absent. She encounters first the grounds of the estate, then praise of her young employer by his veteran housekeeper, Mrs. Reynolds, then his portrait, then the man himself. The content of her emotion from this chance encounter with the man whom she had earlier harshly rejected but whom she will marry, has been prepared, not only by the preceding forty-two chapters, but also by the immediately preceding experience of Elizabeth's excursion to Pemberley:

> Elizabeth was delighted. She had never seen a place for which nature had done more, or where natural beauty had been so little counteracted by an awkward taste. . . . and at that moment she felt, that to be mistress of Pemberley might be something! . . .
>
> In the gallery there were many family portraits. . . . and she beheld a striking resemblance of Mr Darcy, with such a smile over the face, as she remembered to have sometimes seen, when he looked at her. She stood several minutes before the picture in earnest contemplation, and returned to it again before they had quitted the gallery. (*PP*, ch. 43:267, 271)

Her felt disposition toward Darcy becomes gentler from the experience of driving and walking through parts of his estate and of hearing him praised by his housekeeper:

> There was certainly at this moment, in Elizabeth's mind, a more gentle sensation towards the original, than she had ever

felt in the height of their acquaintance. The commendation bestowed on him by Mrs Reynolds was of no trifling nature. What praise is more valuable than the praise of an intelligent servant? As a brother, a landlord, a master, she considered how many people's happiness were in his guardianship!— How much of pleasure or pain it was in his power to bestow! How much of good or evil must be done by him! Every idea that had been brought forward by the housekeeper was favorable to his character, and as she stood before the canvas, on which he was represented, and fixed his eyes upon herself, she thought of his regard with a deeper sentiment of gratitude than it had ever raised before; she remembered its warmth, and softened its impropriety of expression. (*PP*, ch. 43:272)

It is important to appreciate that the ideas of Darcy that are here presented as moving through Elizabeth's mind—some represented by Austen as exclamations—partly *constitute* the very content of the "more gentle sensation towards" Darcy that Elizabeth here feels. This—by today's usage—misnamed "sensation" is actually the emotion of felt gratitude (sensation being only a component of it). She feels new gratitude for having been loved by a man whose temperament and character (and position) she only now begins to see as more worthy of admiration (and consideration) than she had imagined them to be. Her emotion—an experience of felt gratitude toward Darcy—has not only ideas and sensation as components: it has as well a behavioral component that makes her newly "gentle" in her disposition to behave "toward" Darcy; (emotions are, but sensations are not, "toward" something). This "deeper sentiment of gratitude" has a highly civilized moral content that nothing but ideas, of the kind Austen places just now in Elizabeth's mind, can carry. These ideas— of a man generously and conscientiously filling responsible roles in a network of social structures, who, what is more, has wanted to marry *her*—these ideas are the components of Elizabeth's felt emotion toward Darcy that shape *what* it is she feels: her gratitude for his having loved her. Her idea of the weight, as it were, of his proposal of marriage to her is newly minted from the impressions she gains from her new, more direct experience of his social substance and virtue. Both the active deployment of rather abstract ideas of practices and institutions central to English genteel civilization, and the more concrete memory images of a morally complex personal history, enter, literally as ingredients, into the "deeper sentiment of gratitude" she now feels toward Darcy.

Then when they meet by accident on the Pemberley grounds:

> Amazed at the alteration in his manner since they last parted, every sentence that he uttered was increasing her embarrassment; and every idea of the impropriety of her being found there, recurring to her mind, the few minutes in which they continued together, were some of the most uncomfortable in her life. . . . She was overpowered by shame and vexation. Her coming there was the most unfortunate, the most ill-judged thing in the world! How strange must it appear to him! In what a disgraceful light might it not strike so vain a man! It might seem as if she had purposely thrown herself in his way again! Oh! why did she come? (*PP*, ch. 43:273)

Here we can see, if we are willing to, that Elizabeth's thoughts are indispensable elements of the emotion of embarrassment she feels. These thoughts embrace both the personal history of Elizabeth and Darcy and certain conventions peculiar to the particular civilization this man and woman share.

Finally, after enjoying further attention from Darcy that surprises her, Elizabeth's feeling for him is in part summed up by her in this way:

> But above all, above respect and esteem, there was a motive within her of good will which could not be overlooked. It was gratitude.—Gratitude, not merely for having once loved her, but for loving her still well enough, to forgive all the petulance and acrimony of her manner in rejecting him, and all the unjust accusations accompanying her rejection. He who, she had been persuaded, would avoid her as his greatest

enemy, seemed, on this accidental meeting, most eager to
preserve the acquaintance, and without any indelicate display of regard, or any peculiarity of manner, where their two
selves only were concerned, was soliciting the good opinion
of her friends, and bent on making her known to his sister.
Such a change in a man of so much pride, excited not only astonishment but gratitude—for to love, ardent love, it must
be attributed. (*PP,* ch. 44:284–85)

This occurs as part of Elizabeth's effort "to determine her feelings towards" Darcy. The ideas she is examining here are literally components of her feelings. Of course other things than ideas enter into her
new feeling toward Darcy—especially in fixing how intensely and in
what manner she feels what she feels—but nothing is quite so essential in settling *what* she feels as these thoughts she is having now.
These component ideas in Elizabeth's emotion of gratitude—and in-
cipient love—require two-thirds of a novel to accumulate. The target
of her emotion, Darcy as a moral agent and as lover of herself, could
only present himself in these roles through nuanced conduct deployed across an extensive human terrain. Therefore, the coming into
focus for Elizabeth of this object of her romantic emotion—hence
of the emotion itself—must occupy much physical time and social
space.

In contrast, nothing remotely like that complex pattern of
thought and context enters into Tom Brangwen's emotion. Almost no
thought, very little physical time, and virtually no social space are pre-
requisite for it: the idea, "that's her"; two or three minutes in time; a
man leading a horse and wagon, and an unknown woman in a black
cloak and bonnet, walking in opposite directions on a country road.

Because a large proportion of the essential social content and indispensable social context of the emotions that it interested Austen to
explore in her heroines is invariably introduced through the accumu-
lating experience of those heroines, Austen's heroines, in her five most
ambitious novels, are necessarily and emphatically *thinking* beings.
These heroines must comprehend a complex and complexly evolving
society and decipher individual motives, intentions, circumstances,

history, conduct, and character. As well, these women must undertake self-analysis that is no less demanding. And their thinking must be interesting to readers as that.

I have discovered a way readers can convince themselves, with some work, of how exceptionally *thinking* Austen's heroines are. Once when I had been reading through Austen I decided to test how she did her heroines against a Tolstoyan heroine I remembered as especially vivid, Natasha, of *War and Peace*. I put down Austen, picked up an English translation of Tolstoy, and proceeded to read through every passage—from one end of this long book to the other—in which Natasha appeared. Undoubtedly because I had just come from immersion in Austen, I had an altogether new experience of Natasha: it appeared to me that never once in the entire novel was her mind penetrated by an idea. She *never* engaged in thinking! I dare say this is a merely relative fact about Tolstoy's heroine, compared to those of Austen. Jane Austen's heroines *are* exceptionally thinking beings. And this is, according to the socially constructed conception of gender that ruled genteel circles in late eighteenth- and early nineteenth-century England, a more masculine than feminine way of being in the world.

Elizabeth Bennet's embarrassment when Darcy discovers her on his grounds is intensely felt. But it is insufficiently goal-directed to count as a passion (though I suppose it may include a passionate wish to be somewhere else). We shall certainly join Elizabeth in her confidently inferring Darcy's "ardent love" for her from his behavior. Given all we know of their joint history, I should say that Darcy's ardent love for Elizabeth *is* depicted in these Pemberley chapters; but this "all we know" has taken many chapters to accumulate. And Elizabeth's beginning of love for Darcy is not yet a passion.

However, Elinor Dashwood attending her fearfully sick sister does manifest passion—her devotion to Marianne. Eighty percent of the book has been needed to provide the context that will enable readers to situate themselves within Elinor's present experience of Marianne's desperate condition and fully to feel with Elinor her anxiety for her sister. All those chapters of stoical resistance to her own suffering, all those chapters of seeking a balance between wanting for Marianne the happiness natural to her and wanting to reduce Marianne's vulnerability to romantic misadventure, all those chapters of responsible, almost maternal looking out for Marianne without having either the power or information that could protect her—all figure in shaping for us the meaning and hence the content—the *what* she feels—of Elinor's emotion in the face of Marianne's illness. What is more, the content of that emotion is also communicated to us through our accumulated experience of Marianne's devotion, as well, to Elinor, and of the comradeship that—through the give and take of their conversation—engages the mental powers of both: they habitually talk carefully and honestly with each other, especially about people, preeminently Willoughby and Edward but also Colonel Brandon and Mrs. Jennings; and about ways of feeling, speaking, and behaving, especially in matters involving potential mates, but also, for example, in aesthetic matters, such as appraisal of the picturesque or, we surmise, of painting and poetry.

There is grave alarm and foreboding when Marianne takes to her bed. Her hostess, Charlotte Palmer, leaves home with her infant son within an hour of the apothecary allowing the word *infection* to pass his lips. Mrs. Jennings does not expect Marianne to survive. Colonel Brandon fears the worst; when Mr. Palmer is departing to join his wife and son, he is glad to leave Colonel Brandon in residence for an emergency. And the maid who helps Elinor tend her patient echoes Mrs. Jennings's fears for Marianne's life. Yet for days Elinor, while untiringly taking every possible care of Marianne, is undisturbed, confident the apothecary's assurances are reliable. When, after signs of improvement, the crisis in Marianne's illness begins, Elinor is swiftly plunged from the crest of a hopeful wave to a frightening trough:

> Marianne, suddenly awakened by some accidental noise in the house, started hastily up, and with a feverish wildness, cried out—
>
> "Is Mama coming?—
>
> "Not yet," replied the other, concealing her terror, and assisting Marianne to lie down again, "but she will be here, I

hope, before it is long. It is a great way, you know, from hence to Barton."

"But she must not go round by London," cried Marianne, in the same hurried manner, "I shall never see her, if she goes by London." (ch. 43:306)

Readers who remember that Marianne has no reason to believe her mother is on the way and who know Marianne is now situated between Barton Cottage and London not only know she is delirious, we experience her thus. We are therefore ready to believe Austen when she makes a rare (possibly unique) application to a heroine of the word *terror* to describe Elinor's reaction. This we are the readier to receive because Elinor is without help in her late vigil: Mrs. Jennings has gone to bed, her maid is enjoying free time with the housekeeper (near midnight!), and only Colonel Brandon can be expected still to be up and available, but he is downstairs. When Elinor finds Marianne "still talking wildly of mama" and her pulse "lower and quicker than ever!" she hurries downstairs to get Brandon to send for Mr. Harris, the apothecary, and for her mother, whom he offers to go and fetch by carriage:

> She thanked him with brief though fervent gratitude, and while he went to hurry off his servant with a message to Mr. Harris, and an order for post-horses directly, she wrote a few lines to her mother.
>
> The comfort of such a friend at that moment as Colonel Brandon—of such a companion for her mother,—how gratefully was it felt!—a companion whose judgment would guide, whose attendance must relieve, and whose friendship might soothe her!—as far as the shock of such a summons *could* be lessened to her, his presence, his manners, his assistance, would lessen it. (ch. 43:307)

First Austen describes a manifestation of Elinor's emotion of gratitude: her brief but fervently grateful thanks to Brandon. Then the interior content is rendered for us with a kind of imaginary, emotional internal monologue: it's not that we are to believe all the words of the second paragraph are inwardly spoken by Elinor. Inwardly, it is for her *as if* they are.

In that second paragraph, the symmetrical structure, on the one hand, and the evolving rhythm, on the other, give effective expression to Elinor's emotion: the symmetry displays the comforting order offered Elinor by the morally charged emotion of a gratitude felt in the face of the terrifying disorder of her sister's crisis; the evolving rhythm gives expression to the fervency merely asserted of this emotion in the first paragraph. But this grateful emotion can be only briefly indulged: "She returned to her sister's apartment . . . to watch by her the rest of the night. It was a night of almost equal suffering to both. Hour after hour passed away in sleepless pain and delirium on Marianne's side, and in the most cruel anxiety on Elinor's. . . . Her apprehensions once raised, paid by their excess for all her former security" (ch. 43:307).

Because of Marianne's delirious fixation on her mother and because Elinor has failed to bring her mother there earlier, Elinor's suffering is often vicarious, anticipating her mother's:

> Marianne's ideas were still, at intervals, fixed incoherently on her mother, and whenever she mentioned her name, it gave a pang to the heart of poor Elinor, who, reproaching herself for having trifled with so many days of illness, and wretched for some immediate relief, fancied that all relief might soon be in vain, that everything had been delayed too long, and pictured to herself her suffering mother arriving too late to see this darling child, or to see her rational. (ch. 43:307–8).

Elinor's tendency to experience distress in this crisis from her sense of somehow failing an absent family member—rather than simply feeling for Marianne herself—seems to me somewhat surprising. In the following passage I presume that we should give "friend" the usual meaning in that era for such contexts as this one: "family member." The visit by Mr. Harris "concluded with encouraging assurances which reached the ear, but could not enter the heart, of Miss Dashwood. She was calm, except when she thought of her mother, but she was almost hopeless; and in this state she continued till noon, scarcely stirring from her sister's bed, her thoughts wandering from one image of grief, one suffering friend to another" (ch. 43:308–9)

When Elinor's tendency to feel guilt in such a situation reminds me of an even sadder moment in Cassandra Austen's life with her sister Jane, I find myself again speculating that Austen's older sister may have served as a partial model for Elinor. Here is the continuation of the letter I quoted earlier in this chapter that Cassandra wrote to Jane Austen's favorite niece immediately after Austen's death: "I loved her only too well, not better than she deserved, but I am conscious that my affection for her made me sometimes unjust to & negligent of others, & I can acknowledge, as more than a general principle, the justice of the hand which has struck this blow" (*L*, 344).

Whatever it may be that can account for some readers failing yet to feel the passion in Elinor's devotion to Marianne and for their perceiving her still as "a stick," when the crisis of Marianne's illness begins to pass, and then passes, Elinor's emotion is unmistakable. Indeed, I suspect that, as rendered by Austen, Elinor's emotion here is indistinguishable from that of a lover or spouse. Perhaps it is some form of blindness induced by the sexually romantic values of so many readers that interposes a block, here, between Elinor's emotion and its appreciation.

> About noon, however, she began—but with a caution—a dread of disappointment, which for some time kept her silent, even to her friend—to fancy, to hope she could perceive a slight amendment to her sister's pulse;—and at last, with an agitation more difficult to bury under exterior calmness, than all her foregoing distress, ventured to communicate her hope. Mrs Jennings, though forced, on examination, to acknowledge a temporary revival, tried to keep her young friend from indulging a thought of its continuance; and Elinor, conning over every injunction of distrust, told herself likewise not to hope. But it was too late. Hope had already entered; and feeling all its anxious flutter, she bent over

her sister to watch—she hardly knew for what. Half an hour passed away, and the favourable symptom yet blessed her. Others even arose to confirm it. Her breath, her skin, her lips, all flattered Elinor with signs of amendment, and Marianne fixed her eyes on her with a rational, though languid, gaze. Anxiety and hope now oppressed her in equal degrees, and left her no moment of tranquillity till the arrival of Mr Harris at four o'clock;—when his assurances, his felicitations on a recovery in her sister even surpassing his expectations, gave her confidence, comfort, and tears of joy. (ch. 43:309)

Mrs. Jennings soon displayed "unequivocal cheerfulness" at Marianne's recovery. However—

Elinor could not be cheerful. Her joy was of a different kind, and led to anything rather than to gaiety. Marianne, restored to life, health, friends, and to her doting mother, was an idea to fill her heart with sensations of exquisite comfort, and expand it in fervent gratitude;—but it led to no outward demonstrations of joy, no words, no smiles. All within Elinor's breast was satisfaction, silent and strong.

She continued by the side of her sister, with little intermission, the whole afternoon; calming every fear, satisfying every inquiry of her enfeebled spirits, supplying every succour, and watching almost every look and every breath. (ch. 43:310)

There is perhaps in Elinor's joy at her sister's recovery an element we should not expect to find if the sister were instead a lover: she thinks of Marianne restored to everything and everybody but herself. But would Elinor be different in responding later to an analogous situation with Edward as her husband? Possibly not. I remember being surprised, in reading the following mild indictment of Edward by Elinor, that the weight given to "our relations" as injured parties is greater than that assigned to herself! This comes after their engagement; it is part of their joint review of the misbegotten days of their not-quite-courtship. They are happy and all critique is made in a playful spirit.

Nonetheless, I think the special emphasis of Elinor's judgment expresses her characteristic outlook:

> Elinor scolded him, harshly as ladies always scold the imprudence which compliments themselves, for having spent so much time with them at Norland, when he must have felt his own inconstancy.
>
> "Your behaviour was certainly very wrong," said she, "because—to say nothing of my conviction, our relations were all led away by it to fancy and expect *what*, as you were *then* situated, could never be." (ch. 49:357)

Ever ready to focus emotional significance upon some community larger than a mere pair, Elinor imagines some of the grief and the joy of Marianne's crisis and recovery—and some of the injury from Edward's misconduct—transferred from herself to her mother and other relatives of hers, counting herself as affected only so far as she is a member of the group. This tells us how her intellect works within her emotional life rather than how much she herself feels. It is nonetheless possible that this mental habit of hers has misled some readers into thinking her "communitarian" inclinations not only shape the *how* and the *what* she feels but fix as well the *how much* she feels, so that the latter quantity is thought to be less than it is depicted by Austen as being. However, as Spinoza worked so hard to persuade us, the fact that a person's intellect enlarges the scope of an emotion's target, to encompass a larger community than the initially tiny human pair that initiated it, this does not at all entail that the emotion itself will be less powerful; rather the opposite, insists Spinoza. We should probably do well at least to avoid prejudice in either direction. In any event, again we find that for Elinor to feel, even intensely, is also for her to think harder than most, and for her to feel strongly about one is also for her to think about many.

Consistently with the high level of emotional intensity Austen has constructed for Elinor's life from chapter 43, when Marianne becomes ill, to the novel's end, the author has barely allowed Elinor to relax in the conviction of Marianne's recovery when she provides us with a startling ending for this already dramatically strong chapter 43, the very last words of which are those that end the following passage:

> The night was cold and stormy. The wind roared round the house, and the rain beat against the windows. . . . The clock struck eight. . . . The flaring lamps of a carriage were immediately in view. . . . Never in her life had Elinor found it so difficult to be calm. . . . The knowledge of what her mother must be feeling . . . perhaps her despair!—and of what *she* had to tell! . . . she hurried downstairs. The bustle in the vestibule . . . assured her that they were already in the house. She rushed forwards towards the drawing-room,—she entered it,—and saw only Willoughby. (ch. 43:310–11)

In view of what she had just endured with Marianne, Elinor's reaction—which Austen offers us only in the opening words of the next chapter—is to be expected: "Elinor, starting back with a look of horror at the sight of him, obeyed the first impulse of her heart in turning instantly to quit the room" (ch. 44:312).

Both on her own as narrator and through Elinor's reflective judgment, Austen credits Willoughby, early and late in the novel, with being open and affectionate. Now he shows himself to Elinor as having been more genuinely in love with Marianne than Elinor, in view of his brutal behavior, could have believed him. And he is utterly open: he gives as nearly as possible a true confession of all that bears on his conduct toward Marianne. Since the truth he has to tell is in large part ugly, Elinor is at first angry to hear it told and she proposes to put a quick end to the interview: "Such a beginning as this cannot be followed by anything" (ch. 44:314).

But it could. As his "still ardent love for Marianne" emerged, his "open, affectionate, and lively manner" and the "warmth which brought all the former Willoughby to her remembrance" made its impression upon her. She responded also once again to what Austen calls "that person of uncommon attraction," words that from his first appearance conveyed the author's report of his immediate sexual appeal to the three mature Dashwood women. Elinor's feeling for Willoughby is largely returned to its original tender quality: "In spite of all his faults" she now thinks of his being "separated for ever from her family with a tenderness, a regret" she could not have conceived possible half an hour ago. In fact, despite her fatigue from sitting up with Marianne, she does lose sleep that night because "Willoughby, 'poor Willoughby,' as she now allowed herself to call him, was constantly in her thoughts; she would not but have heard his vindication for the world, and now blamed, now acquitted herself for having judged him so harshly before." Even days later, after Mrs. Dashwood has talked at length of her hopes for Colonel Brandon's success with Marianne, Elinor, when reflecting by herself on her mother's remarks, found herself disposed to wish success for Brandon, "and yet in wishing it, to feel a pang for Willoughby" (ch. 45:326–27, 331).

I think that for most of us her way of responding to Willoughby during his visit enlarges Elinor for us. And I think her own consciousness of an enrichment of her life is marked by her thought that she would not "for the world" have missed hearing his vindication— and by that excitement of her "spirits" which kept her awake that night. Elinor's emotional response to Willoughby did not keep her from being hardheaded in analyzing his conduct and character and in positing the influences that shaped these. That he could be guilty of as many moral failures as he was, and responsible through them for so much suffering in Marianne, yet—and this she discovers through her own emotions—yet nonetheless be lovable, be someone to whom she could, after all that, honestly say she "was even interested in his happiness," this is for her something extraordinary, something enlarging to live through (ch. 44:325). And so it may be, as well, for the careful reader. There is nothing else like it in Austen's fiction.

Some readers may be given pause at my assertion above that it is through her own emotional response to Willoughby that Elinor learns something about Willoughby. It is not always acknowledged by the hardheaded that our emotions may mediate for us *knowledge* of things external to us. Yet that this is true for one sort of external thing is a commonplace, if not of common sense at least of poetic criticism. For nearly all critics have over long stretches of intellectual history believed, for example, that an essential ingredient in the warrant with which a critical reader judges a poem successful is the poem's emotional impact upon that reader. A poem is (commonly) meant to elicit a certain emotion, to have an emotional impact. My assurance that a poem is good commonly requires that I experience an appropriate emotion in reading it. Something similar is true of much music and much painting. And there are human traits, too, whose value is to be found—as David Hume liked to put it—in their being agreeable to others. Surely being lovable is that sort of desirable human quality. And a critical observer closely interacting with another human being will rightly find the warrant for a judgment of that person's lovability to reside partly in an emotional response to the other person that has in it at least the "makings" of love.

It is therefore interesting that it is two of the three earliest of Austen's ambitiously conceived heroines who achieved something of this kind of reversal of judgment about an important male figure, partly on the basis of their emotional responses to that person when he is showing new behavior in a new context. What I have in mind is that Austen was more disposed early than late to provide her heroines with the intellectual hardheadedness and clearheadedness to qualify them as, so to say, *critical* readers of human conduct, so that their emotional responses, when based on accumulated experience of their object, could be trusted to constitute components of important new knowledge of another person. Elinor in this late meeting with Willoughby is one instance. Elizabeth Bennet responding to Darcy on his home grounds, Pemberley, is another. For Austen, emotion mediates knowledge only where intellect permeates emotion.[4]

Of course character as well as one's more or less permanently structured emotional disposition, one's temperament, are relevant for Austen as well. We do not believe Fanny Price would have responded as Elinor did, in the same circumstances, to Willoughby—not because of deficient critical intelligence, of which Fanny has plenty; but because she is, in her private mental life, a less generous person than Elinor.

After the chapter given to the intense encounter with Willoughby, a rather relaxed short chapter follows, marked by the lovely opening paragraphs describing Elinor, in the afterglow of that meeting, becoming conscious of how the magic of Willoughby's presence had affected not only her feeling toward him, which she is willing to leave in its revised form, but her moral appraisal of him, which she is not willing to leave so. In the next chapter Elinor's attention is again fully held—and her emotion engaged—by Marianne, as the latter, with assistance from Elinor regarding Willoughby, completes her conversion from (imprudent) sensibility to (hyperprudent) sense. These intensely demanding conversations with Marianne are not concluded until the middle of one more chapter, whereupon Elinor is again hurled into a whirlpool of passionate feeling: almost directly after we are told that "Elinor grew impatient for some tidings of Edward," she receives some (ch. 47:343). They are announced by the Dashwoods' "manservant" Thomas: "I suppose you know, ma'am, that Mr Ferrars is married."

Elinor is living life at much too high a pitch throughout these late chapters of the novel for her to qualify as "a stick": the ordeal of Marianne's illness and crisis; the excitement and challenge, the new knowledge and new tenderness of the meeting with Willoughby; the concentration on her contribution to Marianne's "conversion"; and now the ordeal of Edward's apparent marriage to Lucy Steele. It is, I hope, a mark of how cordially we have come to identify ourselves with Elinor that one may be surprised, in looking back, to discover that Elinor had to endure this latest—and last—of her unhappy times for only five pages. Then Edward himself ends this one with his arrival and the news he bears that Lucy Steele has married not him but his brother Robert.

I am bringing near its end my discussion of Austen's manner of creating Elinor's (critically neglected) emotional life. I have ended my focus upon Elinor's emotional disposition as also contributing, by its rationality, to Austen's reconstruction of feminine gender. I now remark that some readers may fail to become conscious of one device Austen uses to keep alive for us our knowledge of Elinor's feeling for Edward so that Elinor's intense emotion when she learns Edward is free of Lucy does not surprise us. Austen inserts into rather unlikely, out-of-the-way places allusions to Elinor's unbroken preoccupation with Edward Ferrars in both her thinking and her feeling. Here Elinor wonders if her mother has forgotten Edward: "Marianne continued to mend every day, and the brilliant cheerfulness of Mrs. Dashwood's looks and spirits proved her to be, as she repeatedly declared herself, one of the happiest women in the world. Elinor could not hear the declaration, nor witness its proofs without sometimes wondering whether her mother ever recollected Edward" (ch. 45:328).

When for the first time Elinor experiences Mr. Palmer not as unattractive guest of others but as host to her sister and herself, she finds him surprisingly improved: "perfectly the gentleman in his behaviour to all his visitors." Yet she cannot resist a comparison with Edward: "She liked him . . . upon the whole much better than she had expected, and in her heart was not sorry that she could like him no more;—not sorry to be driven by the observation of his epicurism, his selfishness, and his conceit, to rest with complacency on the remembrance of Edward's generous temper, simple taste, and diffident feelings" (ch. 42:301). Those reflections occur, the reader will remember, well after Elinor has apparently lost Edward to Lucy.

Even at the moment of Marianne's most acute suffering, when first Marianne and then Elinor have just read Willoughby's cruel letter of rejection to Marianne, a contrast with Edward, now known also to be engaged to another woman, occurs to her mind: "In her earnest meditations on the contents of the letter, on the depravity of that mind which could dictate it, and, probably, on the very different mind of a very different person, who had no other connection whatever with the affair than what her heart gave him with everything that passed, Elinor forgot the immediate distress of her sister, forgot that she had three letters on her lap yet unread" (ch. 29:196–97).

When Elinor and Marianne set off with Mrs. Jennings for London and (Marianne believes) Willoughby, Elinor envies Marianne her "animated object" and her hope. Then she has this thought about her own loss, in case Marianne's hope about Willoughby is fulfilled: "She must then learn to avoid every selfish comparison, and banish every regret which might lessen her satisfaction in the happiness of Marianne" (ch. 26:175).

The last link in this chain of reminders of Elinor's love for Edward is put in place when she hears, through the servant Thomas's report, that Edward is apparently married to Lucy. As we have observed earlier, she found she could easily imagine Lucy as an efficient wife of Edward who would unite "a desire of smart appearance, with the utmost frugality." But she could not picture Edward married to Lucy: "nothing pleased her; she turned away her head from every sketch of him" (ch. 48:347).

Some readers are surprised that Elinor takes so little serious exception to Edward's having, in effect, courted her while engaged to another. I think we can find at least a partial explanation for this in the fact that in her heart Elinor sustained for Edward an attachment that—somewhat as she judged Willoughby's for Marianne after his marriage—"it was not . . . innocent to indulge" (ch. 45:326). In her view, for some months she has shared with Edward the minor dishonor of enjoying a love it is not innocent to indulge. Since she and he share this guilt, she cannot condemn him more than herself.

Less than fifty pages from the start of the chapter devoted to Elinor's response to Marianne's illness, and less than twenty from the end of the novel, we find ourselves witnessing one more—entirely believable—burst of Elinor's tears, as Edward corrects the servant's mistake about a Ferrars marriage:

> "Perhaps you do not know—you may not have heard that my brother is lately married to—to the youngest—to Miss Lucy Steele."
>
> His words were echoed with unspeakable astonishment by all but Elinor, who sat with her head leaning over her work, in a state of such agitation as made her hardly know where she was.
>
> "Yes," said he, "they were married last week, and are now at Dawlish."
>
> Elinor could sit it no longer. She almost ran out of the room, and as soon as the door was closed, burst into tears of joy, which at first she thought would never cease. Edward, who had till then looked anywhere, rather than at her, saw her hurry away, and perhaps saw—or even heard, her emotion; for immediately afterwards he fell into a reverie, which no remarks, no inquiries, no affectionate address of Mrs. Dashwood could penetrate, and at last, without saying a word, quitted the room, and walked out towards the village. (ch. 48:350)

4

Men and Society: Deception, Formality, Patriarchy, Mobility, and Work

*T*HERE IS MORE to come about Elinor. But not every reader has my appetite for unbroken enjoyment of her variety. So we now take a break from Elinor, turn to a salient feature of the novel's plot—its emphasis on deception—and consider traits of the depicted society that may or may not explain deception's large role in the novel.

More fully than any other Austen novel, the plot of *Sense and Sensibility* is shaped through deception by its characters. Deceptions are negligible in *Northanger Abbey* and *Mansfield Park,* and of little moment in *Persuasion.* In *Emma* one hidden engagement plays a role in the plot, but it does not much affect the heroine. There is the same count in *Pride and Prejudice,* where Wickham's lies about Darcy have an effect Darcy rates as intolerable but the reader experiences as little more than interesting. However, *Sense and Sensibility* imposes upon each of the two heroines a momentum-stopping deception. Throughout a large portion of the book both Elinor and Marianne, each in her distinctive way, suffer from wounds inflicted by a lover's deception. In effect, Willoughby deceives Marianne about his character and entanglements, and Edward misleads Elinor about his marital availability and therefore about what "intentions" he can have toward her.

Deception so permeates the pages of this novel that we can afford a moment to be specific about its incidence and precise about its content.

Edward hides his engagement from Elinor. And from his mother and sister and brother. And from the world. Of course Lucy joins him in her part of that concealment.

When Elinor learns from Lucy of her engagement to Edward, she hides her knowledge from Marianne and her mother, and of course from Edward's sister. She hides from Edward what she learns about Lucy in conversations with her.

Willoughby hides from Marianne his affair with Eliza Williams, his troubles with Mrs. Smith about that affair, his reason for leaving Marianne for London, his engagement to Miss Grey, the fact that Miss Grey authored his brutal letter to Marianne, and the fact of his wanting Marianne during and after his betrayal of her.

Until Willoughby abandons Marianne, Colonel Brandon hides from the Dashwoods Willoughby's seduction of Brandon's ward, and the colonel's duel with Willoughby.

Lucy Steele hides from Edward her coolness toward him.

Robert Ferrars and Lucy conceal from Edward and everyone their courtship. When she marries Robert Ferrars, Lucy Steele contrives to cause Elinor to be misled into thinking Lucy has married Edward.

Marianne in effect conceals from her sister and mother the exact nature of her relationship to Willoughby by not correcting their unavoidable impression that the two are engaged.

Can we say that deception provides the engine that moves, or the energy that drives, the story forward? That image does not satisfy me. There is something it points to, yet the image is false. For surely the author has invested the forward-moving energy for the story principally in the deepest desires of the two heroines: Marianne's for self-expressive self-fulfillment, Elinor's for—what? Let me anticipate later chapters: Elinor's desire for community.

The men's deceptions are a kind of deflecting force tending to block movement toward the heroines' principal goals. Because these goals are less self-centered in Elinor than in Marianne, the obstructing force of the men's deceptions is less effective at undermining healthy purposiveness in Elinor's life than it is at inflicting this damage upon Marianne.

If the power of male deception in the novel can be shown to be an expression of some social force or structure represented in the novel, then the centrality of this deception for the plot may have a deep meaning, possibly sociological, possibly political, possibly both. Austen may be aiming criticism at the social force that sponsors the deception; this would be a political meaning. She might be developing, or even unconsciously manifesting, facts about social causation within her class; that would be a sociological meaning. She may be intending the sociological thesis for the sake of the political thrust. Still other interpretations of the key role of deception in the plot are possible, *if* the proposition can be made plausible that pervasive deception is represented in the novel as an outcome of social forces, institutions, or practices. From the point of view of literary theory, making out the pervasive deception to be a deeply significant trait of the depicted society would be an attractive outcome. Two distinguished literary critics have advanced (different) hypotheses that can be taken as intending to make an outcome of that sort plausible: Professors Claudia L. Johnson and Tony Tanner. I am skeptical about either's success. Yet the effort to find a deeper meaning in the novel's emphasis on deception deserves attention.

Tony Tanner's case seems to me easier both to present and to question than Claudia Johnson's. So I begin with him.

Tanner suggests that the complex deceptions with which Willoughby betrays Marianne are symptoms of a disorder specific to the sort of real society he takes Austen's novel to image. Tanner believes this society's high incidence of deception is a sort of perverse expression of its extreme formality. He remarks that "one can share a good deal of Marianne's abhorrence for all forms of 'concealment' when one sees something of the mischief and misery that can ensue in a world where the truth of things is usually not to be found on the surface." What kind of world is this? At least "as Jane Austen depicts it," he writes, it is "a world completely dominated by forms, for which another word may be screens, which may in turn be lies." [1]

Throughout his extended remarks on the deceptive human surfaces of the novel's formal society, Tanner places his emphasis on the way people's exteriors commonly fail to reflect their interiors, how behavior and expression regularly mask some feelings and simulate others. It was "a society which forced people to be at once very sociable and very private" and therefore to learn to adjust to "a world of . . . many secrets and supposed suppressions," which is to say to "a world of screens." Tanner elaborates:

> There are more secrets than the unavowed deeds and previous commitments of the main eligible males in the novel. . . . There is a much more important kind of secrecy which Jane Austen makes us aware of: the secrecy of everything the heart may not enforce with the hand, display with the face, or express with the voice; that is, the secrecy of those things within, which are struggling to get out and meet with different kinds of restraints or suppressions. Such concealments may be admirable, or sly, or simply all that is possible . . . but in one form or another they recur throughout.[2]

Tanner is mistaken in believing that Austen in this novel made the hiding of thoughts and feelings—the concealing of one's inner life—"much more important" than the hiding of conduct—the concealing of one's "outer" life.

In the novel the deceptions that matter most are those inflicted by Willoughby and Edward upon Marianne and Elinor. But these are misrepresentations of the young men's situation and behavior; these deceptions are *not* in the main a matter of misleading the women as to how the men feel (or think) about them. Elinor, once she discovers how Edward has deceived her about his freedom to court her, never loses her correct belief that he does not love Lucy and does love her. His feelings have made themselves known. And Edward's rapid departure for Barton cottage after his release from his engagement to Lucy shows how much confidence he has in Elinor's feeling for him. Despite her prudent self-restraint, Elinor's feelings had been manifest to Edward, a man not brimming with either vanity or self-confidence.

Marianne's belief that Willoughby loved her was correct—with allowance made for his initial insincerity and for limitations on his capacity for love. (After abandoning and insulting her, Willoughby might be said to conceal from Marianne that her belief in his serious attraction to her, which has now been called in question, is correct. But *conceal* is perhaps the wrong word here, since the two no longer meet or communicate.) This man of whom, late in the book, Elinor is still ready to say that, "to every advantage of person and talents, [he] united a disposition naturally open and honest, and a feeling, affectionate temper" *had* in fact shown to Marianne his true feeling (including his—all too defeasible—intentions) toward her (ch. 45: 324). To say his character did not reveal itself is in large part to say the actions that his feelings for Marianne foretold could not be inferred from those feelings and intentions; and that his history was hidden from Marianne.

What is more, as Elinor discerned from conversation with Lucy and as Lucy's farewell letter to Edward affirms, Lucy Steele knew that Edward Ferrars no longer loved her and did love Elinor. Edward, however, did not know of Lucy's coolness to him: Lucy alone deceived an amatory partner as to true feelings, thoughts, attitudes. This is not a high incidence of deception in regard to lovers' inner life.

In short, Tanner is mistaken in this way: that the novel does *not* render the formality of its society as posing a serious obstacle to lovers discovering one another's feelings and thoughts. Nor does this social formality appreciably increase the suffering caused by revelations of lovers' deceptions. Elinor's need to feign indifference in the face of Lucy's revelations to her is arguably an effect of the society's formality; but for Elinor, feigning composure at this revelation lowers the intensity of her suffering. And if Willoughby, rather than coldly rebuffing Marianne at a party—which no doubt was, as Tanner suggests, all too vivid a model of the way in which the society as a whole could be in every sense stuffy—if Willoughby had, instead, told Marianne in private the whole, stark truth, would her pain at his defection have been much less? It would have been less, yes. But perhaps not, over time, much less.

I have another doubt. Would an actual society that embodied the formality of the fictional society Austen created have a greater tendency than, say, the extreme informality of current American society to encourage concealment of romantically significant conduct? From all appearances, concealed infidelity is as rampant today in informal America as ever it has been in the English-speaking world.

I shall shortly revisit Tanner's "formality hypothesis." First, I want to turn to an alternative account of how individual deception might be an outgrowth of social institutions in the world of *Sense and Sensibility.*

In her chapter on this novel in *Jane Austen: Women, Politics and the Novel,* Claudia L. Johnson has no special preoccupation with deception. Her preoccupation is rather with male decadence generally in the novel, which she takes to be presented by Austen as an outcome of a particular social organization. However, since in *Sense and Sensibility* the most important rendered examples of male moral failure figure as deceptions (and related betrayals) of women, Johnson's claim that the novel exhibits à social explanation for male decadence applies, specifically, to male deception.

Professor Johnson's argument is part of a larger argument to the effect that in this novel Austen is offering an "extremely trenchant and in some ways extremely radical" critique of [the] conservative ideology of the 1790s (the period when she first wrote the book). Johnson holds that Austen develops this critique "largely through an examination of the morally vitiating tendencies of patriarchy." Johnson holds that Austen especially "indicts the license to coercion, corruption, and avarice available to grasping patriarchs and their eldest sons."[3]

According to Johnson, then, *patriarchy* is the social structure in the novel that has for an outcome male corruption, especially of patriarchs in the novel and their eldest sons. One corruption to which Austen gives a major role is male betrayal of women by deception. We now have for our consideration not Tanner's theory of social *formality* as accounting for both sexes' deceptions, but, in its place, Johnson's theory of *patriarchy* as generating the male deception so central to the plot of *Sense and Sensibility.*

On the subject of male deception and betrayal of women as an expression of the corruption inherent in the English patriarchal social structure, Johnson writes:

Gentlemen in *Sense and Sensibility* are uncommitted sorts.
They move on, more or less encumbered by human wreckage from the past. No sooner does Edward, like Willoughby,
bind himself to one woman than he proceeds to engage the
heart of another. . . . While Willoughby at least admits to having amused himself with Marianne "without any design of
returning her affections" (SS 320), Edward never hints at any
consciousness that he may carelessly have created an attachment in Elinor that he had no intention of reciprocating.
As different as Edward and Willoughby are individually, as
English gentlemen many of their failings are identical. In
marked contrast to the Darcys and Knightleys of this world,
they are weak, duplicitous, and selfish, entirely lacking in that
fortitude and forthrightness with which Austen is capable of
endowing exemplary gentlemen when she wishes. In *Sense
and Sensibility* . . . these faults are described as the effects of
established and accepted social practices for men of family,
not as aberrations from them.[4]

My reader will have observed where her thesis about Austen on the
corrupting effects of patriarchy takes Johnson when she makes it concrete: Austen's full characterization of Edward Ferrars is missed, as I
hope my earlier treatment of Edward, written before reading Johnson,
convinces the reader. Edward is made out by Johnson to be such an
abomination that I fail to recognize him. Of course Willoughby does
answer to her denigrating description; but with him Johnson finds
herself transported by a disgust that outstrips the disapproval that
Austen authorized with her completed portrait of Willoughby.

I shan't again give my brief for Edward Ferrars. However, so bril-
liantly persuasive is Johnson's book as a whole, some direct rebuttal of
its attack on Edward may be useful, especially as bearing on the case
for her thesis that Austen means to show patriarchy's social and political hegemony as accounting for male corruption generally, hence for
male deception specifically.

Edward is subsumed by Johnson under the class "gentlemen in
Sense and Sensibility" who "are uncommitted sorts" who "move on,
more or less encumbered by human wreckage from the past." Against

this we set the fact that Edward refused to break his engagement with
Lucy, despite the assurance from his mother that his refusal would
cause him to be cast out from his family, stripped of all his generous
inheritance, and left relatively poor (so much so that kindly Mrs. Jennings is ready to offer him "bed and board" at her house). Mrs. Ferrars also assured Edward that if he persisted in his refusal, then "if he
were to enter into any profession with a view of better support, she
would do all in her power to prevent his advancing in it" (ch. 37:267).
In case we readers should fail to appreciate how heavy is the price Edward must pay for disobeying his mother's command to break his engagement to Lucy, Austen gives us this help:

> Mrs Jennings was very warm in her praise of Edward's con-
> duct, but only Elinor and Marianne understood its true
> merit. *They* only knew how little he had to tempt him to be
> disobedient, and how small was the consolation, beyond the
> consciousness of doing right, that would remain to him in
> the loss of friends and fortune. Elinor gloried in his integrity;
> and Marianne forgave all his offenses in compassion for his
> punishment. (ch. 38:270)

(The reader will remember that "friends" here means "family.")

As to Edward engaging the heart of Elinor "no sooner" than he
had bound himself to Lucy: when Lucy tells Elinor of it, Lucy and Edward had been engaged for four years. Elinor and Edward had been
romantically interacting for about eight months. So it was more than
three years after his engagement to Lucy that he engaged the heart of
Elinor.

Johnson says Edward does not so much as hint at guilt for leading
on Elinor when he was not free to marry her. Here is his reply to that
charge: "I felt that I admired you, but I told myself it was only friendship; and till I began to make comparisons between yourself and Lucy,
I did not know how far I was got. After that, I suppose, I *was* wrong in
remaining so much in Sussex, and the arguments with which I recon-
ciled myself to . . . it, were no better than these:—The danger is my
own; I am doing no injury to anybody but myself" (ch. 49:357). It is
true, this reply is no model of honest inquiry into barely conscious

motives for selfish behavior. But Edward offers more than a mere hint of guilt; he makes, however hesitantly, an admission of it.

I am surprised to find that Professor Johnson's version of a feminist reading of this novel has inflicted a radical distortion on her experience of the two major male characters in the novel. This shows itself compactly in a comparison: she gives Willoughby favorable marks, compared to Edward, for his full, even fluent confession of guilt in regard to Marianne. This unfavorable comparison of Edward to Willoughby is foolishness. Willoughby is suffering from, among other less creditable pangs, a bad conscience about having adopted a deliberately unprincipled course of action toward Marianne. Deliberately acting unconscionably toward women has been a pattern of his. He has no illusions about himself. Although unhappy about his conduct with Marianne, he has for long apparently been almost hardened in his exploitation of women. Elinor already knows the worst about him. It is therefore to be expected that, once Willoughby is motivated to seek out the Dashwoods and set straight the record, he will have no difficulty speaking the full truth about his offenses.

Edward, on the other hand, is a young man of principle who has to work out, with worse than no help from his awful family, how to live by a difficult moral code and still achieve some personal happiness. That he live a principled life matters to him. In falling for Lucy and committing himself to her, he made a mistake that promises to be lethal to his hope of happiness. At his age this is terrible to confront. Placed in the same house with a woman who offers the prospect of a happiness he had ceased to hope for, he is bewildered and morally imperfect. Because fault matters to him, as does continuity of self, when the time comes to review his conduct, he will naturally be more cautious than Willoughby about where exactly to blame himself.

Of course in bringing out Willoughby's failings, Johnson is on firmer ground. However, given, by the author, more than an inch— call it a half-mile—to work with, she has taken a mile. Here she is, on Willoughby's late interview with Elinor downstairs from Marianne's sickbed:

Willoughby makes himself the hero of Marianne's story. . . . [He] treats Marianne's anticipated death as an occasion to solicit sympathy for himself: 'If you *can* pity me, Miss Dash-wood, pity my situation as it was *then*. With my head and heart full of your sister, I was forced to play the happy lover to another woman!' . . . And Elinor does pity him. Though she recognizes his selfishness, she never appears to observe how his self-reproach smacks of vainglory of a peculiarly prurient sort.[5]

Johnson has missed the generosity and the genius in Austen that have partially redeemed Willoughby by creating this remarkable in-terview with Elinor. Johnson ignores the context of Willoughby's ask-ing for sympathy, ignores the motive for his visit: "to offer some kind of explanation, some kind of apology, for the past; to open my whole heart to you, and by convincing you, that though I have been always a blockhead, I have not been always a rascal, to obtain some-thing like forgiveness from Ma—from your sister" (ch. 44:313–14). Elinor accepts this motive as genuine. Nothing in the novel calls it in question.

As to his "prurience," to be prurient is to be lustful, lecherous, lascivious. To write that in speaking of himself as, for the sake of money, having to play the happy lover to a woman he does not love (his wife), Willoughby thereby (boastfully) displays lecherous, lewd lustfulness—I am much afraid this tells us that Professor Johnson's theory of Don Juan–ism is ill-suited to Jane Austen's pluralistic intui-tions of it. Johnson continues thus on Willoughby:

As Willoughby (wrongly) imagines, Marianne's dying breaths pay tribute to his potency: "What I felt on hearing that your sister was dying—and dying too, believing me the greatest villain upon earth, scorning, hating me in her latest mo-ments". . . . Like Brandon then, Willoughby does not find the prospect of an abandoned woman's death displeasing. Recall-ing that his departure almost did Marianne in on the spot— "I had seen Marianne's sweet face as white as death" . . . —he fantasizes about his preeminence at a death scene caused and haunted by his absence: "Yet when I thought of her to-day as really dying, it was a kind of comfort to me to imagine that I knew exactly how she would appear to those, who saw her last in this world."[6]

Johnson's reading suggests that her disposition to accept the mixed moral composition of most humans is less firmly entrenched than Austen's: she cannot imagine how a desperately selfish man, who is nonetheless other things, can play the villain to a woman he desires and yet be horrified at the thought he may have caused her not only to die but to die thinking him to be worse than he is. This is a moral complexity with which Austen has enriched her portrait of Willoughby, only to have Johnson call Willoughby's lament an instance of his imagining Marianne's "dying breaths pay tribute to his potency"! Consider Willoughby's finding a "kind of comfort" in being able to imagine how Marianne looked dying (as he supposed), as he was traveling to reach her before she died. When Johnson takes this to show that "he does not find the prospect of an abandoned woman's death displeasing" (making an unfair comparison with the stilted, conventionalized picture of an unreal Brandon-telling-his-Eliza-stories), I feel compelled to quote again from the letter of Cassandra Austen describing Jane Austen's last conscious hours, written to the niece she believed to be strongly attached to her sister:

> She felt herself to be dying about half an hour before she became tranquil & aparently (sic) unconscious. During that half hour was her struggle . . . she said she could not tell us what she suffered. . . . When I asked her if there was anything she wanted, her answer was she wanted nothing but death & some of her words were "God grant me patience, Pray for me Oh Pray for me." Her voice was affected but as long as she spoke she was intelligible. I hope I do not break your heart my dearest Fanny by these particulars, I mean to afford you gratification whilst I am relieving my own feelings. (*L,* 344)

What can Professor Johnson make of this "gratification"?

Johnson offers other questionable readings of Willoughby. Except for her remark about his "debauching" Eliza and "abandoning her

and his child by her," I pass them by.[7] Willoughby denies to Elinor
that he knew of Eliza's pregnancy; if this is true, he could not be said
to have abandoned the forthcoming child, nor could he be held utterly callous, in his ignorance, for failing to give her his address—he
says common sense would have told Eliza how to reach him. Finally,
as to debauching Eliza, he makes remarks about "the violence of her
passions" and "the weakness of her understanding" which, *unattractive as they are* (and as he recognizes them to be), I am inclined to
credit, not as admirable but as accurate, because first, Elinor seems to
do so, and second, they exactly anticipate Eliza's successor, in Austen's
next novel, Lydia Bennet, who, as Austen's treatment of her appears to
me to declare, has too little character to be "debauched" by Wickham.

Austen has left no doubt that in several respects Willoughby deserves to be heartily despised. But she has also made him more worthy of our sympathy and less despicable than Claudia Johnson is able
to acknowledge. It may be that even here Austen is partly opposing a
patriarchally sponsored gender conception: now a boastful ruling
class's self-representation of its own decadent exercise of male prerogatives. Johnson—more radically feminist than Austen—may be
more disposed than Austen to accept this stereotype of English male
oppressors of the 1790s.[8]

This discussion of Claudia Johnson's moral appraisal of Edward and
Willoughby began by my seeking an explanation for the central role of
deception, especially deception of women by men, in shaping the
structure of this novel. Although in fact she aims at a greater range of
male corruptions, I treated Johnson's thesis as if her answer to my
more limited query is that Austen's fictional representation of rampant male deception places responsibility for this moral failing upon
the patriarchal organization of the society depicted in the novel. I have
suggested here that Johnson's answer loses plausibility from the textual distortion her defense of this thesis requires. (In chapter 6 I develop further the misgivings I have about taking this novel to mount
an attack on patriarchy as such rather than on its miscarriages.) Earlier I had also rejected as a possible answer to my query one suggested
by Tanner's idea that Austen has presented ubiquitous deception, es-

pecially about one's thoughts and feelings, as an outcome of a highly formal society.

I doubt that I can find so juicy an explanation of the thematic and structural preeminence of deception in the novel—specifically of male deception—as either Tanner's or Johnson's theory would provide if either worked as a good explanation. Neither does. Nevertheless, I can see one way a kind of hybrid of Johnson's and Tanner's ideas can help account for the men being the novel's culpable deceivers. It may be a patriarchal (Johnson's idea) formality (Tanner's) of the society within the novel that men of the middle and upper ranks are almost unlimited in their freedom of movement about the nation, whereas women of similar rank are sharply constrained in their mobility. This "favors" male over female deception.

Willoughby and Edward have only to get on their horses to be able to move from one social world to another that is virtually incommunicado with the first. The conduct of gentlemen in one world may be unknown in the other. Deception in one world, as to their behavior and circumstances in another, is easy. The temptation to fractionate their lives into diverse and unrelated erotic liaisons must have been considerable to some young men of means—like the potential of a sailor's life for "a girl in every port." One is led to imagine that where youthful courtship was afoot, so that no children would be making special claims upon the young women, and where horses were available (as they were not for the Dashwood sisters), young gentlewomen could have been nearly as mobile as young men—had they not been embedded in an oppressive social structure. (I say "nearly as mobile" because a measure of protection from male aggression on the open road would have entailed some constraint. Yet young men—at least wealthy young men like Edward—riding horseback often traveled with a male servant in attendance; so could women have done when they could afford it.) With women's mobility freed up, one could perhaps expect the extent of female deception roughly to match the male quantity.

As a principle of organization that helps shape the structure of this early novel, the young men coming and going between a visible and a hidden life fulfills, in a rather primitive way, several novelistic aims Austen will learn to achieve in later work with subtler, more fertile structural devices (although without ever abandoning this one).[9]

By the conventions and expectations developed for the novel and its readers when Austen began to write, she felt compelled to provide something of the adventure story—perhaps even a picaresque dimension—so common to the eighteenth-century novel. The latest development of the "on the road" plot had been the Gothic novel with a woman on the move, a form parodied in *Northanger Abbey*. She was determined to domesticate the drama and suspense of the established forms, not only playfully and fancifully, but seriously and radically. *Northanger Abbey* is divided between the trials and temptations of Bath and the tribulations and revelations of the Abbey. In *Sense and Sensibility* change of location similarly contributes movement to the plot. The Dashwood family is driven from its home by a capricious patriarchal injustice and an evil sister-in-law. At Barton, Marianne faces the hazards of seduction, Elinor encounters a crafty rival and discovers her lover is false. False lovers make startling—even transforming—arrivals and departures on horseback. London becomes a goal promising resumed romance for Marianne, but in the event only despair for her, vicarious pain for Elinor. At Cleveland all trace of Edward is lost, but Willoughby travels with headlamps burning through a stormy night to reach Marianne's presumed deathbed. Instead, he provides surprising revelations and satisfactions for Elinor. The Dashwoods return home to Barton; Edward arrives on horseback after his own long ride and is taken to be someone else, only to reveal that he is now metamorphosed from a captured to a liberated lover.

The structure of deception Austen invented for this novel also allows some improvement upon the sentimental novel's legacy. She uses that structure, through her handling of deceptive action, to correct the unrealities of the novel of sensibility with a major advance in realism for the emerging novel of sense. Willoughby's betrayal causes intolerably intense suffering, which is, however, enacted under strict standards of severely domestic realism. Edward's less decisive defection offers Elinor a nearly novel-length bout of male-inflicted unhappiness, which, however, she stoically refuses to display and almost refuses to suffer. Lucy Steele, with Robert Ferrars's help, offers a concluding, frivolous deception that suspends the moment of tearful relief for Elinor to nearly the end of the story—and the author does in fact limit Elinor's indulgence in tears to no more than a moment.

A structure that provides for growth in moral wisdom for one or more protagonists is a requirement for Austen's novels. The deception plot does not offer the most interesting device for this purpose, but in her hands it is suited to it. Although he is unable to put into practice what he learns, Willoughby does grow wiser through suffering from his self-betrayal, which he sees to be such. Marianne's hard-earned discoveries are the most explicit. Elinor discovers something of both the powers and limits of stoicism. Also, Elinor's experience of Marianne's suffering and of Willoughby's brutality and partial redemption immensely widens her moral horizon. She gains something similar from intensely feeling the complexity of Edward's moral failures and successes. Much vicarious experience fuels Elinor's growth. And her joint role with Colonel Brandon in offering his gift of a living to Edward forces on her a hard maturing (about which more is forthcoming in the next two chapters).

Finally, the deception-structure as Austen shaped it in this novel is used in a penetratingly humanizing way to render two men who are, like so many humans, deplorably weak (Edward) or even evil (Willoughby) yet also good (Edward) or worthy of affection and sympathy (Willoughby). Their deceptions, and thereby their betrayals, of Marianne and Elinor are constructed by Austen to be manifestations not only of a dual life but as well, and more profoundly, of a grievous internal conflict and a divided self. This condition prompts Edward's "I think . . . that I may defy many months to produce any good to me" and accounts for Willoughby's confessing the sad form of relief from guilt's pain he experiences: "Miss Dashwood, you cannot have an idea of the comfort it gives me to look back on my own misery" (ch. 19:128, 44:318). In quite different ways, and at different stages in their relationships with the sisters, each is moved to deceive from a powerful desire to live a richer, happier life than the one in which he has seemed to himself to be trapped. In Willoughby's case it is his loving Marianne that reveals the better self within the decadent one; in Edward it is his refusing to break with Lucy that shows his moral mettle.

In both men, their deception is culpable. Yet early and late, Willoughby's spontaneously open and affectionate nature is affirmed to be genuine and worthy of appreciation for the pleasure it gives, and for the innocence of its basis in the man. Although not grounded in correct principles, his desire to be forgiven and his regret (I do not see remorse) for his offenses against Marianne are nonetheless redemptive in their tendency. And on balance, Edward is made out to be a good person, undistinguished, ordinary in his rationalizing and in his lack of ambition, yet exceptional in his principled conduct, his modesty and his self-knowledge, and engaging in his disposition to truthfulness and gentle wit.

Compared to the young women, one can say the young men have an "advantage" that is also a morally dangerous temptation, in the double lives—the duality of self—their superior freedom of motion opens to them. And the two sisters suffer real oppression from the deception the men use their freedom to practice upon them. The sisters are victims of this unequal distribution among the sexes of the power of movement, and to this extent victims, as deceived, of a socially formal structure with a patriarchal bias. So much one grants to Claudia Johnson's thesis of oppression by patriarchy and to Tony Tanner's of oppression from social formality, theses here blended, revised, and no doubt diluted by me.

While patriarchy aims to suppress young women, young men in turn can be seen to be themselves the unintended victims of a social practice that is also patriarchal in origin. Austen presents this practice as working against young men's freedom of action in ways that cut even more deeply into their character than does male mobility's license for duplicity. A set of interconnected conditions is depicted by Austen as arising from a single social tradition among the gentry, and the whole constellation is presented as deeply afflicting the young male protagonists (among whom I here include Willoughby).

In *Sense and Sensibility* this primordial affliction for the young men is lack of a profession. The socially constructed conception of a gentleman makes it of his essence that he does not work for a living. Being without a profession is part of the definition of the pure, unqualified gentleman. Jane Austen here too, then, is fictionally reconstructing a portion of the patriarchally motivated conception of upper-class masculine gender. In this novel, from the absence in the young men of either an aimed-for or an achieved profession flows, to each man, some share of a mass of grievously damaging effects: lack of purpose; excessive idleness; extravagance, dissipation, and indiscipline if an heir—if not an heir, total economic dependence upon another person; and either way, in regard to personally important matters, severely limited freedom of choice and action.

The father of Elinor and Marianne appears to have been a landed gentleman—and consequently a man without a profession—whose tenure of the land was indeed fragile. The novel's third paragraph develops at length the whimsical foundation upon which the life of a family rests, when it is wholly dependent upon an economics of personal ties:

> The old gentleman [Mr Dashwood's uncle] died; his will was read, and like almost every other will, gave as much disappointment as pleasure. He was neither so unjust, nor so ungrateful, as to leave his estate from his nephew;—but he left it to him on such terms as destroyed half the value of the bequest. Mr Dashwood had wished for it more for the sake of his wife and daughters than for himself or his son:—but to his son, and his son's son, a child of four years old, it was secured, in such a way as to leave to himself no power of providing for those who were most dear to him, and who most needed a provision, by any charge on the estate, or by any sale of its valuable woods. (ch. 1:39–40)

After their father's death in chapter 1, this capricious decision of an old man will reduce the three Dashwood sisters and their mother to a barely genteel form of life without luxury, unless their now wealthy half brother John Dashwood is moderately generous to them. The entire second chapter is devoted to dramatizing the economics of personal caprice. This is where we encounter John Dashwood, moved by his passion for his greedy wife, renouncing his promise to his dying father to provide for his half sisters. Ten paragraphs from the end of the novel, the theme is still being heard: "What Edward had done to forfeit the right of eldest son, might have puzzled many people to find out; and what Robert had done to succeed to it, might have puzzled them still more" (ch. 50:366).

Indeed, this theme of economic dependence upon another's personal caprice pervades the novel, critically shaping its plot. The only route to economic self-sufficiency open to the young women is marriage to someone who has it. Both the preferred lovers of the Dashwood sisters are led into deceptive contortions because of their difficulty dealing in a rational way with the impulses or principles of a relative upon whom they are dependent: both Edward's ferocious mother and Willoughby's scrupulous older cousin, Mrs. Smith, baffle the aspirations of each young man to follow his inclinations—Edward to prepare for the ministry, Willoughby to marry Marianne (although of course here Willoughby's misunderstanding of Mrs. Smith is decisive). Willoughby abandons Marianne because, brought up to be a gentleman without a profession, he knows no means of material support other than dependence upon his wealthy relative or a rich wife. Edward traps himself in a disastrous engagement partly because his widowed and wealthy mother has enforced upon him an idleness meant to be elegant. In part from fear of his wealthy mother's reaction to it, Edward hides his engagement to Lucy Steele, and thereby puts Elinor in a false position.

Perhaps Austen felt she would have cut too uselessly against the grain of current reality if she regretted the absence of professions for women. However, she could distinguish between those women who made productive use of their leisure and those who did not. Lady Middleton is presented (joined with her husband) as part of a vacuously idle couple, whose "want of talent and taste . . . confined their employments, unconnected with such as society produced, within a very narrow compass. Sir John was a sportsman, Lady Middleton a mother. He hunted and shot, and she humored her children; and these were their only resources" (ch. 7:65). On the other hand, the Dashwood women had a different standard for the use of their leisure time. Once they had become well settled in their new house at Barton, "the ordinary pursuits which had given Norland half its charms, were engaged in again. . . . Sir John Middleton, who called on them every day for the first fortnight, and who was not in the habit of seeing much occupation at home, could not conceal his amazement on finding them always employed" (ch. 9:73).

For young men, lack of autonomy and lack of a profession are closely connected—sometimes, as in Edward's case, by a two-way causal interdependence. And in the world depicted in the novel, both are, in turn, connected with dangerously unproductive idleness. I believe there are more disparaging remarks made in this novel about young men's lack of a profession and their consequent idleness than in any other Austen novel.

Since *Sense and Sensibility* has two heroines, it must have two heroes: the two men who marry the heroines, Edward Ferrars and Colonel Brandon. (I had never done this novel's hero-arithmetic until I encountered it in Alison Sulloway's book.) [10] Never mind that Colonel Brandon is artistically a failure; formally he is the second "hero." This novel is, therefore, the only one Austen wrote in which there are two heroes both of whom follow a profession: Brandon is an army officer with service in India behind him, Edward becomes a minister. Nor are these facts treated as irrelevant to their lives. When Brandon reveals to Elinor that he had met Willoughby in a duel over the latter's seduction of his ward, "Elinor sighed over the fancied necessity of this; but to a man and a soldier, she presumed not to censure it" (ch. 31:220). When Marianne and Willoughby together express their low valuation of Brandon's company, Elinor's defense of him suggests her esteem for his profession, and part of it invokes by implication some of the gains she believes may accrue from the pursuit of soldiering: "He has seen a great deal of the world; has been abroad; has read, and has a thinking mind. I have found him capable of giving me much information on various subjects, and he has always answered my inquiries with the readiness of good-breeding and good nature" (ch. 10:82). After his marriage, and at the very end of the book, Edward, at last liberated from dependence on his mother, is notable for "the ready discharge of his duties in every particular . . . an increasing attachment to his wife and his home, and . . . the regular

cheerfulness of his spirits" (ch. 50:366). And the two professional
men—as they are by this time, since Edward has undertaken the rec-
torship Brandon provided for him—are explicitly said to be alike in
character: "The gentlemen advanced in the good opinion of each
other, as they advanced in each other's acquaintance. . . . Their resemblance in good principles and good sense, in disposition and
manner of thinking, would probably have been sufficient to unite
them in friendship, without any other attraction" (ch. 49:359).

Nowhere else in Austen's fiction is the importance of having a
profession so explicitly developed as in two conversations involving
Edward. The first is opened by Mrs. Dashwood "as they were at break-
fast the last morning" of his first visit at Barton cottage:

> "I think, Edward, . . . you would be a happier man if you
> had any profession to engage your time and give an interest
> to your plans and actions. . . ."
> "I do assure you . . . that I have long thought on this
> point, as you think now. It has been, and is, and probably will
> always be a heavy misfortune to me, that I have had no
> necessary business to engage me, no profession to give me
> employment, or afford me anything like independence."
> (ch. 19:127)

As we saw earlier, Edward continues for many lines explaining why,
since his family found his preferred profession, the church, "not
smart enough," and he found objections to both the army and the law,
and the navy did not occur to any of them until he was too old for it,
"I was therefore entered at Oxford and have been properly idle ever
since." This leads Mrs. Dashwood to speculate that "since leisure has
not promoted your own happiness, . . . your sons will be brought
up to as many pursuits, employments, professions, and trades as
Columella's."[11]

That exchange occurs fairly early in the story. In case we should
have forgotten this important theme—and perhaps as well to correct
anyone who may think Edward is masking the true source of his unhappiness (his engagement) by invoking his lack of a profession as the

source—the entire thesis is restated by Edward near the end of the book, this time with culpability for his unfortunate engagement itself ascribed by him to his lacking a profession. Of his attachment to Lucy in earlier years he says:

> "It was a foolish, idle inclination on my side, . . . the conse-
> quence of ignorance of the world—and want of employ-
> ment. Had my mother given me some active profession when
> I was removed at eighteen from the care of Mr. Pratt, I
> think,—nay, I am sure, it would never have happened; for
> though I left Longstaple with what I thought, at the time, a
> most unconquerable preference for his niece, yet had I then
> had any pursuit, any object to engage my time and keep me
> at a distance from her for a few months, I should very soon
> have outgrown the fancied attachment, especially by mixing
> more with the world, as in such a case I must have done. But
> instead of having anything to do, instead of having any pro-
> fession chosen for me, or being allowed to choose any my-
> self, I returned home to be completely idle; and for the first
> twelvemonth afterwards I had not even the nominal employ-
> ment, which belonging to the University would have given
> me, for I was not entered at Oxford till I was nineteen. I had
> therefore nothing in the world to do, but to fancy myself in
> love." (ch. 49:352)

This repetition of a thesis is conspicuously placed—it is Edward's first expansive utterance after Elinor's acceptance of his proposal; and it occurs in the next-to-last chapter of the book. It is also long—it con-tinues for many more lines, and thus shares with its predecessor, also only partly quoted above, the dignity of making up one of Edward's longer "speeches." The thesis is not only cogently propounded by Ed-ward but is also asserted, and first, by Mrs. Dashwood, who can seem to express the combined wisdom of herself and her two elder daugh-ters on this masculine subject matter, because she seems to give vent to an impatience with Edward's mode of life that they too feel. It will be remembered that for Elinor, Edward's "want of spirits, of open-ness, and of consistency, were most usually attributed to his want of independence"—an attribution that turns out to be sound though not in the way intended (ch. 19:126).

Turning now to Willoughby: Elinor's explanation of Willoughby's deficient character suggests Austen is here applying to an early-inheriting heir her idea of the moral price often paid for reaching manhood without having prepared for a profession: "Her thoughts were silently fixed on the irreparable injury which too early an independence and its consequent habits of idleness, dissipation, and luxury, had made in the mind, the character, the happiness" of Willoughby (ch. 44:324).

In a thought of Elinor's purportedly about her host, Mr. Palmer, a young man in his mid-twenties who is running for Parliament, she condemns with a casual generalization a rather large portion of the young male gentry: "For the rest of his character and habits, they were marked, as far as Elinor could perceive, with no traits at all unusual in his sex and time of life. He was nice in his eating, uncertain in his hours; fond of his child, though affecting to slight it; and idled away the morning at billiards, which ought to have been devoted to business" (ch. 42:301).

All too often, in Austen's view, lack of a profession brings with it lack of purpose, vacant time, and either an income demoralizingly dependent on personal ties or, if the young man with no profession is independent, egotism, lack of discipline, extravagance, debt, and finally in both cases: the absence of true freedom in some major choices. In this novel an appropriate share of these afflictions directly exerts an oppressive force on the early life of Edward and on the entire life of Willoughby. Of the two heroes, one, Brandon, is saved by his having pursued the soldierly profession, the other, Edward, is saved at the end of the novel by his entering the clerical profession. I find it impossible to resist the perception that Austen knew her mind on the subject of male practice of a profession remarkably early in her life: she was emphatically in favor of it.

It may well be true, as Jane Nardin has argued, that in her later novels Austen was more disposed than in her earlier ones to embody the "work ethic" in conspicuously working men.[12] This is certainly true in her last novel, *Persuasion,* where not only Captain Wentworth but his navy associates as well, especially Admiral and Mrs. Croft and

Captain and Mrs. Harville, are so redolent of the sea that, for convincing us of their working lives, they might as well be sailing on it. Mr. Knightley in *Emma* does indeed seem to be more at work at Donwell Abbey than Mr. Darcy does at Pemberley. And if Sir Thomas Bertram deserves little credit for anything else, he is entitled to acknowledgment for his possibly arduous and surely dangerous years spent away from home and in some sense (the slaves give pause) "at work" on his estate in Antigua. If I am right, however, this is at most an artistic, not an ideological development. In *Sense and Sensibility*, the low density of genteel male characters with palpably manifest work under way is balanced by the highest density of Austen's stated demands that a gentleman needs a profession.

To me it is interesting to view *Persuasion* and *Sense and Sensibility* as exemplifying two different modes of fictionally developing the same reforming ideas about gentlemen and work. For example, notice that the "price" Austen pays in *Persuasion* for so emphatically portraying the hero as a working man is that she must settle for less reconstruction of masculine gender than in our earlier novel: for Wentworth is an almost swashbuckling naval officer. Conversely, if Austen is to make both heroes in *Sense and Sensibility* so effectively gender-reforming males as they are, she cannot afford to make Brandon a vivid soldier or, for most of the novel, to give Edward any masculinity-enhancing professional place in a world of work that is infinitely less accessible to gentlewomen than to gentlemen.

Nevertheless both her high rate of praising, even demanding, professions for men in the early novel and her increasingly vivid rendering of gentlemen at work in her later ones do figure as identically targeted, fictional reconstructions of the concept of *genteel* masculine gender. For it was still a part of the definition of a gentleman that he did not work for a living. A rural clergyman who was not noted, as Edward was, for "the ready discharge of his duties in every particular" (ch. 50:366), but was noted for the quality of his hunting dogs, his stable, and his wine cellar was more likely to be taken for a gentleman than his hard-working clerical counterpart. If this definition was already weakening its hold on the ruling classes by the time Austen attacked it, she was part of a progressive movement whose good works were far from finished.

5

Elinor's Character: A Heroine
as Public Servant (1)

LINOR DASHWOOD'S CHARACTER—the ethical foundation of her conduct—is a puzzle. With no proof possible, yet with some plausibility, it has been held to be devoutly Christian. On the other hand, appealing to virtually perfect consistency with all explicit evidence, Elinor's moral foundation has been read as secular—only to find the motivational source of her selflessness a puzzle. This may be prime territory for a deconstructive analysis. I am not the one to give it. However, the reading I do give I can understand being viewed as more constitutive than explicative. This is to say, I intend to find a solution for the conundrum of Elinor's character, and of course I think Jane Austen provided the answers I discover; but although I believe the secular resolution I offer is more reasonable, it is no more capable of conclusive proof than the religious thesis.

Probably no serious detective work is needed to identify the specific rules guiding Elinor in situations for which she adopts the moral point of view. One keeps promises, even when made to a rival in love. One treats obnoxious—even malicious—relatives and acquaintances with steady civility. Whenever it is consistent with friendship, one refrains from inflicting upon others the pains of one's own disappointments. Where judgment is necessary concerning others' actions that work against your own interest, you make every effort to judge with disinterested impartiality. Where doing the right thing is in question, one's own interest counts for no more than anyone else's. And so on.

On the other hand, it is no easy matter to work out to everyone's satisfaction the outcome to a more probing inquiry. From what deeper principles, if any, does Elinor derive her ethical rules? From what source does Elinor draw the motive force to sustain her most scrupulously self-denying courses of action?

What is the right way to proceed in answering these questions? This methodological query is puzzling in a special way because of the peculiar division between the role of religion in Austen's life and in her writing. It is reasonable to believe religion's role in her personal life was explicit, overt, and important. So is the role of religion in the "conversion to sense" of Marianne Dashwood during and after her serious illness. But I am not now concerned with Marianne, but with Elinor: it is she, not Marianne, whom some readers—to mention only extremes—experience as either anxiously or starchily conforming, while others find her to be nearly a saint. For some readers she is so good that her characterization falls short of full credibility. And her way of goodness coheres so well with Christian teachings which—we infer from the author's biography—Jane Austen personally believed in, that it is natural Elinor should be experienced by some readers as Austen's most emphatically Christian heroine. Yet Austen the author never offers an explicitly religious account of Elinor's thoughts, feelings, attitudes, choices, actions, words, or patterns of conduct.

A simple explanation can be advanced for the author's intending Elinor to be conscientiously Christian (if she did intend this) and yet never saying so. This explanation makes at least superficially intelligible that odd literary gambit by Austen: religious decorum requires that an author not introduce serious piety into literary comedy. Yet even if we accept that Austen privately thought of Elinor as Christian but refrained, out of a sense of religious decorum, from explicitly introducing pious motivation into Elinor's character, the text itself remains nonetheless problematic. Shall the author's private intention for pious Elinor, when presumed, override for the reader her achieved secular effect? Even if one should be inclined to answer yes, one has to decide how to negotiate *two* somewhat plausible but opposed authorial intentions, the first manifest, the second hypothesized. First, the manifested intention: that no religious motivation for Elinor's actions shall be discernible in the novel, that is, none shall even be inferable with certainty from the text of the novel alone. Second, an intention hypothesized from the author's personal life: that Elinor's actions shall be religiously motivated.

At this point the dialectic of a critical confrontation can begin to seem incurably metaphysical.

One side argues: there is nothing *to* a fictional character beyond what is to be found in the text of the novel. To believe (as an inept amateur might) that, despite a certain trait for a fictional character being nowhere discernible in a text, nevertheless, because during the writing the author has thought of the trait as belonging to this fictional character, therefore the trait *does* belong to it—this is belief in magic! Beliefs like this are not an uncommon superstition of incompetent, amateur writers. The belief is a superstition because, of course, since a novel's whole universe is contained exclusively in its text, if a trait is not visible in or implied by a novel's text, it cannot belong to any character in the novel.

Now, if that principle holds for the ignorantly superstitious amateur, it equally holds for the sophisticated critic interpreting the text of a novelist of genius. If a novelist did not explicitly write a certain motive for a character into her text, or imply it from circumstances she did write in, then the critic is subscribing to magic to believe that the author's merely intending the motive to be there has the effect of investing the character with that motive. Neither a novelist of genius who wishes to avoid public display in a fictional character of a sort of feature (say, a religious motive), nor an amateur who lacks, say, the skill to embody such a feature in an invented character—neither can invest a fictional character with a feature of this sort merely in virtue of *thinking* of the character as having that feature.

So speaks one voice of the dialectic.

However, another argues: to think of a text without a presupposed reader is to think of a merely physical object. If no human (or comparably thoughtful) imagination is supposed to be brought to bear on this object, then no meanings and so no fictional persons are being supposed to exist in connection with the text—indeed, it is not being conceived as a *text*. This is to say that of course what brings into being the imaginary—the fictional—characters of a novel is the response of reading the text with understanding. If this is so, then fictional characters can be said, strictly speaking, to have being only in the imaginations of a text's readers. So those characters' features depend, for their being, upon the imaginations of readers. By some definition of "what readers imagine," therefore, it must be that what sort of character a fictional character *is* is determined by what the (competent) readers of a fictional work imagine (or would if they were to read it). Surely critical readers are entitled, then, to give special weight to the imagination of the person who in reading the text was also creating it and thus to accept the character as it existed in the author's imagination. (Her biography may strongly suggest how she imagined it.) If the description an author has embodied in her text *is consistent with* how she in her private thinking imagines a character, then, concerning any feature that the author imagines belonging to that character, readers who know what she imagines are entitled to believe that in (fictional) fact this features *does* belong to this fictional character.

So speaks a second voice in this exchange.

Let us move away from the potential impasse of abstract dialectic and consider an important moment in Elinor's story.

When Lucy Steele tells Elinor of her secret engagement to Edward, she asks Elinor to keep the secret. Elinor replies, "Your secret is safe with me," thereby promising to tell no one (ch. 22:153).

Keeping this promise will require "unceasing exertion" because it means she must not let her sister or mother see her distress at the loss of Edward (ch. 23:159). This exertion is, as it happens, "a relief to her" because it saves her from the emotional stress that telling them would entail for her. However, once Elinor has mastered her grief from apparently having lost Edward, she pays a painful price for keeping this secret when Marianne misunderstands, and even becomes alienated, because of her ignorance of the basis for some of Elinor's behavior.

When Elinor in London tries to get Marianne to speak more openly of her relationship to Willoughby, Marianne retorts "with energy," "We have neither of us any thing to tell; you, because you do not communicate, and I because I conceal nothing."[1] Elinor was "distressed by this charge of reserve in herself, which she was not at liberty to do away" (ch. 27:184). Later, when Marianne joins the unhappy trio of Lucy, Edward, and Elinor and then afterwards, when alone with Elinor, expresses her disgust that Lucy would not leave them alone with Edward, Elinor again must suffer Marianne's reproach in silence:

> "What can bring her here so often!" said Marianne, on her leaving them. "Could she not see that we wanted her gone!—how teasing to Edward!"
>
> "Why so?—we were all his friends, and Lucy has been the longest known to him of any. It is but natural that he should like to see her as well as ourselves."
>
> Marianne looked at her steadily, and said, "You know, Elinor, that this is a kind of talking which I cannot bear. If you only hope to have your assertion contradicted, as I must suppose to be the case, you ought to recollect that I am the last person in the world to do it. I cannot descend to be tricked out of assurances, that are not really wanted."
>
> She then left the room; and Elinor dared not follow her to say more, for, bound as she was by her promise of secrecy to Lucy, she could give no information that would convince Marianne; and painful as the consequences of her still continuing in an error might be, she was obliged to submit to it. (ch. 35:248–49)

Elinor would like to break her promise for the sake of her relationship to Marianne. However, there is never a hint that she would like to break it by getting information to Edward's sister or mother in the hope of undermining the engagement. Of course Elinor would understand she could not know for sure what effect this would have on the engagement. In any event, we all understand that the dishonor of such an interference in the lives of the engaged couple, quite apart from consideration of her promise, makes it an action the very thought of which would not cross her mind.

Elinor had learned from her conversations with Lucy a good deal Edward does not know about Lucy. For one thing, that Lucy does not love Edward. Also that Lucy knows Edward loves Elinor. Some of this knowledge, if he could accept it, would, in Edward's possession, lead him to break the engagement: "He had always believed her to be a well-disposed, good-hearted girl, and thoroughly attached to himself. Nothing but such a persuasion could have prevented his putting an end to an engagement, which, long . . . had been a continual source of disquiet and regret to him" (ch. 49:356). So one might suppose the thought could enter Elinor's mind to speak directly to Edward of what she had learned of Lucy. To be sure, she might dismiss it on the practical ground that it would be embarrassingly difficult to make Edward certain that Lucy does not love him. Yet in the light of the cost to Edward and to her of his ignorance, she might at least *consider* the attempt. Notice that telling Edward what she learned from talking to Lucy would break no promise to Lucy. The promise was to keep the engagement secret, no more. (Elinor lost no confidence in Edward's feeling for her after her conversations with Lucy: "Elinor remained . . . well assured within herself of being really beloved by Edward" [ch. 23:159].)

Imagine Marianne in the same situation. Would she not think herself honor bound, from a duty to her lover and to their love for each other, to tell her lover what she had learned about how he was being duped?

It is explicit that Elinor's sense of honor has a sharply different content from that. In regard to Lucy, Elinor was "firmly resolved to act by her as every principle of honour and honesty directed, to combat her own affection for Edward and to see him as little as possible" (ch. 23:160). Here Elinor's resolution goes beyond anything entailed by her promise to Lucy of secrecy about their engagement. Elinor has taken on three distinct obligations bearing upon Lucy's engagement: first, to tell no one of it; second, to see Edward as little as possible; third, to attempt to suppress her own affection for Edward. Only the first arises from the commitment openly made to Lucy. The other two, with their corollary of noninterference with the engagement, these two purely private undertakings are more momentous for Elinor, since it is they, more than the promise of secrecy, which strip her of all power of fighting against Lucy through a direct approach to Edward.

Here is the interesting commentary on this stance of Elinor's by the critic Gene Koppel, who, following the illustrious example of Stuart Tave, defends a religious interpretation of Elinor's character:

> To explain Elinor's conduct strictly in terms of moral commitment—[for example:] "She has a very high standard of conduct and lives up to it"—is possible, but is such an explanation really plausible? Elinor is, after all, merely an upper-middle-class girl of nineteen. Her grace under the pressure of sustained, vicious psychological attack is not even perceived, much less admired, by those around her. She has no one to support her in the face of her attacker. Yet she continues to reject the temptation that has to be constantly drumming in her consciousness—to turn on Lucy, to repay her malice with righteous indignation . . . and sweep her vulgar assailant, who holds her in contempt as an honorable fool, from her life.
>
> But nineteen-year-old Elinor, isolated from all those who might encourage her, perseveres in doing the right thing. Can a simple moral commitment really explain this? . . . Elinor's strong emotions, her need and her ability to love and to be loved, her fulfillment in serving others, even in sacrificing herself for them, all point to a young woman who is passionately living her Christianity, rather than doggedly following a moral code. The inspiration for Elinor's treatment of Lucy lies, I believe, . . . in . . . Matthew: "But I say unto you, Love your enemies, bless them that curse you, do good to them that hate you, and pray for them which despitefully use you, and persecute you." (5:44) And while I believe that all of Jane Austen's heroines are in an important sense Chris-

tian heroines, only Elinor is called upon to bear the malice of
a merciless enemy in complete silence (even Fanny has Edmund to sympathize with her about Mrs. Norris's abuse),
and to "do good to them that hate you" even to the point of
destroying her own happiness.[2]

Do let us get age and class out of the way. Supposing that nineteen
years in Austen's time equals nineteen now is rather like thinking five
pounds then equals five now. And in this context, introducing the upper middle class commits several fallacies unworthy of Koppel's high
purpose. But he doesn't, anyhow, need for his argument invidious
discriminations based either on age or class.

As a device of exposition, let me speak of two Austens: Austen the
author, who is defined by her writing; and the private Austen. And let
us suppose the private Austen's religious disposition is, roughly speaking, captured by the following words of David Cecil:

> Jane Austen's religion, so her biographer discovers as he stud-
> ies her, is an element in her life of the highest significance and
> importance. The Austen reticence kept her from ever talking
> much about it. But the little she did say, and what her inti-
> mates said about her, show that she grew up to be deeply re-
> ligious. She actively practised her faith and her moral views
> were wholly, if unobtrusively, determined by the dictates of
> the Christian religion as interpreted by her church. The seeds
> of her faith were sown early and at home by her father's
> teaching; it was developed and strengthened by private devo-
> tions and by the services she went to at the little Steventon
> church.[3]

Why I accept this as only "roughly speaking" accurate is in part because I do not consider it at all likely that a woman of Austen's genius,
not to mention worldly wisdom, should have had her moral views
wholly "determined by the dictates of the Christian religion as interpreted by her church." Indeed, is it likely Cecil would have made *that*

remark about a male writer of comparable genius and piety (say, of Samuel Johnson)?

If, with that qualification, we suppose Cecil's account to be roughly accurate of the private Austen, it will be reasonable to suppose, as a consequence, that Koppel's way of construing Elinor—as an emphatically Christian heroine—roughly coincides with how the *private* Austen imagined Elinor. On the supposition that the private Jane Austen imagined Elinor as emphatically Christian, if we wish to understand Elinor as she in (fictional) fact is, are we readers of Elinor's story required to imagine her as Koppel does?

I doubt that either yes or no can be proved to be the correct answer to this question. I shall, however, offer suggestions tending to support a negative answer. But in doing so I shall make one more supposition which is not unarguably true: that Austen puts nothing in the text that makes it *certain,* from the text alone, that Elinor is pious. In the latter portion of his chapter on this novel, in *Some Words of Jane Austen* Stuart Tave has called attention to some uses of the words "exertion" and "serious" in connection with Elinor that are plausibly, though I think not necessarily, construed as having a religious reference. And there are moments when Elinor is so much reassured about Marianne by Marianne's late, pious utterances that one could argue that Elinor could only be so if she herself were pious. This is reasonable, but not, I think, conclusive: she *could,* for the sake of a sister with very different vulnerabilities from her own, be pleased by Marianne's pious reform without being pious herself—perhaps being only conventionally churchgoing. However, I shall simply ignore these rare and bare intimations, and I shall treat the text as consistent with but neither affirming nor entailing religious motivation in Elinor.

Many readers of Austen have no desire to find a Christian interpretation of Elinor's story. For example, there must be (I presume) Hindu, Buddhist, Muslim, Jewish, Confucian, and Taoist readers of that inclination. Agnostics and atheists—whose view of religion coincides, for example, with David Hume's—also read Austen. For such readers, a Christian interpretation of Elinor need not enrich the novel. Many of these readers will not have read critics or biographers

disposed to read Elinor Dashwood religiously. It will not have occurred to them to read her in that way. Not every one of these readers
will find Elinor credible; shortly I shall take this fact seriously. Yet
quite a few doubtless do find her credible. If we rush to a religious
reading, we may fail to look closely enough at the moral texture of Elinor's story to discover how Austen succeeded in so rendering Elinor's
self-denying conduct that she is credible to many readers without appearing pious.

We have seen that Elinor assumes not merely the obligation to
Lucy that Koppel mentions and that is founded on a promise to keep
Lucy's engagement secret but also two more that are undertaken as
private resolutions: to see Edward as little as possible and "to combat
her own affection for Edward." The passage that mentions the second
two commitments also describes motivation Elinor found for taking
them on: they figured for Elinor as entailments of the obligation she
assumed "to act by her *as every principle of honour* and honesty directed" (ch. 23:160; my emphasis).

According to official patriarchal ideas, when it is personally momentous, a matter of honor is a masculine concern. More than that, it
is a matter involving gentlemen only; strictly speaking, a man who is
not a gentleman has no honor to be upheld or offended. Interpreters
of fiction have largely followed patriarchal rules in being readier to ascribe to a sense of honor the actions of men in novels than those of
women. No critic is likely to overlook Willoughby's recognizing that
in putting off from day to day his proposal to Marianne, he had been,
as he confessed to Elinor, "scrupling to engage my faith where my
honour was already bound" (ch. 44:315). Apart from the ridiculously
narrow and essentially vulgar equation of her "honor" with her chas-
tity, a woman is not assigned a place on the field of honor. Women do
not bind their honor by spending more time with one man than with
any other. Women do not fight duels. And so forth.

But this construction by the patriarchy of a profoundly ethical
form of gender differentiation may be rejected by a woman as if it
were a piece of social legislation that is made void by the obsolescence
of its tunnel vision. We need to be able to imagine that Austen held
this view and that she meant in this novel to make sure the motiva-

tional force of a sense of honor in women could be seen to be quite as effective as it may be in men—*and* that the contexts in which women might engage their honor matched in breadth of ethical interest the men's field.

In this novel Jane Austen chose to make their sense of honor a strongly motivating force in the psychology of the novel's three favored women.

In speaking to Marianne of what troubles she might have encountered in a marriage to Willoughby, Elinor attributes to Marianne the same sense of honor she herself is moved by in response to Lucy: "His demands and your inexperience together on a . . . very small income, must have brought on distresses . . . entirely unknown and unthought of before. *Your* sense of honour and honesty would have led you, I know, when aware of your situation, to attempt all the economy that would appear to you possible" (ch. 47:341). Compare with that the occasion of Colonel Brandon's sense of honor being brought into play by Willoughby's seduction of his ward. He told Elinor they fought a duel, "he to defend, I to punish his conduct," and Elinor reluctantly realized that "to a man and a soldier, she presumed not to censure it" (ch. 31:220). Brandon's sense of honor as a gentleman requires that he personally try to punish Willoughby for the injury inflicted on Eliza Williams: this is a kind of meting out of justice. The imagined operation of Marianne's sense of honor would have been an undertaking to give to creditors their due; this too is a way of doing justice.

No readers are likely to suppose that Brandon's sense of honor could operate as a motive in his challenging Willoughby to a duel only if it were backed by religious conviction. Perhaps a gentleman could scarcely fail to discover, willy-nilly by a kind of osmosis from the community, something of a gentleman's code of honor, and to find its motivating force in a desire like Darcy's to be respected as a gentleman. No doubt Colonel Brandon's experience as an army officer is relevant. Where should we look for the source of the Dashwood sisters' sense of honor? Austen is explicit about one likely source:

No sooner was [John Dashwood's] father's funeral over than Mrs John Dashwood, without sending any notice of her intention to her mother-in-law, arrived with her child and their attendants. No one could dispute her right to come; the house was her husband's from the moment of his father's decease; but the indelicacy of her conduct was so much the greater, and to a woman in Mrs Dashwood's situation, with only common feelings, must have been highly unpleasing. But in *her* mind there was a sense of honour so keen, a generosity so romantic, that any offense of the kind, by whomsoever given or received, was to her a source of immoveable disgust. (ch. 1:41)

Mrs. Dashwood proposed to leave the house immediately—an obvious rebuff to her daughter-in-law—so acutely did she "feel this ungracious behavior and so earnestly did she despise her daughter-in-law for it." Her sense of honor made her acutely aware of the consideration due to her in light of her loss of both a beloved husband and a treasured estate.

Although the deliverances of Elinor's and Marianne's sense of honor would often doubtless be different, it is understandable that each daughter should have been influenced by her mother's example to develop her own variant. We should expect Marianne's code to give priority to the values of individualism, Elinor's to manifest a strong disposition to take up the point of view of a community with which she identifies.

If we later readers are to eschew gender bias, we have no more reason to refuse a merely familial and communal origin for these fictional women's sense of honor, and instead to seek a religious source for it, than we have to do the same for fictional Colonel Brandon's sense of honor in regard to his ward Eliza. If one would appeal to pride as a motive especially natural to Brandon's situation, this is equally natural in the imagined case of Marianne (regarding debts) and in the actual case of Mrs. Dashwood (regarding her daughter-in-law's insulting behavior); and it is equally natural for Elinor in her conduct toward Lucy Steele: all of these can be "natural" targets of pride's reaction if they can be so viewed by a group or a community with which each proud agent identifies. Since Elinor is our present concern, let us consider more closely the operation of her resolution, in relation to Lucy, "to act by her as every principle of honour and honesty directed" (ch. 23:160).

We remember that when Marianne had been most painfully injured by Willoughby's letter, Elinor urged her sister to be moved by a "reasonable and laudable pride" (ch. 29:201). And we remind ourselves that in the very passage that invokes Elinor's sense of honor in regard to Lucy, pride is clearly the moving force when she is also said to be intent on dissembling before Lucy, unwilling to "deny herself the comfort of endeavoring to convince Lucy that her heart was unwounded" (ch. 23:160). We know that Elinor believes Lucy lacking in "delicacy . . . rectitude . . . integrity of mind" and that she takes note of the absence of these qualities precisely because she values so highly their presence in herself (ch. 22:149). The pride that leads Elinor to pretend to be unwounded can move her to invoke her sense of honor against using tactics she knows Lucy would use if in Elinor's shoes.

However, those tactics would not be dishonorable unless there is a principle of honor that applies to the situation and that they would violate. For Colonel Brandon, in his situation with Willoughby, the principle is something like "Punish a man who violates a woman in your care." For Mrs. Dashwood's position, the applicable principle (violated by Fanny Dashwood) is "Be kindly before grief." For the position imagined for Marianne as Mrs. Willoughby, "Pay your debts, and do not live beyond your income." And for Elinor's situation with Lucy? "Respect another woman's engagement." This principle of feminine honor implies a certain solidarity with one's sisters in a shared and sometimes desperate dependence. It is no harder to understand that a woman should acquire, without the aid of religion, the power to pay a high personal price to live by this principle than it is to understand how a Brandon could do the same for his honor at the possible price of paying with his life in a duel.

In short, Elinor's conduct in relation to Lucy Steele is easily intelligible, and Elinor in this respect entirely credible, without introducing a religious motivation that is never offered to us by Austen. What is required of us to feel quite comfortable with this reading is that we imagine it to be as natural for Austen to wish to celebrate a woman's

independent sense of honor as to acknowledge a man's. In a patriarchal social order, men are more likely than women to be conceived as
not requiring a higher authorization for their honor: the ultimate
source of moral authority is a father, and because each man is capable
in principle of becoming one, each can be treated as such. We must
imagine Austen to be unwilling to accept that invidious undervalua-
tion of the moral quality of womanhood. Quite as naturally as Colonel Brandon (and far more vividly, for his duel is offstage) Elinor
Dashwood is to be experienced (with a bow to another woman, her
mother) as having within her secular self—partly in her personal
pride—the motivating force of her own sense of honor.

However, to this reader, it is in another situation that a secular reading of Elinor's motivation is more problematic. This situation extends
through two chapters, 39 and 40, which I find among the most striking and significant—and enjoyable—in the book. Here coherence of
explanation requires us to uncover the redrawing of gender boundaries that is more camouflaged yet perhaps in some ways bolder than
any so far located. I shall therefore take some time with these two
chapters.

   When, near the end of the book, Elinor believes she has virtually
been told by the bride herself that Edward Ferrars has just married
Lucy Steele, she "found the difference between the expectation of an
unpleasant event, however certain the mind may be told to consider
it, and certainty itself" (ch. 48:347). One of the earlier moments when
Elinor's mind was told to become more sure of this event was the occasion, in chapter 39, of Colonel Brandon's making it possible for Edward to marry Lucy by offering him the rector's living at Delaford.
More precisely, the occasion was Brandon's informing Elinor of his
intention to make this offer, and asking *her* to extend it to Edward on
his behalf! That this occasion made Elinor more confident in her expectation of that marriage is of present interest only as it makes more
extraordinary her full response to this communication.

   Of course Elinor would rather not accept the charge. She tries to
get Brandon himself to make the offer to Edward, but, from "motives
of equal delicacy" to her own, Brandon is so insistent on Elinor's be-

ing the instrument of his good works "that she would not on any account make farther opposition" (ch. 39:282).

Elinor accepts the commission, and, after Colonel Brandon's departure, she is just congratulating herself on being able to do it by letter rather than in person when Edward himself is announced and appears. This is their first meeting since he has known her to be aware of
his engagement; and she is charged with conveying to him, as a reward for his loyalty to Lucy, the wherewithal to marry Lucy! All of this

> made her feel particularly uncomfortable for some minutes.
> He too was much distressed, and they sat down together in a
> most promising state of embarrassment. . . .
>
>   "Mrs Jennings told me," said he, "that you wished to
> speak with me, at least I understood her so,—or I certainly
> should not have intruded on you. . . ."
>
>   . . . "Mrs Jennings was quite right in what she said. I have
> something of consequence to inform you of, which I was on
> on the point of communicating by paper. I am charged with
> a most agreeable office, (breathing rather faster than usual as
> she spoke.) Colonel Brandon, who was here only ten minutes
> ago, has desired me to say that, understanding you mean to
> take orders, he has great pleasure in offering you the living of
> Delaford, now just vacant, and only wishes it were more
> valuable. Allow me to congratulate you on having so re-
> spectable and well-judging a friend, and to join in his wish
> that the living—it is about two hundred a year—were much
> more considerable, and such as might better enable you to—
> as might be more than a temporary accommodation to your-
> self—such, in short, as might establish all your views of
> happiness." (ch. 40:286–87)

Colonel Brandon thinks of Elinor and Edward as friends only. He had
asked Elinor to convey to Edward his wish that the living were
sufficient to enable Edward to satisfy what he takes to be Edward's desire to marry Lucy. This desire is also describable, by the convention
of the time and in Elinor's words, as Edward's "view of happiness," or

in Brandon's words, Edward's "only object of happiness" (ch. 39:282). In joining in this wish, Elinor in effect says to the man she loves, "Let me join Colonel Brandon in wishing the living were sufficient to allow you to marry Lucy Steele."

What in the world are we to make of this behavior? To start with, she need not have accepted the commission from Brandon. Why did she? Having accepted it, perhaps she was obliged to pass on to Edward Colonel Brandon's regret that he could not also provide for Lucy, although one might think this obligation could have counted as sufficient reason not to accept the commission in the first place. But *that* obligation did not in the least require that she should join herself to the colonel's wish. Yet she did. Nor was this a matter of getting tangled in difficult words and saying more than her cooler mind would have expressed. For after quite enough conversation for her to have achieved composure, she *in effect* again wishes him happiness in his forthcoming marriage to Lucy Steele:

> They parted, with a very earnest assurance on *her* side of her unceasing good wishes for his happiness in every change of situation that might befall him. . . .
>
> "When I see him again," said Elinor to herself, as the door shut him out, "I shall see him the husband of Lucy."
>
> And with this pleasing anticipation she sat down to reconsider the past, recal the words, and endeavour to comprehend all the feelings of Edward; and, of course, to reflect on her own with discontent. (ch. 40:289)

In the interest of keeping track of Austen's realism at a fictional moment that puts it in question, we need to be sure to remark how this entire action of Elinor's closes: Elinor is reflecting with discontent on her own feelings. She achieved by her immersion in this action at best a brief respite from the inevitable distress this new boost in Lucy's prospects must cause her to feel.

I want to draw an analogy with the psychology of sense perception. I believe Austen has created in these two chapters, 39 and 40, an Elinor who is truly a "reversible figure," like the Necker cube, a set of lines that looks now to be a cube having one orientation, then to be one having another; or the rabbit-vase figure, a set of lines that one now sees as a rabbit profile, then as a vase, now again as a rabbit, and so on. I can understand a way of seeing Elinor in these Brandon-to-Elinor-to-Edward scenes that makes Elinor superciliously polite and spinelessly insincere. This is not at all the perception I have. Yet, especially on first reading, and especially if one takes Elinor in the secular way, this unfavorable perception is all too natural as one way of experiencing Elinor here. How does this perception go?

On the unfavorable reading of Elinor, she is guilty of grotesque contortion of herself in dissimulation before Edward, from two motives, neither of which is sufficient to justify radical dishonesty in so close a personal relationship. (I ignore here the theoretical possibility that Elinor can't think of a nonembarrassing excuse for refusing Brandon's request—Austen's portrait of Elinor does not support slow-wittedness under stress as an explanation for something momentous that Elinor does.) First, she accepts from Brandon a commission that, out of loyalty to the love that she knows Edward and she have for each other, she should never have undertaken; she accepts it because she lacks the courage to amend, when she should, her "plan of general civility," which means *too* much to her (ch. 17:119). Second, in carrying out the commission, she exceeds its requirements, by presenting herself to Edward as if she were at one with Colonel Brandon in the wish to help him marry Lucy Steele. She thus dissembles, as earlier with Lucy, in order to hide from Edward, if not her affection (too late), at least her vulnerability. On this reading, her present behavior is meant by her to suggest to Edward that her affection has been superficial and ephemeral. She wishes to suggest this from motives of personal pride: it is the highly civilized but nonetheless defensive and contorted behavior of a woman who has lost out.

Now I reverse the figure, and offer a favorable reading of Elinor's behavior with Brandon and Edward.

In the Lucy-Elinor "battle scene" of chapter 24 Austen gives explicit indication of her intention to present Elinor as descending from her usually superior altitude to Lucy's level of almost-open combat. That descent is a marked exception to the author's habit with Elinor.

But here, in the text of chapters 39 and 40, there is no sign that Austen intends to show Elinor to disadvantage. Rather the opposite. Almost any reader coming to the text with the Christian interpretation of Elinor's character that Gene Koppel has offered would find this action of Elinor's a confirming example. Austen writes without irony in presenting as exemplary Elinor's performance of her duty, first to the extraordinarily generous but reticent Colonel Brandon, and then to the so honorably self-denying, and so painfully embarrassed, Edward. Such a Christian-leaning reader would therefore plausibly find it compelling to view Elinor in her present actions as selflessly conscientious in her will to do good for these two men who are themselves so admirably doing good (Brandon) or right (Edward); and that reader would find the favorable interpretation far more coherent with the full portrait of Elinor than the unfavorable one.

I am in essential agreement with a *secular* version of the favorable reading of Elinor Dashwood in Chapters 39 and 40. But the secular version of this reading, which I think correct because it limits itself to the text Austen created for us, faces its own special challenge. To phrase its problem in an acute form: how shall Elinor be found credible as figuring, at least on this occasion, as something close to a secular saint? Although I disavow that oxymoronic formulation of her moral achievement, I find the difficulty it points to formidable indeed. My effort to resolve it will be proportionately strenuous.

My first step in meeting this challenge for the favorable yet secular interpretation of Elinor's conduct is to provide explanatory background for her accepting and executing Colonel Brandon's commission. The unfavorable interpretation ascribes her accepting it to her inability to amend her "plan of general civility," amend it on behalf of loyalty to romantic love. I think this is mistaken: her accepting Brandon's commission is *not* done as a matter of civility. Nevertheless, understanding Elinor's acceptance of Brandon's commission does require a clear view of the place in Elinor's moral economy of her policy of general civility. It is because *both* that policy *and* her acquiescence in Brandon's request concerning Edward spring from similar motivation that critical discriminations can get muddled. So I turn first to Elinor's policy of general civility. Her "plan of general civility" does *not* pertain to her Brandon-Edward transaction. Yet her passion for general civility *does* share a psychological source with her unexpected Brandon-to-Edward mediation. Hence these two self-expressions of Elinor do figure similarly in composing her character.

It was Edward who offered as a description of Elinor's social practice the phrase "plan of general civility" (ch. 17:119). Marianne offers another apt phrase when she equates practicing "the civilities" with performing "the lesser duties of life" (ch. 46:338). That Marianne (until late in the novel) agrees with some readers in thinking Elinor attaches too much importance to general civility is evident from her once remarking, facetiously, "But I thought it was right, Elinor, . . . to be guided wholly by the opinion of other people. I thought our judgments were given us merely to be subservient to those of our neighbors. This has always been your doctrine, I am sure" (ch. 17:119). Of course, as Elinor promptly asserts, she holds no such doctrine. Yet it is likely that the source of the impression of Elinor's caring *too* much about civility is that she is in fact moved by something close to a passion both to practice it and (especially but not only in regard to Marianne) to promote it. Suppose this is so. Then we need to understand the nature of this passion. Let us try.

It could be that Elinor's drive for civility manifests a passion for pleasing others, or at least for avoiding offense, that springs from a timid and fearful nature, so that her reward for the practice is her pleasure from others' approval and her relief from anxiety or fear. For me this interpretation works too much against the upbeat tone of Austen's treatment of Elinor: it does not cohere with the authorial intention that seems manifest in the text to present Elinor as an admirably strong young woman.

Or Elinor's passion for general civility could be the one natural to "a young woman who is passionately living her Christianity, rather than doggedly following a moral code," as Gene Koppel describes her, thus reading into Elinor the religion of the private Jane Austen. I have already accepted the idea of a passionately motivated practice, so a "doggedly followed" one is certainly to be rejected. And this Christian interpretation is, I say again, surely *consistent with* what we are told about Elinor: that is to say, it does not contradict anything we find in the text of the novel. My problem with it is that it goes way beyond what is given there. Where no religious thought or motive is ever ascribed to Elinor, to invent a passionate Christianity for her is to undercut the author's extraordinary achievement, *if it is achieved:* namely, having created a heroine whose behavior is such that she *could* be a passionately Christian protagonist but who is made credible to us as a purely secular heroine.

My objection, then, to the religious explanation for Elinor's passion for strenuous civility has force *only if* that passion is credible when it is read in a way that is both nonbelittling and nonreligious. This brings me to my own explanation of the passion with which Elinor supports the general practice of the civilities and lesser duties. My interpretation is based on an analogy. There exists a purely secular vocation that may be invested with ideal content and pursued with passion and that enables those who follow it to find satisfaction in being agreeable to disagreeable people, being friendly to unfriendly people, being kindly to persons who are unkind to them, polite to persons who are rude to them, and helpful to persons who hinder them. I mean the sometimes splendid calling of the dedicated statesperson-politician. Elinor's practice of difficult civilities among her acquaintances is of the same species as the practice by public-spirited statespersons of uncommon friendliness toward their constituents and associates. Her policy of general civility springs from a passion and gives a satisfaction of the same species as those that move and reward the elected official whose life is genuinely devoted to the service of the public.

Having stated my conclusion, I shall shortly go back and develop its grounds by using, as a representative instance, Elinor's practice of a difficult civility on the occasion of Edward Ferrars's first visit to the Dashwoods at their new home, Barton Cottage. However, before doing this, I have a preliminary matter to dispatch.

That Elinor finds it *difficult* to undertake those lesser duties that many of us would find downright repellent is left understated, or shown indirectly, by an author more interested in displaying Elinor's mastery of her civic vocation than its difficulty for her; then too, from the habit of conceiving Elinor as stoical—or worse, impassive—we sometimes simply overlook the evidence. For example, when Mrs. Dashwood was disgusted by Fanny's cruelly quick arrival to take possession of Norland after Mr. Dashwood's death, Elinor "could struggle, she could exert herself" to "receive her sister-in-law on her arrival, and treat her with proper attention" and urge her mother "to similar forbearance" (ch. 1:42). Much, much later, in London, after Elinor has received—through omissions and by indirection—various insults from this same Fanny Ferrars Dashwood, when Marianne insists Elinor therefore not visit Fanny to inquire about a bogus health problem, and not even good-natured Mrs. Jennings's "strong desire to affront [Fanny] by taking Edward's part, could overcome her unwillingness to be in her company again," nonetheless "Elinor set out by herself to pay a visit, for which no one could really have less inclination, and to run the risk of a tête-à-tête with a woman, whom neither of the others had so much reason to dislike" (ch. 41:291–92). Another example we have noted in another connection. When Elinor decided to accompany Marianne to London where they would stay with Mrs. Jennings, part of her reason was that she did not think "Mrs Jennings should be abandoned to the mercy of Marianne for all the comfort of her domestic hours" (ch. 25:173). At the start of their three-day journey to London

> Elinor could not find herself in the carriage with Mrs Jennings, and beginning a journey to London under her protection, and as her guest, without wondering at her own situation . . . so wholly unsuited were they in age and disposition, and so many had been her objections . . . and Elinor . . . could not witness the rapture of delightful expectation which filled the whole soul and beamed in the eyes of Marianne, without feeling how blank was her own prospect, how cheerless her own state of mind in the comparison. (ch. 26:175)

Let us continue to observe Elinor in the pursuit of her program of general civility, now without regard to whether or not it looks hard for her. When Edward Ferrars makes his first visit to the Dashwoods after they have moved from Norland to Barton Cottage, he is no amiable lover. He arrives unexpectedly on horseback and is at first mistaken by Marianne for Willoughby returning from London. Here rereaders of the novel understand, as the two sisters do not, that his coming directly to Barton Cottage from a visit to "friends near Plymouth" is for him an uneasy transition after spending two weeks with Lucy Steele at her uncle's. Marianne is dismayed by Edward's cold behavior to Elinor, for "there was a deficiency of all that a lover ought to look and say on such an occasion" (ch. 16:113). Elinor too felt Edward to be cold:

> Elinor . . . endeavored to support something like discourse with him by talking of their present residence, its conveniences, &c extorting from him occasional questions and remarks. His coldness and reserve mortified her severely; she was vexed and half angry; but resolving to regulate her behavior to him by the past rather than the present, she avoided every appearance of resentment or displeasure, and treated him as she thought he ought to be treated from the family connection. (ch. 16:115)

Although significant conduct toward Edward is not normally part of "mere" civility, in this instance he has so distanced himself from the role of her lover that, for Elinor at least, the "lesser duties" come into play. The reason this performance of a lesser duty is useful for my purposes is that there is more analysis of Elinor's mode of thought than Austen usually offers for similar performances; and this way of thinking seems singularly expressive of Elinor's characteristic subordination of the personal to a distinctive form of the impersonal.

Elinor's personal emotion on this occasion is strong: she is vexed, she is half angry, she is severely mortified. But instead of reacting to Edward's coldness and reserve toward her, she subsumes his conduct under general concepts that suggest a rule by which to govern her behavior. She categorizes his manner toward her as an unaccountable deviation from a lover's form, so she invokes the form for another aspect of their relationship: warmth toward a family friend. By an act of will—"resolving"—that is characteristic of Elinor, she suppresses her personal emotion and chooses to regulate her behavior to him according to rules governing the merely family aspect of their connection. To apply to herself Elinor's own earlier words of praise of Colonel Brandon, this is the work of "a thinking mind" (ch. 10:82). It is also the work of a mind much disposed to view its own situation from an impersonal perspective: again and again, in situations in which she has a personal interest she ignores this interest by adopting a disinterested viewpoint. But this viewpoint she so often adopts can also be thought of as belonging to some human group larger than herself, as expressing the interest of a family, it may be, or of a community that is as fluid as an evening party in London, as stable as a village, or as tradition-bound as a social class.

Let me pick one noun—let it be *community*—for the generic idea here, and say that when Elinor is deliberating about her own actions, it seems almost more natural for her to take up a point of view expressive of the interest of some community than it is to be guided by her personal interest. And let me use in my own sense, as a term conveying no more meaning than flows naturally to it from my broad use of the noun *community,* the adjective *communitarian:* Elinor has a strongly communitarian ethical outlook. Edward is a presumptive lover, and also the brother of the wife of Elinor's half brother. When her personal interest in the first relationship is vexed and even mortified, she disconnects herself from that interest and acts from the perspective of this extended family's common good.

Endowed with a thinking mind and as highly discriminating a sensibility as Marianne, Elinor nonetheless eschews elitism in her daily life and, on grounds of propriety, extends essentially equal courtesy to Anne Steele, Mrs. Palmer, and Lady Middleton, to Mrs. Ferrars, Fanny Dashwood, and Mrs. Jennings. This suggests that she is moved not merely by kind consideration for a likeable, good-hearted person such as Mrs. Jennings, but also—even toward Mrs. Jennings— by the interest that she believes the community as a whole has in a "plan of general civility" for its members.

The fact that, despite the ugly egoism and materialism and the depressing shallowness of so much of the novel's population, we nonetheless do experience them all as constituting a *community* in which Elinor is immersed is, in no small measure, explained by this fact: that the central consciousness through whose experience we readers encounter the novel's population, Elinor's, faithfully and articulately affirms the interest of that community—does it ever so tactfully by invoking the genteel euphemism "propriety"—and subordinates, sometimes poignantly, her own desires to the requirements of responsible citizenship. Rather than think of Elinor, in this aspect, as the moralist (not to mention religionist), compare her project to that of the pursuit of public-spirited politics by the conscientious public servant who, to serve usefully, needs the good will of both her colleagues and her constituents. That public servant too suppresses her simply personal emotions in favor of a steadily friendly "address" to constituents she might, as to personal feeling, prefer to avoid or even attack. This is an artifice, but one that she may come to find natural and even gratifying, and through which she expresses her recognition that her vocation is to serve the common good.

My use of feminine personal pronouns just above is of course unhistorical, since a political career was closed to the women of Jane Austen's world. So, largely, was public economic life, for women of the ranks Austen depicted. However, if the cement that held that world together was not only political and economic but also social, as seems certain, then it is to be expected that, without always being conscious of the analogy, there should be women who took with such seriousness this socially binding function that it had for them the quality of a professional commitment like that of the public servant. Elinor would be quite conscious of nursing, through her civilities, the ties binding her extended family. To stretch this consciousness farther is for her little more than to make it comprehend the extended families of her extended family. When a Mrs. Jennings, with her tendency to treat as family anybody she can both visit and be fond of, is a member of that already large group, we can suppose the community whose interest Elinor can make her own has no fixed boundaries. We remember Mrs. Jennings's proclivity for friendship with servants—when the Dashwood sisters finally take leave of her, we recall her taking "comfort in the gossip of her maid for the loss of her two young companions"—

and we realize that, once Mrs. Jennings is within this hyperextended superfamily, it might happen that not even social class could fix the boundaries for Elinor's community of constituents (ch. 46:333).

Jane Austen's religion is not, by the way, the only side of the author's personal life to which a reader may appeal in seeking a biographical source for Elinor's communitarian outlook. Austen's power of expanding the idea of family loyalty so that it embraces public service to both local and national interests could be grounded both in her father's life as Church of England rector at Steventon, and in her two brothers' very long wartime naval service, hazardous duty that held her sisterly attention for most of her adult life. We see her joining the domestic and the patriotic in the concluding words of her last completed novel, speaking of Anne Elliot's marriage to Captain Wentworth: "She gloried in being a sailor's wife, but she must pay the tax of quick alarm for belonging to that profession which is, if possible, more distinguished in its domestic virtues than in its national importance." In a well-known scene in *Emma,* long before the heroine has the thought of marrying Mr. Knightley, Emma mixes English patriotism with family pride in her connection, through her sister's marriage, with Knightley's Donwell Abbey, whose eventual heir, should Knightley remain unmarried, would be Emma's nephew. She begins with purely family feeling: "She felt all the honest pride and complacency which her alliance with the present and future proprietor could fairly warrant. . . . It was just what it ought to be, and it looked what it was—and Emma felt an increasing respect for it, as the residence of a family of such true gentility, untainted in blood and understanding. . . . Isabella had connected herself unexceptionably" (*E,* ch. 42: 353). Although there may be for the author something congenial in this viewpoint, it is a display of Emma's snobbishness, a fact that is marked by its ironic contrast with the ensuing view of Abbey-Mill Farm, and of Knightley in conversation with Harriet helping her to appreciate "all [the Farm's] appendages of prosperity and beauty, its rich pastures, spreading flocks, orchard in blossom, and light column of smoke ascending" (*E,* ch. 42:355). This farm, and Knightley's advocacy of its "mere" farmer Robert Martin as a young man whose social position is quite adequate to marry Emma's protégé is a symbol of

English social mobility, and so of at least a Tory kind of democracy that Knightley stands for. Emma opposes Knightley in this; on another occasion she declares to him:

> "Nothing but a gentleman in education and manner has any chance with Harriet."
> "Nonsense, errant nonsense, as ever was talked! . . . Robert Martin's manners have sense, sincerity, and good-humour to recommend them; and his mind has more true gentility than Harriet Smith could understand." (*E,* Ch. 8:91)

So Emma is not only connecting attachment to family with attachment to England but unwittingly and ironically supporting a kind of English democracy she does not accept, when she relishes the view looking out from the Donwell grounds to where:

> Favourably placed and sheltered, rose the Abbey-Mill Farm, with meadows in front, and the river making a close and handsome curve around it.
> It was a sweet view—sweet to the eye and the mind. English verdure, English culture, English comfort, seen under a sun bright, without being oppressive. (*E,* ch. 42:355)

Both in this her next-to-last novel, and in her last one, *Persuasion,* it is the men—Knightley as embodying the best of the Tory egalitarian spirit, Robert Martin as a yeoman who justifies it, and Captain Wentworth and his fellow naval officers as at once exemplary husbands and patriots—it is chiefly the men in whom the public-spirited impulses of the author find expression, although both Mrs. Croft's and Anne's identification with the navy is important. I suggest that at the start of her most serious writing, Austen was prepared to conceive a woman who came closer than most fictional heroines did to assuming the role of public servant. Further grounds for this reading will develop as we pursue to its next stage our present inquiry.

I have undertaken to understand the motivation behind Elinor's program of general civility as my start in explaining both her difficult willingness to serve as Colonel Brandon's emissary to Edward and her surprising way of conveying Brandon's offer of a living to Edward. I anticipated a similarity in motivation but a difference in quality between her program of general civility and her performance as Brandon's emissary in assisting Edward to marry Lucy. I have interpreted her plan of general civility as motivated by the passion natural to her communitarian vocation, which resembles that of a dedicated public servant. I think neither her acceptance of Brandon's commission nor her way of handling herself with Edward in executing it is a matter of civility. The difference in quality shows there. But I think the motivation behind her delivering Brandon's offer to Edward is like that of her project of general civility: her social-stateswomanly passion is decisively brought into play on behalf of each course of action.

To do justice to this hypothesis about the explanation of Elinor's acting for Brandon on behalf of Edward, I need again to back up, this time in order to gain perspective on Colonel Brandon's offering the Delaford living to Edward. I want to outline for this action a context that should shape our understanding of Elinor's participation in it. And I propose to use a new chapter for these concluding portions of my argument.

6

Elinor's Character: A Heroine
as Public Servant (2)

WANT TO show that the same secular ideals and aspirations that
I have argued underlie Elinor's plan of general civility also do
much to account for her carrying out Colonel Brandon's commission regarding Edward: she is guided by communitarian principles, and she is moved by an impulse to public service.

To reach this endpoint of my inquiry, I need first to clarify the
moral import of Brandon's giving to Edward the Delaford living. I
mean to try for this clarity indirectly, by again considering critically a
thesis from Claudia L. Johnson's stimulating and often illuminating
book *Jane Austen: Women, Politics and the Novel.*

In my earlier discussion (chapter 4) of some of Johnson's ideas
about the failings of Edward Ferrars and Willoughby, I remarked that,
in her chapter on *Sense and Sensibility,* she argues that Austen's harshly
unfavorable rendering of much of family life aligns her with the progressive social critics of the 1790s in England. I also noted that Johnson believes that *Sense and Sensibility*'s "extremely trenchant and
in some ways extremely radical" critique of conservative ideology is
"proffered largely through an examination of the morally vitiating
tendencies of patriarchy."[1] In Johnson's hands, this second thesis
amounts to construing the novel as largely a satirical critique of the

patriarchal organization of the English family. I think this overestimates Austen's hostility to familial patriarchy as such. I believe Austen felt this structure *need* not entail the fatuous and damaging gender distortions she meant to satirize. More pertinent to my present objective, Austen seems to me to have judged that a patriarchal family structure *need* not nurture either male narcissism or an ideology of "family-ism," that is, taking as one's moral imperative "My family first, right or wrong." My dissent from Johnson's reading of the novel aims to bring into focus Austen's separation of good from bad family heads and her use of positive communitarian rather than antipatriarchal principles in making this separation. My goal is thereby to provide a persuasive context for appreciating Austen's—and explaining Elinor's—high valuation of Colonel Brandon's gift of the Delaford living to Edward, when, as John Dashwood put it, there was "no relationship! no connection between them!" (ch. 41:292). My hope is that the psychology of Elinor's participation in Brandon's action can then become accessible to us.

No doubt in the novel's first two or three chapters Austen does attack the rule of male inheritance and disposal of estates. And throughout the novel either second sons (Brandon) or disinherited first sons (Edward) are favored over inheriting sons (Willoughby, and Brandon's elder brother as well as Edward's). But where, in the novel's rendered states of affairs, is the patriarchal family whose patriarch is under attack as patriarch or whose patriarchal structure—simply as such—appears to be the subject of criticism? Sir John Middleton is a patriarch. As I shall shortly observe more closely, however, Austen's treatment of him is not, on balance, dismissive. I suppose the young Mr. Palmer counts officially as a patriarch. But Mr. Palmer moves from being a boor early to being a kind host, and in the end is made out at worst as harmless, at his best as benign. John Dashwood is no doubt another young patriarch. But he stands in awe of his mother-in-law, Mrs. Ferrars, and figures as her abject follower. When he is not taking direction from the mother, he is being dominated by her daughter, his wife, Fanny. His "governance" of his family is presented as a bare formality. Not merely Fanny's dominance but her vicious rule is demonstrated in chapters 1 and 2, when she takes instant possession of Norland upon her father-in-law's death and when she talks her husband out of keeping his promise to his father to provide for his sisters; it is reaffirmed in chapter 36, when she persuades her husband the Steele sisters matter more to him than his own. The only match to Fanny as the satirically most vilified head of a family is her mother, Mrs. Ferrars, a matriarch for sure. Young Willoughby is an eventual patriarch, but he is first ruled by Mrs. Smith and then by Miss Grey. Because of Mrs. Smith, he gives up Marianne, and because of Miss Grey, he brutally insults her. Embracing his disinheritance, Edward Ferrars gives up the patriarchal role, as Claudia Johnson herself observes. That leaves only Colonel Brandon, of whom I shall speak in a moment, but we know Austen does not hold *him* up for rebuke.

In short, among rendered patriarchal families the patriarch is presented either as servile, harmless, or benign. Certainly a reader might see the author as using her portraits of these weak male heads of family in order to subject patriarchy to ridicule. (To their number might be added the emasculated or ineffectual Woodhouse and Bennet patriarchs, as fathers fashioned for the ridicule or contempt of readers.) But I do not find this a compelling defense of the thesis that Austen's manifest dissatisfaction with things as they are in her society has singled out its patriarchal family structure for its focus. It is not possible for me to experience as an attack upon a presumably oppressive family structure a rendering of that institution's male leaders as weak, harmless, or benign. On the other hand, the one truly vicious, official head of family in the book is a matriarch, Mrs. Ferrars. It is, to my perception, an empty gesture of Professor Johnson's to try to claim Mrs. Ferrars for Austen's attack on patriarchy by speaking of her as behaving "like an anxious father" and being "utterly collusive with patriarchal interests."[2] That is not Austen's notation, it is Johnson's. So far as we can see, Mrs. Ferrars is reprehensible not because she participates in patriarchal institutions but because of the appalling way she does it. Nor is Johnson persuasive in speaking, as she does in her introduction, of an author's "acts of displacement" of her aggression against fathers onto a "powerful female figure" whom the author is more willing to assault.[3] I suppose Mrs. Ferrars would be such a displaced patriarchal target. Again I do not find this in the novel, only in

Johnson's own Freudian plot, which demonstrates her justified hostility to the patriarchy she postulates but does not describe the novel. Austen presents two heads of family who are vicious, and both are vicious matriarchs, presented as such. One is Mrs. Ferrars and the second is her daughter, Fanny Ferrars Dashwood, the unofficial head of her family, whom her husband cannot match in aggressive greed.

Nevertheless, Johnson seems to believe Austen intended to present in the novel an alternative family structure to patriarchy. Whereas I believe not exactly that, yet something similar: that a reformed social morality is intended. This is not Johnson's alternative. Hers is a more comprehensive social restructuring: a benign form of *matriarchy*.

Johnson's first example is Willoughby's aunt, Mrs. Smith, who "stands in perfect opposition" to Mrs. Ferrars as "a model of radical authority attempting unworldly and morally corrective coercion" by threatening "to use her power to disinherit Willoughby in order to persuade him to behave honorably and marry the woman he has wronged." [4]

Her second illustration is Mrs. Dashwood, who has no money to withhold and "whose authority is entirely noncoercive," who has been "generally viewed as . . . little more than one of the girls herself," but who "actually presides over a remarkable little establishment," Barton Cottage, which "does present an alternative society" and "the redemptive possibilities of retirement" from "the world and its accustomed dissipations and artificiality." [5] Persuasively, Johnson points out the power of Barton Cottage to improve the characters of Edward and Willoughby during the time it holds them.

It is valuable to have pointed out for us the politically radical character of Mrs. Smith's stance. Yet I find her too far offstage to serve a function so important as Johnson assigns her: I think this needs a rendered personage. As to Barton Cottage, I find Claudia Johnson's remarks about this "remarkable little establishment" a potent example of the value of her feminist sensibility. For me the phrase just quoted adheres to the novel and thereby changes it. And she *may* be right about Austen's intention. My dissent is grounded in the very quality it is necessary for Johnson to emphasize to make her point:

that Barton Cottage is "isolated from the world."[6] I think Austen could be serious about an ideal alternative to the dominant domestic structure of her society only if it might be imagined affecting this society's current of feeling in its mainstream. In family arrangements so isolated from the world she would not see that possibility.

Austen's criticism of the family ethos she depicted does not strike me as aimed chiefly at paternal leadership and male decadence. I think her blows descend upon *family* chauvinism. My own suggestion for Austen's alternative to the aspects of family life she satirized is a more communitarian vision, with the emphasis falling on "general benevolence" (to quote Elinor on a Brandon motive for his gift to Edward).

I think I find a recent ally in the book mentioned earlier, by Gene W. Ruoff, *Jane Austen's Sense and Sensibility.* Following Claudia Johnson's lead, but developing further than she did the peculiar virtues of Johnson's discovery, that is, of the "remarkable little establishment" presided over by Mrs. Dashwood, he uses Mrs. Dashwood's example to sketch what he takes to be Jane Austen's alternative social ideal:

> While other heads of family think linearly, in terms of rank, priority and temporality, Mrs Dashwood, concerned more with the present than the past or future, thinks laterally. She is most concerned to make her home a pleasant place for her daughters at a given moment. She graciously entertains three men who are apparently suitors for her daughters without placing them under the slightest pressure. . . .
>
> On balance . . . *Sense and Sensibility* embraces the implicit social model found in Mrs Dashwood's idea of the family: a group of friends concerned more with living equitably and harmoniously in the present than with projecting themselves into futurity.[7]

What Ruoff conceptualizes as a social ideal that gives priority to "lateral" concerns over "linear" ones roughly corresponds, I think, with what I have in mind in calling attention to Austen's sympathetic presentation of a communitarian social ideal through her depiction of

Elinor Dashwood. Reading Ruoff late in the process of composing the present work, I was surprised to find him able to use Mrs. Dashwood as he has done. Although I am impressed with Ruoff's argument, I do not find that Mrs. Dashwood's personal horizon extends sufficiently beyond her own family for her to serve—to my perception—as the model Ruoff makes her out to be. I am, however, more than happy to accept her as a late addition to my own list of the characters support-ing the communitarian vision Austen pursues in this novel.

The chief figures in Austen's picture of this ideal company are Ed-ward, somewhat obliquely; on one occasion Brandon centrally; and Elinor ubiquitously. However, these three are reinforced by a sup-porting cast of patriarchs and matriarchs who, if not full-fledged com-munitarians, are at least on the side of "general benevolence" and add realistic third-dimensional depth to Austen's political landscape. I start with brief notice of the background figures and work my way to the figures in the foreground and the subjects of original interest in these remarks, Brandon and Elinor acting together on Edward's behalf.

Always keeping in focus what she takes to be Austen's critique of the patriarchal family, Claudia Johnson reminds us of "the total want of talent and taste" that Austen ascribes to Sir John and Lady Middle-ton (ch. 7:65). Johnson insists that with the author's partly favorable portrait of Sir John, Austen is "not so much mollifying her critique of the gentry family as she is extending it." Johnson writes: "The hos-pitality they practice . . . is not a tribute to patriarchal munificence, but rather an antidote to domestic boredom."[8] Indeed, Austen is as explicit as one could want: "Continual engagements at home and abroad, however, supplied all the deficiencies of nature and educa-tion" (ch. 7:65).

Nevertheless, I find that Johnson's emphasis misses the richer and more generous achievement of Jane Austen. In the very next para-graph from the one just quoted, a paragraph not overlooked but un-derestimated by Professor Johnson, Austen continues:

> Lady Middleton piqued herself upon the elegance of her
> table, and of all her domestic arrangements; and from this

kind of vanity was her greatest enjoyment in any of their parties. But Sir John's satisfaction in society was much more real;
he delighted in collecting about him more young people than
his house would hold. . . . The arrival of a new family in the
country was always a matter of joy to him. . . . The friendliness of his disposition made him happy in accommodating
those, whose situation might be considered, in comparison
with the past, as unfortunate. In shewing kindness to his
cousins therefore he had the real satisfaction of a good heart.
(ch. 7:65–66)

Just a couple of pages earlier she had written: "His countenance was
thoroughly good-humored; and his manners were as friendly as the
style of his letter. Their arrival seemed to afford him real satisfaction,
and their comfort to be an object of real solicitude to him. . . . His
kindness was not confined to words" (ch. 6:63). His reaction, later, to
Willoughby's rejection of Marianne shows both his limited talent and
his loyal disposition:

Sir John could not have thought it possible! "A man of whom
he had always had such reason to think well! Such a good-
natured fellow! He did not believe there was a bolder rider in
England! It was an unaccountable business. He wished him
at the devil with all his heart. He would not speak another
word to him, meet him where he might, for all the world! No,
not if it were to be by the side of Barton covert, and they were
kept waiting for two hours together. Such a scoundrel of a
fellow! such a deceitful dog! It was only the last time they met
that he had offered him one of Folly's puppies! and this was
the end of it!" (ch. 32:223)

Deficiencies of nature and education have left Sir John wanting in talent and taste. But the charter members of Jane Austen's good society
will surely include persons of mediocre powers whose good-humored
countenance, friendly disposition, kindness, good heart, and delight
in bringing together an entire neighborhood in a single gathering
make them, in our actual, imperfect world, much needed cohesive

forces for a social order so vulnerable to the atomizing effects of insecurity, ambition, arrogance, and greed.

Even the Palmers, initially presented in so unfavorable a light, undergo transformation when Marianne's unhappiness penetrates their rather sluggish consciousness. They are tenuously related to the Dashwoods. (Mrs. Palmer's sister is wife to Mrs. Dashwood's cousin.) Yet Marianne and Elinor "received a very warm invitation from Charlotte to go with them" to Cleveland for the Easter holidays. This was "reinforced with so much real politeness by Mr Palmer himself, as, joined to the very great amendment of his manners towards them since her sister had been known to be unhappy, induced [Elinor] to accept it with pleasure" (ch. 39:278).

At Cleveland, Elinor found Mr. Palmer, "perfectly the gentleman in his behavior to all his visitors . . . and very capable of being a pleasant companion" (ch. 42:301). Of Charlotte Palmer's vulgarity and imbecility, the narrator is, through Elinor, more than merely forgiving:

> Nothing was wanting on Mrs Palmer's side that constant and friendly good-humour could do, to make them feel themselves welcome. The openness and heartiness of her manner, more than atoned for that want of recollection and elegance, which made her often deficient in the forms of politeness; her kindness, recommended by so pretty a face, was engaging; her folly, though evident, was not disgusting, because it was not conceited; and Elinor could have forgiven every thing but her laugh. (ch. 42:300)

When Mrs. Palmer and baby had left Cleveland to escape the contagion of Marianne's "infection" and wished Mr. Palmer to join them, he was "very unwilling to go, as well from real humanity and good-nature, as from the dislike of appearing to be frightened away by his wife" (ch. 43:304).

Mrs. Jennings's widowed leisure is grounded in the money her husband made "in a low way." Her matriarchal kindliness, her generosity, her expansive friendliness provide a more vulgar manifestation of that same "general benevolence" the author has proffered in Sir John, as an alternative to the narrow, and so often corrupt, affections contained within the family. Mrs. Jennings seems so nearly to adopt Elinor and Marianne that John Dashwood infers they may expect an inheritance from her. And, as noted earlier, she offers to provide Edward with "bed and board at my house" when he is cast off by his mother for engaging himself to Lucy and refusing to abandon her (ch. 37:269). None of these actual and potential recipients of Mrs. Jennings's generosity think of themselves as connected to her as family. But her disposition is to treat as family those she cares for. Several times throughout the novel the author and Elinor, between them, either express warmth toward Mrs. Jennings or praise her because of her inclusive generosity. The most impressive tribute has already been noticed, but will perhaps bear repetition: "Mrs Jennings . . . with a kindness of heart that made Elinor really love her, declared her resolution of not stirring from Cleveland as long as Marianne remained ill, and of endeavoring, by her own attentive care, to supply to her the place of the mother she had taken her from" (ch. 43:304).

I hope that my making a case for Edward as democrat will have already softened the reader's resistance to perceiving him as on the side of a communitarian vision—if only in his modest and unobtrusive manner. We must of course ascribe to his honest belief in the righteousness of his church the "ready discharge of his duties in every particular" once he is rector of Delaford. His chief claim to belong to the communitarian party is his figuring as the unyielding and—thanks to the author's Olympian intervention—finally victorious antagonist to the party of family greed, the party of his mother and sister. He is, in short, morally allied with the creative communitarians, Elinor and Brandon, and spiritually in harmony with them.

It is Brandon's creative action, with Elinor's cooperation, that provides the material support for Edward's final victory over his greedy family. However, when we look for the ideal content of this novel, the quality—more than the upshot—of Brandon's and Elinor's action claims our attention. And Jane Austen offers solid evidence of her view of the quality of Colonel Brandon's gift of a church living to Edward.

Six paragraphs before the end of the novel Brandon becomes patriarch of a family. Austen of course will not attack this new patriarchy in which Marianne at nineteen—half the age of her husband—will find herself "placed" as "a wife, the mistress of a family, and the patroness of a village," with an income (2,000 pounds) that Mrs. Jennings "with all her money" considered "rich" and that Marianne had earlier considered a "competence" and Elinor wealth, living in a house that has "five sitting rooms on the ground-floor, and . . . could make up fifteen beds" (ch. 50:367, 8:70, 40:290). Brandon's gift to Edward, however, occurs well before he has achieved such happiness with Marianne or even has hope of it. It is a gift of one bachelor who has the disposal of a living at his command to another whom he barely knows.

One piece of evidence for the author's high valuation of Brandon's action is the response to it by John Dashwood. Of course he is no reliable judge of values, and his incredulity is doubtless partly intended to further devalue his character and understanding. Yet it coheres with other evidence and deserves consideration:

> "This living of Colonel Brandon's—can it be true?—has he really given it to Edward?—I heard it yesterday by chance, and was coming to you on purpose to inquire farther about it."
>
> "It is perfectly true.—Colonel Brandon has given the living of Delaford to Edward."
>
> "Really!—Well, this is very astonishing!—no relationship!—no connection between them!—and now that livings fetch such a price!—what was the value of this?"
>
> "About two hundred a-year."
>
> "Very well—and for the next presentation to a living of that value—supposing the late incumbent to have been old and sickly, and likely to vacate it soon—he might have got I dare say—fourteen hundred pounds. . . . I suppose, however . . . that the case may probably be *this*. Edward is only to hold the living till the person to whom the Colonel has really sold the presentation, is old enough to take it.—Aye, aye, that is the fact, depend upon it."

Elinor contradicted it, however, very positively; and by

relating that she had herself been employed in conveying the offer from Colonel Brandon to Edward, and therefore must understand the terms on which it was given, obliged him to submit to her authority.

"It is truly astonishing!"—he cried, after hearing what she said—"what could be the Colonel's motive?"

"A very simple one—to be of use to Mr Ferrars." "Well, well; whatever Colonel Brandon may be, Edward is a very lucky man!" (ch. 41:292–93)

Within the novel the astonishment all round over Brandon's gift to Edward tells us the action is extraordinary: this isn't *done*. When Edward gets the news from Elinor, he is no less astounded than John Dashwood:

He *looked* all the astonishment which such unexpected, such unthought-of information could not fail of exciting; but he said only these two words,

"Colonel Brandon!"

"Yes," continued Elinor. . . .

"Colonel Brandon give *me* a living!—Can it be possible?" (ch. 40:287–88)

Perhaps counting more than either of these is Elinor's reaction when *she* hears the news from Brandon: "Elinor's astonishment at this commission could hardly have been greater, had the Colonel been really making her an offer of his hand. . . . She thanked him for it with all her heart"; she said: "I shall always think myself very much obliged to you" (ch. 39:281, 280). The allusion to a marriage proposal refers of course to Mrs. Jennings's comical misunderstanding of this conversation as involving a proposal from Brandon to Elinor. We have also Elinor's own description of her reaction, when she misunderstands Mrs. Jennings's remarks and replies to them as if Mrs. Jennings knew Brandon had just offered the Delaford living to Edward: "It is a matter of great joy to me; and I feel the goodness of Colonel Brandon most sensibly. *There are not many men who would act as he has done. . . . I never was more astonished in my life*" (ch. 40:284; my italics).

Austen in her own voice—or at any rate in that of the narrator of the novel—expresses, in the very last sentence of chapter 39, a valuation of Colonel Brandon's action that is as high as that of any one of her fictional characters: "After this narration of what really passed between Colonel Brandon and Elinor . . . the gratitude expressed by the latter on their parting, may perhaps appear in general, *not less reasonably excited, nor less properly worded than if it had arisen from an offer of marriage*" (ch. 39:282–83, my italics). Colonel Brandon is acting from a motive—compassion—and with a quality—generosity—and under a principle—general benevolence—and to an end—support of self-sacrificing fidelity—and with an effect—a rare affirmation of fellowship within a community defined by its members' moral qualities, whereby he counters one ugly instance of a socially pervasive family chauvinism. These features of Brandon's action surely bring him into alignment with the highest aspirations of Elinor's ideal self. His action, therefore, is morally heartening to her, as it manifestly is to the author of the novel. And Brandon's insistence upon bringing Elinor in as collaborator in this exemplary performance is (among other, "less pleasing" effects) exhilarating to her in a degree proportionate not only to the measure it bespeaks of his regard for her but also, we must believe, to its congruence with her own rare standards. (Chief among the other "less pleasing" effects is of course her dismay at being asked to contribute to the decisive undermining of her own romantic hopes.)

But let us have the gist of Colonel Brandon's offer in his own language:

> "I have heard," said he, with great compassion, "of the injustice your friend Mr Ferrars has suffered from his family. . . .
>
> "The cruelty . . . of dividing, or attempting to divide, two young people long attached to each other, is terrible—Mrs Ferrars does not know what she may . . . drive her son to. I have seen Mr Ferrars two or three times in Harley-street, and

am much pleased with him. He is not a young man with
whom one can be intimately acquainted in a short time, but
I have seen enough of him to wish him well for his own sake,
and as a friend of yours, I wish it still more. I understand that
he intends to take orders. Will you be so good as to tell him
that the living of Delaford, now just vacant, as I am informed
by this day's post, is his, if he think it worth his acceptance—
but *that*, perhaps so unfortunately circumstanced as he is
now, it may be nonsense to appear to doubt; I only wish it
were more valuable.—It is a rectory, but a small one; the late
incumbent, I believe, did not make more than 200£ per an-
num, and though it is certainly capable of improvement,
I fear, not to such an amount as to afford him a very comfortable income. Such as it is, however, my pleasure in presenting him to it, will be very great. Pray assure him of it."
(ch. 39:280–81)

And the part of Elinor's response not already reported: "Her emotion
was such as Mrs Jennings had attributed to a very different cause;—
but whatever minor feelings less pure, less pleasing, might have a
share in that emotion, her esteem for the general benevolence, and her
gratitude for the particular friendship, which together prompted
Colonel Brandon to this act, were strongly felt, and warmly expressed" (ch. 39:281). The "particular friendship" for which she is
grateful is doubtless Brandon's for herself, as her acknowledgment of
its contribution to his action shows when she later says to Edward, "As
a friend of mine, of my family, he may perhaps—indeed I know he
has, still greater pleasure in bestowing it; but, upon my word, you owe
nothing to my solicitation" (ch. 40:288). Yet the strength of her emotion of gratitude suggests that it is partly also on behalf of the man she
loves: that *he* should be so respected, and so generously treated,
warms her heart. She also strongly feels and warmly expresses "her esteem for [Brandon's] general benevolence." And this element in her
emotion—an emotion that comprised, as well as her gratitude, also
"minor feelings less pure, less pleasing" as elements—this strongly
felt esteem for Brandon's general benevolence must surely play no

small part in warranting the narrator's extraordinary valuation of the grounds for Elinor's gratitude: Elinor's appreciation is justifiably equal to what would be appropriate to a proposal of marriage from this man whom Elinor admires! (And from whom she might even have welcomed—I do not say accepted—a proposal, when Edward seemed so close to marrying Lucy.)

Elinor's gratitude must be in part for Brandon's general benevolence, his communitarian spirit, his disinterested virtue. But this is the gratitude of an equal, in this special sense: it is the grateful appreciation one social idealist has for another, and moreover for a fellow practitioner who includes her as collaborator in his exemplary action. The "less pure, less pleasing" feelings express Elinor's personal interest in the matter, which has to mean her regret for Edward's sudden empowerment to marry Lucy. Even for Edward's sake, she has no reason to be pleased, since she knows he cannot be well married to Lucy, and Elinor also knows herself, not Lucy, to be his beloved; moreover, she is quite incapable of losing her grasp of these two facts. If she is to feel so strongly as she does her satisfaction, even excitement, from Colonel Brandon's action, it is really necessary to imagine her motivation rising, for the occasion, to a higher level of abstraction. And we have learned that this is a level of abstraction at which it is natural for Elinor to live: it is the level of impersonal, disinterested evaluation—even choice—of action; the level at which one judges—or chooses—an action from the point of view of how its underlying principle furthers the common good. Unwittingly, Colonel Brandon has called upon Elinor to meet him with a high purpose of her own to match his, and her passion for disinterestedly communitarian principles of action has enabled her to respond to his call.

I find it interesting that when disavowing to Edward an active role in Brandon's decision to offer him the living, Elinor says, "Nor had it ever occurred to me that he might have had such a living in his gift" (ch. 40:288). Brandon is so self-effacing, so little given to displaying his status as lord of the manor, that not even his having been "an object of interest" for Elinor since her move to Barton cottage could produce in her the idea of him as dispensing church patronage (ch. 10:81). She is not alone. When shrewd Lucy Steele, soliciting help for Edward, mentions persons acquainted with Mrs. Jennings who might "have a living to bestow," she names Mr. Palmer (who is running for Parliament) and Sir John Middleton (a baronet), but not Colonel Brandon (ch. 38:276). So a part of Elinor's surprise at Brandon's offer is from his suddenly displaying a status she had failed to remark. And it does appear to me that Austen meant Brandon's offering words, spoken to Elinor, to show him quite comfortable in the exercise of one of the prerogatives of his membership in the ruling class. The confident flow of his speech as he sketches Edward's situation, action, and character and moves on to his own offer to Edward of the living, and to his startlingly brief, trusting, and even collegial request of Elinor to stand in for him in making the offer to Edward, this easy fluency so defines his membership in that privileged order that Elinor in this situation will *actively* share with him that membership if, in reply, she acts empathically, cooperatively, and with equal ease. In this event, she will occupy the highest office of an almost literally political sort that she attains in the novel. To this dimension of Colonel Brandon's invitation to her cooperation, too, Elinor is responsive.

A multiply determined momentum of motivation is thus built up in Elinor that can carry her forward—against the tug of personal dismay—through the interview with Edward, especially since this interview comes quickly and right after she has felt her way into comfort with her task by sitting down to do it in the less painful way, by writing. This motivational momentum, both ethical and quasi-political, bears within its core an identification with Colonel Brandon that she carries over into her unexpected meeting with Edward. Her identification with Brandon accounts in no small part for her finding herself, when conversing with Edward, seconding Colonel Brandon's wish that the living were adequate to fund Edward's marriage to Lucy Steele—doing this, to be sure, with a slight indirection of language that betrays her unease but does not modify this message one jot (or at most a bare jot). The social stateswoman in Elinor has taken charge—not totally of her feelings but (almost) totally of her conduct.

One strategically central element of Jane Austen's reconstruction of Elinor's gender, her portrait of a young woman as an intellectual, is fully out in the open, provided we have the unbiased eyes to see it. Elinor's gender-dissonant emotional temperament is a secondary element in this reconstruction in that it is a product jointly of her intellectuality and her character. And this emotional disposition too is quite visible to the reader, although accurately perceived only with care. The second central feature in Elinor's portrait as gender reforming is the one I am now examining—Elinor's character, which I identify as largely constituted by her vocation as communitarian stateswoman, a vocation taken as embracing her special sense of honor, her passion for general civility, and her power to join Brandon in his offer to Edward. This gender-reforming element in Elinor's portrait falls under the concealment pole of that alternation with revelation ascribed by Sulloway to the political thrust of Austen's fiction. This concealment of Elinor's stateswomanly function figures for the reader as a puzzlement. The revelation enters the reader's experience only as the unearthing of a nearly inscrutable motivation in Elinor to join Brandon in verbally wishing Edward power to marry Lucy, while conveying to Edward the offer that bestows that power. The unearthing has taken some rather hard work on the reader's—this reader's—part. I think nothing less would successfully resolve, along secular lines, the conundrum of Elinor's character.

There remains unresolved a certain conflict between the realism to which Austen is committed in this novel and the sense readers may have that, despite all the work we may do at grasping Elinor's motivation, she still comes through to us at moments as something of an idealization. Because the secular reading I have just given of Elinor's conduct in chapters 39 and 40 implies a near-heroic self-denial on her part, it will be useful to examine some elements of that art of persuasion through which Austen has made Elinor, in these two chapters, as believable as she is, in spite of her almost too noble action. How does Austen integrate an idealization into a realistic canvas?

Dramatic irony plays a part in persuading the reader to accept this veering from a realistic convention toward an idealization. The immediate context of Elinor's action is, of course, Brandon's doing something for Edward that he believes will contribute in a minor way to Elinor's personal happiness. Since anyone who knows all the relevant facts would believe, as Elinor does, that Brandon's action could enable Edward to marry Lucy, it can be expected to contribute in a major way to Elinor's personal *un*happiness. Therein the dramatic irony. An effect of this irony is to cause in some readers—especially in those with an appetite for the ideal made real and realized—so much sympathy with Elinor that they are relieved to find her stronger than themselves and are therefore more ready to believe her so. Since she is stronger because she is better, these readers are also disposed to accept the way she is better than themselves. For this protagonist to escape suffering over a powerful blow from another's ironically misdirected goodness by drawing upon even more goodness (of her own) is aesthetically so fitting that the rightly disposed readers can be ensnared in something close to belief: an imaginative acceptance of fitness and coherence and hence of the kind of reality artistically embodied ideals can gain. The dramatic irony of the gods, so to say, is contested, and bested, by the heroine's purity of heart.

Balancing the impulse toward belief, however, is this dynamic: precisely because the threat to Elinor's happiness from Brandon's generosity *is* ironic (comically so, since this is a comedy, hence must come out right in the end), the reader is authorized to experience something less than a fully serious belief in that threat. This cognitive release in turn authorizes the reader's belief that the author's rendering of Elinor's heroic spiritual poise may be, at the moment, somewhat playful: because of the comic context for the dramatic irony, Elinor's loftiest performance can inspire our imagination even as our reason remains subliminally skeptical. At this moment, as perhaps at others, Elinor has herself become something of an idealization, yet an acceptable one. We can here gain insight into how idealization in fiction can effect a persuasive vision of a somewhat unrealistically high moral good: an idealization operating in the right artistic environment can gain the power of inspiring our imagination without needing fully to persuade our reason that it is realizable.

A part of that artistic environment is a fictional context that is in several ways massively realistic. A curious dimension of Austen's realism, in the present fictional moment, is the way the same elements that create the dramatic irony count for realism, when the *irony* of the opposition of those elements is ignored. Colonel Brandon's offer to Edward is one element of an ironic pattern: ill comes to Elinor from the good guys doing good. Here, Brandon's goodness toward Edward brings much closer the day Elinor fears. And in general, Edward's high-minded fidelity toward Lucy causes misery for Elinor. Taken together, these good men's seemingly unfortunate virtue also works for realism (when its irony is ignored): misfortune resulting from innocent intentions is commonplace; not even exemplary prudence can defend against bad luck. Elinor as idealization gains credibility, not only from the liberating powers (for the reader) of dramatic irony, but as well from the sense of tough-minded realism enjoyed (by the reader) in experiencing the hard knocks Elinor takes from an almost perversely unjust world: since that world is grimly real, she is real. On the one hand, the playfulness implicit in the comic irony of Brandon's doing harm by doing good offers the reader's imagination some freedom from the rigid control of reason, so that it can embrace, for inspiration, Elinor rendered as idealization. On the other hand, the injustice of Brandon's aiming at good but effecting harm makes Elinor's world toughly real, and herself correlatively real: an exemplary episode of artistic economy.

No less vividly presented in these two chapters than the two aspects of dramatic irony, as devices for embedding Elinor-as-idealization in a context that enhances her acceptability as real, is the interweaving throughout of Mrs. Jennings's comic misreading of the Brandon-to-Elinor-to-Edward exchanges. Right off, let me expose my taste: for me this interweaving is not merely comical, it is hilarious; it is, I think, the only place, in this entire black comedy of a novel at which, every time I come back to it, I laugh out loud. Something of the role of this juxtaposition of sublime and ridiculous has been noticed by Stuart Tave. However, I find myself, again, not very close to him: "It is one of the few times that we do not see things through Elinor's eyes. The comic cross-purposes at this moment seem rather mistimed, though they do keep the scene and its effect from becoming heavy and potentially sentimental; but they do so only because Elinor's character makes it possible by converting the scene dramatically."[9]

Certainly I agree that the "comic cross-purposes" keep the scene from becoming heavy and sentimental, but they do more than that. The smiles—even laughs—that they generate undercut the reader's attempt to ascend the heights to Elinor's true elevation, with the upshot that he experiences her at a more plausible altitude than the one to which her performance would otherwise be seen to vault her. Similarly, of course Elinor's character is dramatically pivotal, but it is much more than that: its overreaching heroism threatens verisimilitude through two chapters. So far is Mrs. Jennings's comical misreading from being mistimed, its timing is masterly: it is carefully plotted so that it can be suspended after clouding the otherwise too shiny gold of Elinor's first earned medal, her agreeing to act for Brandon; and it is resumed just in time to tarnish with hilarious nonsense Elinor's second, all but too high-toned self-conquest in her scene with Edward.

Recall that Colonel Brandon has engaged Elinor in such unsettling conversation at the window that Mrs. Jennings sees it cause Elinor to blush, to attend "with agitation," and stop her "work" at measuring a print. So much disruption of Elinor's customary poise suggests to the interested Mrs. Jennings that Brandon is proposing marriage to Elinor! Although Marianne's piano playing obscures most of it, a few snatches of the conversation reach Mrs. Jennings. She takes Brandon's words about the condition of the parsonage house to refer to the manor, and she takes his remarks about the low income from the rectory requiring delay of Edward and Lucy's wedding as indicating delay in Brandon and Elinor's wedding:

> In the interval of Marianne's turning from one lesson to another, some words of the Colonel's inevitably reached [Mrs Jennings's] ear, in which he seemed to be apologizing for the badness of his house. This set the matter beyond a doubt. She wondered indeed at his thinking it necessary to do so;—but supposed it to be the proper etiquette. . . . another lucky stop in Marianne's performance brought her these words in the Colonel's calm voice,
>
> "I am afraid it cannot take place very soon."
>
> Astonished and shocked at so unlover-like a speech, she was almost ready to cry out, "Lord! what should hinder

it?"—but checking her desire, confined herself to this silent ejaculation.

"This is very strange!—sure he need not wait to be older." (ch. 39:280)

A bit later, as they ended the conversation and parted, Mrs. Jennings heard Elinor telling Brandon how she would always feel herself "very much obliged" to him, and she saw Brandon leave without replying to that remark: "She had not thought her old friend could have made so indifferent a suitor" (ch. 39:280). These and other parts of the conversation between Elinor and Brandon are thus anticipated by comical commentary (*how* comical only the rereader realizes right off), so that when we do read the fuller version of their talk, our balking at Elinor's heroism is deflected by amusement at the contrast between it and Mrs. Jennings's misunderstanding. Moreover, not an instant elapses after the author has concluded with Elinor and Brandon, and thus no time is allowed us to reflect skeptically about Elinor's present performance, before Mrs. Jennings begins chapter 40, "Well, Miss Dashwood . . ."; and the amusing exchange at cross-purposes between the two of them has begun, including this confusion between the manor house and the parsonage:

> "And as to the house being a bad one, I do not know what the Colonel would be at, for it is as good a one as ever I saw."
> "He spoke of its being out of repair."
> "Well, and whose fault is that? why don't he repair it?—who should do it but himself?" (ch. 40:284)

When Elinor says she should write Mr. Ferrars to give him the news before anyone else, and immediately, too, because he will have to proceed with his ordination, Mrs. Jennings puzzles out that Edward is to be the minister performing the wedding of Elinor and Brandon. But in that case, is the bride the person to be writing the minister?

> "But my dear, is not this rather out of character? Should not the Colonel write himself?—sure, he is the proper person."
> "Colonel Brandon is so delicate a man, that he rather

wished any one to announce his intentions to Mr Ferrars than himself."

"And so *you* are forced to do it. Well, *that* is an odd kind of delicacy!" (ch. 40:284–85)

Their conversation was happily interrupted by Mrs. Jennings's carriage being ready to take her out; on the way she met Edward coming "to leave his farewell card" and told him "that Miss Dashwood was above and wanted to speak with him on very particular business," with the effect that Elinor's still more challenging scene follows immediately upon this comical introduction of it. What is more, this hilarity with Mrs. Jennings resumes almost directly after Elinor has done her duty with Edward. Mrs. Jennings returns home and, after a few preliminary miscommunications, we enjoy the following consummation of Austen's splendid tomfoolery—here only slightly shortened:

> "Well, my dear," [Mrs. Jennings] cried. . . . You did not find him very unwilling to accept your proposal?"
>
> "No, ma'am; *that* was not very likely."
>
> "Well, and how soon will he be ready?—For it seems all to depend upon that."
>
> ". . . I suppose two or three months will complete his ordination."
>
> "Two or three months! . . . Lord! my dear, how calmly you talk of it; and can the Colonel wait two or three months! Lord bless me!—I am sure it would put *me* quite out of patience!—And though one would be very glad to do a kindness by poor Mr Ferrars, I do think it is not worth while to wait two or three months for him. Sure, somebody else might be found that would do as well; somebody that is in orders already."
>
> "My dear ma'am . . . what can you be thinking of?—Why, Colonel Brandon's only object is to be of use to Mr Ferrars."
>
> "Lord bless you, my dear!—Sure you do not mean to

persuade me that the Colonel only marries you for the sake
of giving ten guineas to Mr Ferrars! (ch. 40:290)

Embedded in this comical context, Elinor's action may find readers'
minds relaxed, and so fill their imaginations that it inspires in them a
will to believe, and, perchance, to raise their sights.

7

---◆◆◆---

Problematic Marianne

WHY DO PROFESSORS of literature puzzle over and disagree about the meaning of Marianne's fictional life? The provocative power of Marianne as a problem for critical reflection springs from the many ways in which she is an anomaly in Austen's fiction.

With Marianne, Austen escaped from constraints she imposed upon herself in composing all her other heroines. All are genteel, but *only* Marianne rejects the genteel code of general civility in favor of either speaking the blunt truth or nothing; hence *only* she practices rudeness in respectable company. Among all Austen heroines *only* Marianne reciprocates the sexually aggressive behavior of a man she finds attractive: *only* she displays the same freedom of affectionate expression and amorous initiative that her unabashed male lover shows, and *only* she feels the same freedom from concern about onlookers' ideas of propriety. *Only* she among Austen's heroines would follow to London an unaccountably absent and noncommunicating lover in order to seek reunion with him. *No other* heroine nearly dies, as Marianne does, from a depicted (or for that matter an undepicted) illness; nor could any other be imagined bringing herself to the brink of death by her despairing response to rejection by a lover. *No other* Austenian heroine past childhood undergoes a metamorphosis that involves a transformation in her character and personality; and of course since no others are rebels, *none* could metamorphose as Marianne does from romantic rebel to quiescent subject of patriarchal rule. How should professors of literature—how should any of us—not be puzzled about the full meaning for Austen of this heroine who is so incongruent with her fellows?

Disagreement about Marianne has sources other than the difficulty of consensus on solutions to real puzzles. Some critics are more sympathetic to rebels than to conservators, some are the opposite. (So too for readers generally.) And Marianne is a rebel against much of the prevailing social order, who yet becomes in the very end of the novel a nineteen-year-old conformist. Austen thereby shows herself—at least in a simple literal sense—of two minds: of the mind that created the rebel and of the mind that created the conformer. So rebel-sympathizing readers may look to the rebelling Austen mind for the author's intended statement through Marianne; whereas conservatively disposed critics may look to the conserving mind of the author to fix the full meaning of Marianne's story.

Other disputable territory draws attention. For some readers, Marianne's ending seems artistically a failure and morally a cop-out. However, for critics who especially prize historical realism, her marriage to Brandon shows moral courage in the author. They read Austen as telling a woman's story as it often would have happened; for these critics the ending even figures as artistically sound.

How, then, shall we think of Marianne?

I find that she is presented to us as exhibit B in Austen's fictional case for feminine gender reform, Elinor being exhibit A. Indeed, I suspect that for much of the novel some readers might (though I do not) experience Marianne as exhibit A, giving Elinor second place in this "competition." In sharp contrast with Elinor's general compliance with conventions of courtship, Marianne openly resists the patriarchal presumption that, between the sexes, men are active and pursuing, gentlewomen either fleeing or passively receptive; men uninhibited, genteel women suppressed; men openly in love, respectable women modestly in doubt; men the teachers, proper women the pupils; unmarried men free agents, decent young women held in bondage to their parents until transferred to their husbands' rule. In respect to all these binary oppositions, Marianne in love with Willoughby exhibits by her behavior her determination to align herself with the sexually adventurous male.

She largely succeeds. But unlike Fanny Burney's Elinor Joddrel in *The Wanderer*, Marianne's personal rebellion is socially reformist in conception, never revolutionary: she courts disapproval but she shows no readiness to cross (though she may tread) the line that separates the respectable young woman from the outcast. This restraint in Marianne manifests a sensible avoidance of the dangers of radical isolation. It keeps Marianne well clear of that suspicion of female hysteria that undercuts the effort Burney's Elinor makes to appropriate for herself male freedom. If Marianne's demonstration finally fails, it is not from a "feminine" excess of sensibility but from Willoughby's cowardly flight from hardship. So far, then, we can imagine that Marianne's resistance to patriarchal definitions of the feminine may be a statement by Austen.

Marianne's attractive prizing of spontaneity, of sincerity, of what a later age would call authenticity leads her to be sometimes inconsiderate or even rude to those who do not share her notions of frank fellowship. This too aligns her with the masculine gender and so, strangely enough, can contribute to an authorial brief for reform. For it is Mr. Palmer who, in his first meeting with the Dashwoods, at their own cottage, demonstrates a genteel masculine right to social arrogance by acknowledging none of the women as worth his notice and directly sitting down to read the newspaper in their very drawing room. To be sure, there are older women who are also rude—Mrs. Ferrars in this novel, Lady Catherine in *Pride and Prejudice*, for example—but each of these is a woman who, from having replaced a patriarch, is released from normal female subordination. In *Sense and Sensibility* we do not see young women other than Marianne in that mode: for example, Mrs. Ferrars's daughter Fanny Dashwood encourages her mother's rudeness but does not quite dare to join in it. (Her rage at house guest Lucy Steele when she discovers Lucy's engagement to Edward exceeds rudeness.) Furthermore, toward counting Marianne's rudeness as a point in favor of gender reform, we note the charm it holds for most readers. We find its motives attractive and its targets deserving what they get.

In debating Edward Ferrars about the picturesque in landscape, Marianne takes on for herself the male gentry's right to full public expression of polemical powers of judgment and taste, including the power of spirited argument with Oxford-educated males. Here the claim of equality of the sexes is only implicit for Marianne; yet one is ready to call it explicit on Austen's part because of her consistent advocacy of this female freedom in all her subsequent novels.

Even Marianne's running down a hill (to stumble and fall at the feet of Willoughby), her enthusiasm for riding, her desire to accept a horse from her new lover, and her identification with Willoughby's interest in hunting—we imagine her imagining herself, when married, joining him in the hunt—all this athleticism coheres with her rejection of her society's patriarchally inspired intention to suppress female vitality.

For Burney's Elinor Joddrel, at least in her conversation, the act of suicide was an expression of strength, not weakness. Accepting it as an admirable choice in some circumstances could be another form of liberation for women from the oppression of patriarchal conventions, not to mention from misery in an unjust world. In this view, as Margaret Drabble notes, Burney's fictional Elinor followed two famously liberated women of her era who also attempted suicide and failed— Madame de Staël (who died, at fifty-one, four days before Austen) and Mary Wollstonecraft—and all three could be said to follow Goethe's famously influential, fictional young man, Werther, whose suicide first fascinated Europe in 1774, the year before Austen's birth. When we accept Marianne's convalescent judgment that if her illness had been fatal she would have been guilty of suicide, we can also subsume her illness-inducing conduct under her rejection of female gender constraints; for she was appropriating a right that was perceived as radical even when offered only for men, as in Goethe's novel.

Against the case I have been giving for Marianne as gender reformer we shall have to place the narrator's report of Marianne's metamorphosis into a young woman who voluntarily gives her "hand" to

Colonel Brandon. We have to try to adjudicate that opposition. Such an ending for Marianne surely does both embody her metamorphosis and oppose my argument, since, on Marianne's side, marriage to Brandon springs from "no sentiment superior to strong esteem and lively friendship" (ch. 50:366).

Before turning to that problem, I want now to profit from the fact that the discussion of Marianne has become especially interesting in recent decades as new psychological, social, and literary theories, a new outlook among female critics, as well as new historical approaches to Austen's times and her place in them, have developed new ways to think of the most openly passionate heroine Austen ever invented. I want to set before the reader, and assess, several professorial ways of seeing Marianne that, even without citing her ending, do not fit with the representation I have just made of her as, in this novel, Austen's Exhibit B in her "case" for reconstruing current ideas of the feminine.

The most influential academic reading of Marianne in recent decades is Tony Tanner's. He has established nearly a critical orthodoxy about Marianne through his fresh and stimulating analysis of the novel, first published in 1969 as an introduction to the Penguin edition (the edition from which I have been quoting), then republished ("in somewhat altered form") in his 1986 book on Jane Austen. He develops two theses about Marianne that tend, as I read them, toward finding her classically "feminine," even hyperfeminine, though he does not explicitly tie them to gender. Let me put the crux of his two theses in two nutshells, and then try to crack them for our intellectual nourishment. Here is Tanner on his widely accepted "Thesis 1" (my label): "The Rousseauistic idea that innate human impulses are good and that it is society that obstructs or corrupts these has certainly reached Marianne, and she . . . would be happy to 'tear away' much of that 'system of opinions and observances' which more sober spirits such as Elinor . . . see as the necessary 'collateral influences' on good conduct. Marianne is a woman of whom it may be said, 'Her motives are just her passions,' as Henry James said of Hedda Gabler." [1] (Hedda Gabler!) In support of his formulation of this thesis, Tanner quotes what seemed to him a decisive passage from the novel. In it Elinor has expressed shock that Marianne would let Willoughby, alone, show her the house of his elderly cousin, Mrs. Smith, since Marianne is unacquainted with Mrs. Smith. Marianne replies.

> "I never spent a pleasanter morning in my life."
>
> "I am afraid," replied Elinor, "that the pleasantness of an employment does not always evince its propriety."
>
> "On the contrary, nothing can be a stronger proof of it, Elinor; for if there had been any real impropriety in what I did, I should have been sensible of it at the time, for we always know when we are acting wrong, and with such a conviction I could have had no pleasure." (ch. 13:97)

Here is Tanner's conclusion from this passage: "The point is that she . . . believes that the feelings that well up spontaneously inside a person are inherently moral and therefore the best possible motives for action."[2]

A more recent critic, Gene W. Ruoff, quotes some of those same lines from Marianne and agrees with Tanner that for Marianne "the only possible arbiter of behavior in love is feeling. . . . The danger of her ideology of romantic love, of course, is precisely the conviction that pleasure is all. . . . There is ultimately no place it could not lead her, because it acknowledges no limits." In short, by strict implication though not explicit statement, Ruoff infers from Marianne's argument that unmarried Marianne is ready to go (with a clear conscience) to bed with Willoughby![3]

Professor Tanner and his allies read Marianne's ethical reasoning as if it shows she believes that her feeling pleasure in an action either constitutes or founds the rightness of that action; as if her argument says or implies that her *feeling pleasure* at the time of acting *makes* her action right.

In fact her argument—and it *is* a cogently structured argument—neither says nor implies that; nor does it imply anything like it.

The only feeling Marianne mentions in her short clear argument or by implication alludes to is pleasure, pleasure found in an action.

She reports that her *knowing* an action is wrong precludes her taking pleasure in it. *How* would she know it is wrong? *She never says.* She merely asserts that people of her sort—that is to say, people of the right upbringing—"we"—"always know when we are acting wrong." There is not even a hint from her that how wrong action is *known* to be wrong is by appeal to one's feelings.

Marianne's reasoning goes thus: she *always knows* what is wrong; once she knows an action is wrong, she *cannot* take pleasure in it; therefore, since she *did* take pleasure in this action, it was not wrong.

This argument has no tendency whatever to claim that what *feels* right *is* right. Nothing in the quoted passage or elsewhere in the novel even suggests that for Marianne, as Tanner believes, "her motives are just her passions" or that she thinks that "the feelings that well up spontaneously . . . are inherently moral," or, as Ruoff claims, that "the only possible arbiter of behavior in love is feeling" or "that pleasure is all." [4]

Austen writes, with her usual care to be precise, that Marianne "abhorred all concealment where no real disgrace could attend unreserve; and to aim at the restraint of sentiments which were not in themselves illaudable, appeared to her not merely an unnecessary effort, but a disgraceful subjection of reason to common-place and mistaken notions" (ch. 11:84). By implication, there *are* for Marianne sentiments (feelings) which *in themselves* are illaudable—contrary to our critics' readings.

Elinor had once or twice tried to persuade Marianne to subdue public display of her affection for Willoughby. Yet all the Dashwood women, at that time, found Willoughby worthy of love. Since, therefore, there could be nothing wrong in loving him, Marianne's reason told her there could be nothing wrong in showing this love.

Marianne here accepts two principles of right conduct that make her a social rebel: one, that the moral acceptability of one's romantically loving someone follows from the beloved's worthiness-to-be-loved-in-that-way; and two, that if it is morally acceptable to love a person, then so is it morally acceptable to display that love. These two principles of Marianne's philosophy of romantic love figure centrally in Austen's remodeling of feminine gender through her charac-

terization of Marianne Dashwood. For, as practical guides, the second rule is congruent with the patriarchally constructed *masculine*
gender-concept but not with its female complement; and the first
contradicts both concepts, a more grievous offense in a young woman
than in a young man. But these ethical principles by which Marianne
is guided in matters of the heart do not associate her even remotely
with the belief that it is morally right to act upon *whatever* sentiment
or impulse one spontaneously feels.

That Marianne's ideas of loveworthiness, and generally of moral
soundness, fit the family code, hence agree with Elinor's, is evident
when she describes, early in the novel, her ideal lover: "He must have
all Edward's virtues, and his person and manners must ornament his
goodness with every possible charm" (ch. 3:51). And we know full well
that Marianne believes that Edward's virtues are inconsistent with accepting impulse (let alone pleasure!) as the guarantor of an action's
moral quality; for later in the novel she says of him: "I really believe he
has the most scrupulous conscience in the world; the most scrupulous
in performing every engagement however minute, and *however it may
make against his interest or pleasure*" (ch. 35:248, my emphasis).

So much for the Marianne Thesis 1, which Tony Tanner and his
fellow professors profess. Tanner's Thesis 2 brings Sigmund Freud to
bear upon poor Marianne. Tanner invokes the theory of neuroses as
manifestations of repressed sexual desire: "*Sense and Sensibility* may
be said to look forward to Freud's *Civilisation and Its Discontents*. . . .
Marianne does suffer from neurosis brought on by repression and her
sickness is precisely the cost of her entry into the sedate stabilities
of civilized life envisaged at the end."[5] It is plausible to say that *how*
Marianne's passion for Willoughby is frustrated—by his brutal rejection of her—causes her to become physically ill. However, Freud's
"repression" plays no role here. For Freud, a repressed desire is an
unconscious desire. The repressing is also unconscious. Marianne's
desire for Willoughby—which is of course, among other things, the
sexual desire of a country girl who, like Austen, has grown up knowing about such matters (and can be expected to have read *Tom Jones,
Pamela,* and *Clarissa*)—this sexual desire is fully conscious; that is
precisely the health, by Freudian standards, of Marianne's tempera-

ment. And nothing could be more conscious for a sufferer than the frustration of that desire is for Marianne.

If there is repression in a Dashwood sister, look to Elinor for it. Tanner does not look there, of course, because when Elinor's love for Edward is frustrated, she does not become ill. To be sure, one could argue that Marianne's "conversion to sense" involves libidinal desires being newly repressed, going underground. But Austen presents this conversion as a consequence of Marianne's illness, effected through the insights this illness gives her into the self-indulgent behavior that made her vulnerable to illness. If there is late repression ingredient in Marianne's conversion to sense, then clearly, since the conversion develops from the illness, *this* repression cannot cause the illness.

One wonders whether Tanner would ever ignore in a male lover the evidence of full awareness of desire that Marianne's openly affectionate behavior with Willoughby provides. It's as if, despite Austen's emphatic efforts to show Marianne does *not* meet the standard of repression that English patriarchy expected from its maiden ladies, this male critic is determined to find that Marianne met that standard, and got sick from it.

I suppose few would doubt that Austen herself believed that Marianne's form of openness has in general to be subordinated, if not to Elinor's at least to Elizabeth Bennet's level of self-restraint and of tact. One can even say *this* novel favors Elinor's level. Tanner goes further and claims that Austen "makes it clear that Elinor and Marianne do embody slightly but crucially different notions about how to live and that society will only tolerate one of these notions."[6] Tanner's last proposition here is just plain false: *Sense and Sensibility* does not show that society will not tolerate Marianne's way. The novel "shows" that for a woman, openness in love is dangerous. Openness makes her vulnerable to one of the many forms of bad faith to which some formally respectable men are disposed. Excessive sensibility in a young woman increases the danger of ill effects if she has the bad luck to be betrayed. But Willoughby's late meeting with Elinor shows that he was, from the perspective of Marianne's *perceptiveness,* a "near miss." It is bad luck that Willoughby was not, say, *Persuasion*'s Captain Benwick. Nevertheless, her way of life is dangerous in a way Elinor's is not (though it is only good luck that keeps Elinor from a loss of love). Marianne's way is therefore imprudent; hence it is not to be commended. But Austen has too much good sense to think "society will only tolerate" Elinor's way.

It is unfortunate for me that my rescuing Marianne from the Tanner school's too zealous concern for her emotional and moral health may appear, upon reflection, to do no more than move her, considered as a puzzle, from the frying pan into the fire. For if she registers such a repression-free foundation for mental health as I have made out for her, how come she dissolves at nineteen into the wife of a pallid man twice her age for whom she has only "strong esteem and lively friendship"? On the one hand, her not being a Rousseauist rescues her—as respectable enough—for the fictional function that Burney's bizarre Elinor Joddrel could not play, of embodying a progressive and feasible revision of patriarchal gender conceptions. On the other hand, what use is that rescue, when in her youth (however late in the novel) she succumbs to patriarchal oppression by marrying, without loving, a colorless man old enough to be her father? The opposition between Marianne as I find her rendered and the conclusion of her story, as Austen wrote it, is a problem for me. A big problem.

I think it evident that the author's specification of Marianne's degree of fit with the socially constructed concept of genteel feminine gender divides, differentially, into two parts: the first part develops mainly before Marianne's illness, but most vividly before her rejection by Willoughby; the second begins after her illness—I shall inquire later exactly when. I hope it is by now clear that in a large portion of the novel Marianne deviates so radically from the patriarchal rules for young ladies that, if only she had prospered as the rebel she there shows herself to be, then the proposition that feminine gender reform is an important part of Marianne's reason for fictional being would be at least plainly plausible.

However, Marianne did not prosper. She came to grief. And her dissenting ways played a part in bringing about her misery.

Even so, if in defeat and pain and illness, or in recovery from these, the author had left Marianne's spirit as it had been—however much Marianne improved in prudence and in her consideration for other persons—the case for gender reform would remain persuasively present in Marianne. For the world would be at fault, to be sure, and she would have been reckless and inconsiderate; but there would be time enough for someone so young to give the world another chance, and neither a healthy new prudence in Marianne nor a reasonable new civility need extinguish her original spirit.

But Marianne's "voluntarily" deciding (as we are merely *told* she did) to "give her hand" to Colonel Brandon, a man not only twice her age but with no lively spark, toward whom she had no more than the friendly and respectful sort of feeling she had long felt for Edward Ferrars—this constitutes a change in her spirit (ch. 50:366–67). This is in fact another Marianne. The dissonantly gendered Marianne has not only been defeated; at the end of the novel, and quite outside the reader's presence, the author has replaced her with a different, patriarchally sanctioned Marianne.

Can Austen, then, plausibly be read as embodying in Marianne an attempt at reforming socially constructed gender? If so, how can we make the absent yet story-ending Marianne *cohere* with such reform work?

The answer to the second question is that we cannot. Yet I propose an affirmative answer to the first question—barely affirmative, indeed, because highly qualified. Yet affirmative.

In *rendering* Marianne for us, Austen deploys, almost without faltering, all her artistic impulse and power for constructing a passionate rebel against the gender restrictions of her era. What is more, to my perception, she constructs not only a passionate but an intelligent rebel and even (once Marianne has gained wisdom from her illness) a rebel who might prosper within the uncongenial world Austen made for her. This means that, to my sensibility, as long as Marianne is *present* for us, she embodies a feasibly reshaped conception of feminine gender. Once the author has taken Marianne off the stage—has ceased to make her present to us—we have reports of another Marianne and, in a useful sense of the phrase, we have another story. However, for the moment I want to stay with the Marianne who *is* made present to us.

How complete, or how qualified, does Austen intend our approval of the gender-dissonant Marianne to be? Am I justified in saying that for a reader of the right sensibility the rendered Marianne exemplifies a persuasively reconstructed concept of genteel feminine gender? To some extent, how we answer that question depends on how morally attractive we find Marianne to be. Here again enter varied voices of professors, not all speaking of Marianne as I do.

Consider Professor Margaret Anne Doody's acid remarks about Marianne in her provocative 1990 introduction to the World's Classics edition of the novel: "Marianne . . . cannot see for herself how lacking in originality she is, how slavishly she is following a certain set of conventions. Her own genuine 'sensibility' has been bent to rules, stipulations of romanticism which Marianne accepts, not recognizing that she is merely duplicating someone else's prescription. Her aesthetic sense, her love for wild trees, rugged hills, and dead leaves, is a mediated and artificial sense."[7] I am unmoved. Romanticism was a rebellion against an older ordering of sensibilities, ideas, attitudes, and actions; to join the rebellion is of course to "buy into" new conventions. If this participation in new ways of taking the world is sincere and grounded in one's own temperament, it is not "slavish." We have no evidence that Marianne is meant to think herself "original" or to be so: this is a novel of ordinary people, not of leaders of revolutions. Besides that, where has Professor Doody encountered an "aesthetic sense" that is *not* "mediated" and in that sense "artificial"? In Blake? In Wordsworth? Would not, say, Harold Bloom disagree with any example one proposes? And wouldn't he be right?

Doody is herself surely original in another charge she brings against impulsive Marianne Dashwood:

> Marianne becomes greedy and predatory. She goes with Willoughby to look over the mansion of his relative Mrs Smith. . . . She prowls about noting the details of the "charming house". . . . Calculating the value to herself of this property that is sure (she thinks) to fall to Willoughby, she can happily assume the death of the woman whose demise will give Marianne (as Willoughby's wife) the enjoyment of the

"pretty sitting room".... She bears in this instance a horrid
likeness to her half-brother [John Dashwood].... She...falls
into very unromantic sins of insensitivity, greed and callous
calculation.[8]

To believe Marianne stands for the poetry of Scott and Cowper over
Pope, for the picturesque over the useful in landscape, for moderate
liberation of women in preference to their intemperate suppression, is
not to believe that she must renounce realism about the desirability of
affluence and about its common dependence upon the death of relatives. Part of my thought in response to Doody's remarks is that perhaps Marianne has her feet more solidly planted on the earth than
some critics acknowledge. Closer to the crux of my difference with
Doody, I think, come the alleged "sins" of a very young woman in love
for making that exuberant excursion to (and through) Allenham: I
find Doody's curious language too gratuitously moralistic to fit the
case. I place Marianne's tour in a category not wholly dissimilar to
Elizabeth Bennet's "prowling" through Darcy's grand estate in the absence of an owner whose proposal of marriage she had angrily refused, but now begins to have second thoughts about. Although Marianne as reported in Professor Doody's language does sound like John
Dashwood—so might Elizabeth Bennet. In Austen's language, neither
sounds so to me.

Some readers considering Professor Doody's and my differences
may be reminded of something they know but do not always keep in
mind: that it is not only one's sense that determines one's interpretation of Marianne but one's sensibility as well. Doody and I very likely
differ more along the latter dimension than along the former. Is this
difference at all tied to gender? I doubt it. Consider a male critic who
has written as fine an essay as any published on the moral content of
Pride and Prejudice—Stuart Tave in his chapter on that novel in his
book *Some Words of Jane Austen*—but whose response to Marianne
differs from mine even more abundantly than Doody's does. For
fifteen pages he deplores what he perceives as Marianne's multitude of
failings. I feel little connection to the sensibility in Tave that provokes
the disciplined fervor of his attack. One of the (to me) more demon-
strably wrongheaded readings of Marianne in his chapter on *Sense*

and Sensibility concerns Marianne's behavior on the one occasion of Mrs. Ferrars's making a personal appearance before the novel's readers. I shall let my readers decide between us.

The scene is a dinner party of the John Dashwoods at which the Dashwood sisters meet for the first time Mrs. Ferrars, Edward's mother. Except for Edward, virtually everyone who is anyone in the novel is there. Mrs. Ferrars pointedly ignores Elinor and, with her daughter Fanny, wife of John Dashwood, is especially gracious to Lucy Steele and her sister. Mother and daughter have of course no hint that Lucy, secretly engaged to Edward, is the true obstacle to their scheme for marrying Edward to the daughter of a rich peer (one Lord Morton). Their purpose in this attention to the Steeles is to give emphasis to their slight to Elinor, whom they believe to obstruct their plans for Edward. This misdirected courtesy toward the Steele sisters (with its reception) and Mrs. Ferrars's wasted rudeness toward Elinor is a source of malicious amusement to both Elinor and the narrator. However Marianne, who does not know what the narrator and Elinor know about Lucy and Edward, is deeply offended when praise of some screens done by Elinor is deflected by Fanny and her mother to praise of the absent "Miss Morton":

> "They are very pretty, ma'am—an't they? . . . Do you not think they are something in Miss Morton's style of painting, Ma'am?—*She does* paint most delightfully!—How beautifully her last landscape is done!"
>
> "Beautifully indeed! But *she* does every thing well."
>
> Marianne could not bear this.—She was already greatly displeased with Mrs Ferrars; and such ill-timed praise of another, at Elinor's expense, though she had not any notion of what was principally meant by it, provoked her immediately to say with warmth,
>
> "This is admiration of a very particular kind!—what is Miss Morton to us?—who knows, or who cares, for her?—it is Elinor of whom *we* think and speak."
>
> And so saying, she took the screens out of her sister-in-law's hands, to admire them herself as they ought to be admired.

Mrs Ferrars looked exceedingly angry, and drawing herself up more stiffly than ever, pronounced in retort this bitter phillippic; "Miss Morton is Lord Morton's daughter."

Fanny looked very angry too, and her husband was all in a fright at his sister's audacity. . . .

Marianne's feelings did not stop here. The cold insolence of Mrs Ferrars's general behaviour to her sister, seemed, to her, to foretel such difficulties and distresses to Elinor, as her own wounded heart taught her to think of with horror; and urged by a strong impulse of affectionate sensibility, she moved, after a moment, to her sister's chair, and putting one arm round her neck, and one cheek close to hers, said in a low, but eager, voice,

"Dear, dear Elinor, don't mind them. Don't let them make you unhappy."

She could say no more; her spirits were quite overcome, and hiding her face on Elinor's shoulder, she burst into tears. (ch. 34:241–42)

Now let us hear Professor Tave on Marianne's actions in this scene:

She cannot bear that Mrs. Ferrars should praise Miss Morton's art at the expense of Elinor. . . . Neither knowing nor caring to know anything of Miss Morton or what it is that her name means to several people present and the relationships among these people, she stirs up anger, bitterness, and fright in what is already a most unpleasant collision. . . . What her sensibility misses for all its touching affection, is that Elinor's heart and mind and circumstances differ from hers and that for Elinor she has worsened the moment by taking it in the only way that she can, as her own. The impulse concludes with the dominance of her own feelings when . . . she becomes not the comforter of Elinor but, as usual, the one in need of comfort.[9]

It is true that Austen wrote, in a sentence I omitted, "Elinor was much more hurt by Marianne's warmth, than she had been by what produced it" (ch. 34:242). But Tave ignores a remark of the narrator's concerning the earlier moments that evening of Mrs. Ferrars's un-friendliness to Elinor, milder than the attack from mother and daughter that provoked Marianne: "A few months ago, it would have hurt [Elinor] exceedingly"—that is, before Elinor discovered Edward was engaged to Lucy (ch. 34:239). Not knowing of this engagement, Marianne has very good reason to believe mother and daughter are *now* hurting Elinor exceedingly, and Tave has no good reason for ignoring this decisively important fact. That Tave should judge it a matter of regret that Marianne's effect on Mrs. Ferrars's malicious hostility toward Elinor is that Marianne "stirs up anger" in Mrs. Ferrars toward herself surely expresses, not the author's valuation, but solely (and inscrutably) Professor Tave's. And he has (yet how *could* he have?) missed the irony in Austen's ascription to Mrs. Ferrars of a "bitter phillippic," as well as the amused contempt in Austen's remarking John Dashwood's "fright at his sister's audacity." And as for Tave's finding that Marianne is "as usual the one in need of comfort"—when I consider the only cause of her needing much comfort in this story (Willoughby's monstrous betrayal), I want to say about Professor Tave here what Mrs. Jennings said of another elsewhere: I have no notion of men going on in this way!

There are other situations in which it is certainly possible for an acute reader to find Marianne's character defective. Her treatment of Mrs. Jennings is one. Consider their trip in a coach from Barton to London: On the three-day journey of the two sisters and Mrs. Jennings, Marianne "sat in silence almost all the way, wrapt in her own meditations, and scarcely ever voluntarily speaking," except for occasional remarks on the view "exclusively addressed to her sister. To atone for this conduct therefore, Elinor . . . behaved with the greatest attention to Mrs Jennings, talked with her, laughed with her, and listened to her whenever she could" (ch. 26:175–76).

We have to remember that shortly before this, Elinor had complained of Mrs. Jennings that "she is not a woman whose society can afford us pleasure" (ch. 25:173). We hear that Mrs. Jennings "was an everlasting talker, and from the first had regarded [Elinor] with a kindness which ensured her a large share of her discourse. She had already repeated her own history to Elinor three or four times; and had

Elinor's memory been equal to her means of improvement, she might have known very early in their acquaintance all the particulars of Mr Jennings last illness, and what he said to his wife a few minutes before he died" (ch. 11:85). How much countenance should Marianne be expected to give to such repetitive, tasteless, painful conversation? (How much would Jane Austen in person have given to a real-life copy of Mrs. Jennings?) Is there any evidence that Mrs. Jennings was ever offended by Marianne's neglect of her? None. Mrs. Jennings was not in this way a sensitive person.

I want to believe that Austen's treatment of Marianne is neatly divisible into a rendered presence (most of the novel) working persuasively *for,* and a merely reported absence (with concluding marriage) working (only formally) *against* a portrait of an admirable and lovable young woman fit to be accepted as Austen's Exhibit B for feminine gender reform.

Marianne's story is not so conveniently split in two. Curiously enough, the fact that it isn't makes the novel morally somewhat more integrated: Marianne is prepared for her final surrender to the patriarchal establishment by being made to seem, occasionally, more deserving of such a fate by virtue of being sometimes delinquent, sometimes—as every critic seems to have pointed out—a caricature of herself.

Even here there is distinguished dissent: not every professor of literature perceives Marianne's end as an abandonment by her author. Writing in an often profound book on Austen's novels, here is Julia Prewitt Brown in rebuttal to those who think Jane Austen's nerve failed her in her concluding disposition of Marianne:

> I do not agree . . . that Austen lacked the courage to investigate the fate of passion existing in society. . . . Austen never injured the complexity of her story through . . . taking the central problem out of the hands of the characters and solving it on another level. At the end of *Sense and Sensibility* Marianne's heart is broken, but she is still alive, thinking. There is a horror in this conclusion that we may not wish to contemplate. It is not the conclusion of a writer who lacks courage.[10]

My response to this interesting perspective is the simplest rebuttal I can imagine: we do not know what Marianne's mental life is like at the very end of the novel, because the author is unwilling—indeed, unable—to show us Marianne in the course of becoming the person who would succumb to Brandon's courtship. The reason Austen is unable is that the Marianne she rendered for us would not have so succumbed. And this is to say that although at the end of the novel the Marianne who has been alive *is* still so in us, she is not "still alive" in that ending.

At times Marianne seems so foolish as to appear a caricature of herself. This self-caricaturing Marianne is a failure of Austen's art. As when, for example, Marianne denies to Edward taste in art because his response to it falls short of "rapturous delight" (ch. 4:53). Or when she remarks that "a woman of seven and twenty . . . can never hope to feel or inspire affection again" (ch. 8:70). These snapshots of Marianne as caricature of Marianne constitute an artistic failure deliberately accepted by Austen for the sake of improvement in the moral coherence of the *plot's* ending. If the character, temperament, and thinking of the gender-dissonant Marianne show some signs not only of possible delinquency but also of absurdity, then her replacement by an absent, passive Marianne who accepts the lusterless Brandon without loving him renders a kind of justice: capital punishment for an unassimilable rebel! Given Austen's personally limited power of public rebellion, her compromises in composing the rendered Marianne were necessary. I acknowledge the necessity; I am not willing to celebrate it.

I have just ascribed to Austen a limited power of public rebellion. Few would question the vague idea of such a circumscription, though no consensus exists about how to define those limits. I do believe we need a partially biographical explanation for what I perceive to be the artistic failure marked by young Marianne's metamorphosis at the end of the novel from spirited dissenter to pallid conformist.

The first version of *Sense and Sensibility,* probably called "Elinor and Marianne," possibly an epistolary novel, is believed to have been written in 1795. Since Austen did not turn twenty until mid-

December of that year, the novel was probably first written by a nineteen-year-old younger sister of an admired prototype of Elinor: Cassandra Austen, three years older than Jane. One can imagine that the nineteen-year-old Jane Austen felt many more of the nonconforming impulses of seventeen-year-old Marianne than her elder sister Cassandra did. Yet Jane must play safe in the risky project a very young lady undertakes by publicly appearing for the first time as an author. She could express her own wild, inner self by creating, in Marianne, a fictional distortion of the rebellious self within her. She could assure her own safety as respectable young lady by letting that "more than rational distortion" of herself—that multiply liberated self, Marianne—be defeated by an ugly, fictional world.[11] And she could at once loyally celebrate her elder sister and reassure all her family, for whom she initially wrote, by letting that defeated self be converted to her sister's deliberating reason, as embodied in Cassandra's fictionally idealized double, Elinor Dashwood.

Did the young Jane Austen feel many more of the nonconforming impulses of a Marianne than her elder sister did? *Did* she have a wild, inner self? And *was* young Cassandra Austen notably rational in her conduct—was she rather more like Elinor than young Jane was? Curiously, apart from letters from Jane in her early twenties, our best basis for inference about the Austen sisters' personalities as girls is not direct evidence about them as very young but evidence about the adult Jane and Cassandra provided in retrospective pictures by women who were children when the Austen sisters were adults. One of these, who played with Jane's nieces and nephews when they visited their two aunts at Chawton, has written that Jane's "sister Cassandra was very lady-like but *very prim,* but my remembrance of Jane is that of her entering into all Children's Games & liking her extremely."[12] Jane Austen's niece Caroline writes as follows:

> Of the two, Aunt Jane was by far my favorite—I did not *dislike* Aunt Cassandra—but if my visit had at any time chanced to fall out during *her* absence, I don't think I should have missed her—whereas *not* to have found Aunt Jane at Chawton, *would* have been a blank indeed. . . .

> When staying at Chawton, if my two cousins . . . were
> there, we often had amusements in which my Aunt was very
> helpful—*She* was the one to whom we always looked for
> help . . . and *she* would often be the entertaining visitor in our
> make believe house—she amused us in various ways.[13]

When I combine this evidence with Austen's early letters, with her authorial narrative voice, and with the portraits of sisters in both *Sense
and Sensibility* and *Pride and Prejudice,* I am satisfied that my questions, above, about young Jane Austen deserve positive answers: she
did have more of Marianne's nonconforming impulses than her sister,
she did have a wild inner self, and young Cassandra Austen was more
rationally deliberate in the affairs of everyday life than Jane. So I think
it probable that Marianne and Elinor are, in a fashion, offspring of
Jane and Cassandra, conceived in the former's adolescence, written in
her youth, and rewritten again and still again in later years.

We have been told by some who were there that the elder sister
was viewed within the Austen family as more important, at least by
their mother, who outlived Jane by ten years. Of course this would
have begun with the observance of precedence for the eldest daughter,
a strong tradition of the time. That Jane Austen herself shared in *some*
way this deference to Cassandra, even into adulthood, is implied by
another remark by her niece Caroline about Aunt Jane: "When I was
a little girl, she would frequently say to me . . . that Aunt Cassandra
could teach everything much better than *she* could—Aunt Cass. *knew*
more—Aunt Cass. could tell me better whatever I wanted to know . . .
I truly beleive she did always *really* think of her sister, as the superior
to herself."[14] My caveat is this: a child's memory cannot inform us
how often Aunt Jane's elevation of the other aunt in the house might
have manifested a desire to shunt the children's attention toward her
sister in order, for the sake of her writing, to be free from distraction.

In the course of the sixteen years during which at least two revi-
sions of *Sense and Sensibility* were written, one must believe that
something substantial in the deference of the younger sister for the
elder would have long since dropped away from the private belief of
this genius who had already also written the unpublished *Northanger*

Abbey and *Pride and Prejudice.* The victory awarded to Elinor's temperament by the (annihilating) defeat of Marianne's is the fictional image in *Sense and Sensibility* of Jane Austen's early sisterly deference. So this question arises: why shouldn't we expect that once the deference had been reduced, this image of deference would be modulated, in revision, by Marianne's being made consistent with herself (and therefore present *as* herself) to the very end of the novel?

Perhaps the reason is that this advance in Jane Austen's self-appraisal had found *its* fictionally corresponding progression in the novel she had gone on to write in 1796–97, right after finishing the first version of *Sense and Sensibility.* This next novel was called "First Impressions"; it was the first version of *Pride and Prejudice.* Her father so admired it he attempted to have it published. It too was revised over the years, until it was published in 1813 as "by the author of *Sense and Sensibility.*" In this novel Austen moves the Cassandra figure, Jane Bennet, into the background of the author's second fictional self-projection, Elizabeth Bennet, endowing Jane Bennet with a far fainter, more washed-out presence than Elizabeth's. Elizabeth, whom I conceive as a fictional idealization of Jane Austen as love object, combines in herself some of the spontaneity of Marianne and the sense of Elinor. The movement beyond obeisance to Jane Austen's elder sister having, we imagine, found its artistic expression in the novel written directly after the first version of *Sense and Sensibility,* this vicarious self-elevation was not required in her revision of the latter: Cassandra Austen's way can still triumph; the Marianne we know can be replaced in the very end with an absent stand-in, who may have been a bland abstraction of Cassandra's way.

When, then, is the dissonantly gendered Marianne replaced? The answer is precise and decisive: not until she has left the scene, not until she is offstage. We are *merely told about* the "Marianne" who marries Colonel Brandon feeling for him only "strong esteem and lively friendship." She is never made present to us. Even at second hand we never "hear" her speak, nor ever read a written word of this Marianne who "gives her hand" to Colonel Brandon.

Some readers may question my latest assertion. For they will believe the replacement-Marianne, the one who at nineteen *could* marry

Brandon, is rendered for us in the few pages Austen gives us of what I call Marianne's "conversion to sense," an outcome of her dangerous illness. It is true this conversion to sense—rather, its articulation by Marianne—is rendered for us in conversations she has with her sister. I think we see Austen developing for us in these "conversion" conversations precisely the Marianne I could wish had ended the story: a Marianne who is improved, who is kinder, more tolerant, more prudent, more sensible, but who has *not* lost her original spirit. Let us look at the key moments in Marianne's very last personal appearances before us, all of them in conversations with Elinor, when Marianne is successfully convalescing from her illness.

Because Elinor brings these conversations to an end with a rather powerful indictment of Willoughby and because Marianne is still weak from illness, the reader may later seem to remember Marianne's new views as passively received from Elinor. They are not. Indeed we are surprised to discover—believing we shared Elinor's constant attendance upon her sister—that Marianne's illness had been used so productively by her that she can report to Elinor that, "long before I was enough recovered to talk, I was perfectly able to reflect" (ch. 46:336–37). Her illness brought an unwonted "calmness" that helped reflection. While still ill, she came to realize that her illness "had been entirely brought on by myself, by such negligence of my own health, as I had felt even at the time to be wrong. Had I died,—it would have been self-destruction" (ch. 46:337). Although we learn with surprise of Marianne's self-criticism while she was ill, we find it believable. Her illness was, in the minds of everyone, including herself, life-threatening. Surely it could have been psychologically momentous for her. Retroactively this self-revelation improves Marianne in our eyes. It continues: "How should I have lived in *your* remembrance!—My mother too! How could you have consoled her!—I cannot express my own abhorrence of myself" (ch. 46:337). Once we have sympathized with Marianne's self-abhorrence, we are ready to follow her when she moves directly from it to this painful confession: "Whenever I looked towards the past, I saw some duty neglected, or some failing indulged. Every body seemed injured by me" (ch. 46:337).

It is Marianne's romantically ascetic plan for the narrow life she

now fancies herself required to live—as if in compensatory expiation
for her self-indulgent past—which convinces us that, despite her
physical weakness and retrospective self-disgust, Marianne is pos-
sessed of the same spirit we have known: "You, my mother, and Margaret, must henceforth be all the world to me; you will share my affections entirely between you. From you, from my home, I shall never
again have the smallest incitement to move" (ch. 46:338). Despite this
burst of enthusiastic unrealism, which manifests the old Marianne
setting out on a new (morally reforming) sort of romantic adventure,
she talks honestly of her feeling for Willoughby. This too bespeaks
continuity with the Marianne we have known: "As for Willoughby—
to say that I shall soon or that I shall ever forget him, would be idle"
(ch. 46:338).

Equally believable and rather more interesting is her feeling
that she could now have peace of mind in regard to Willoughby,
"if I could be assured that he never was so *very* wicked as my fears
have sometimes fancied him, since the story of that unfortunate girl"
(ch. 46:336). By this she means she wishes she knew he hadn't meant
to seduce her: "For not only is it horrible to suspect a person, who has
been what *he* has been *to me*, of such designs,—but what must it make
me appear to myself?" (ch. 46:336).

Few attentive readers will miss the respect with which Austen
treats Marianne's attachment to Willoughby and the tenderness with
which this author for the last time enters into Marianne's painful experience of Willoughby's deserting her:

> She paused—and added in a lower voice, "If I could but
> know *his* heart, everything would become easy."
> Elinor, who had now been for some time reflecting on
> the propriety or impropriety of speedily hazarding her nar-
> ration [of Willoughby's recent visit with her], without feeling
> at all nearer decision than at first, heard this; and perceiving
> that as reflection did nothing, resolution must do all, soon
> found herself leading to the fact.
> She managed the recital, as she hoped, with address; pre-
> pared her anxious listener with caution; related simply and

honestly the chief points on which Willoughby grounded his
apology; did justice to his repentence, and softened only his
protestations of present regard. Marianne said not a word.—
She trembled, her eyes were fixed on the ground, and her lips
became whiter than even sickness had left them. A thousand
inquiries sprang up from her heart, but she dared not urge
one. She caught every syllable with panting eagerness; her
hand, unknowingly to herself, closely pressed her sister's, and
tears covered her cheeks.

Elinor, dreading her being tired, led her towards home;
and till they reached the door of the cottage, easily con-
jecturing what her curiosity must be though no question
was suffered to speak it, talked of nothing but Willoughby,
and their conversation together; and was carefully minute in
every particular of speech and look, where minuteness could
be safely indulged. As soon as they entered the house, Marianne with a kiss of gratitude and these two words just articu-
late through her tears, "Tell Mamma," withdrew from her
sister and walked slowly up stairs. (ch. 46:338–39)

I may be mistaken—so early in the novel's history is their creation—
yet I cannot help thinking these are among the finer passages of intimacy in the fictional literature of the English language. To be sure,
some of us might wish Elinor could have seen her way clear to telling
Marianne the whole truth of Willoughby's visit, by not "softening"
his expressions of present "regard." But we have no responsibility for
Marianne's health.

Later in the day when their mother has joined the two sisters,
Marianne again brings up the subject, and we hear what are almost
her last words:

"It is a great relief to me—what Elinor told me this morning—I have now heard exactly what I wished to hear."—For
some moments her voice was lost; but recovering herself, she
added, and with greater calmness than before—"I am now
perfectly satisfied, I wish for no change. I never could have

been happy with him, after knowing, as sooner or later I must have known, all this.—I should have had no confidence, no esteem. Nothing could have done it away to my feelings." (ch. 47:341)

Having shown that the earth moves around the sun, Galileo Galilei was required, by the pressure from social forces inhering in *his* circumambient patriarchy, formally to accept the socially constructed concept of a fixed earth at the center of the universe.

"Eppur si muove"—"And yet it moves"—legend has it that he quietly declared, just after his recantation.

With a replacement Marianne relegated to an offstage story ending, Austen formally acquiesces—on behalf of her one overt rebel—in another patriarchy's damping of feminine spirit.

"Yet she lives," insists her vivid depiction of the resisting Marianne Dashwood.

Notes

INTRODUCTION

1. Margaret Drabble, introduction to *Lady Susan / The Watsons / Sanditon,* by Jane Austen (Harmondsworth: Penguin Books, 1974), 7–8.

2. For an exciting presentation of *Northanger Abbey* as an engaged novel of progressive political advocacy, read Claudia L. Johnson's chapter on that work, especially pp. 32–48, in her *Jane Austen: Women, Politics and the Novel* (Chicago: Univ. of Chicago Press, 1988). I, on the other hand, am here classifying this novel solely on the basis of its author's limited ambition in creating its heroine, Catherine Morland—a limitation that has, of course, consequences.

3. Alison G. Sulloway, *Jane Austen and the Province of Womanhood* (Philadelphia: Univ. of Pennsylvania Press, 1989), 180.

4. Margaret Drabble, introduction to *The Wanderer: or, Female Difficulties* (1814; rpt. London: Pandora, 1988), xii.

5. Claire Tomalin, *The Life and Death of Mary Wollstonecraft* (New York: Mentor, 1974), 291.

CHAPTER 1. ELINOR DASHWOOD: THE HEROINE AS AN INTELLECTUAL

1. Stuart Tave, *Some Words of Jane Austen* (Chicago: Univ. of Chicago Press, 1973), 96–97.

2. Since Austen was born in December 1775, she would not have been twenty until the last month of 1795. She rewrote the novel in 1797 and revised it again in her mid-thirties before submitting it to the public in 1811.

3. Julia Prewitt Brown, *Jane Austen's Novels: Social Change and Literary Form,* (Cambridge: Harvard Univ. Press, 1979), 45. My epigraph for the present book can be found on p. 155.

4. Sulloway, *Jane Austen and the Province of Womanhood,* 167.

CHAPTER 2. EDWARD FERRARS AND JANE AUSTEN'S DEMOCRACY

1. Quoted in Hesketh Pearson, *Sir Walter Scott: His Life and Personality* (New York: Harper, 1954), 191.

CHAPTER 3. ELINOR'S EMOTIONS

1. Stella Gibbons, introduction to *Sense and Sensibility,* by Jane Austen (New York: Heritage Press, 1957), x.

2. Ibid., xiv.

3. D. H. Lawrence, *The Rainbow* (New York: Penguin Books, 1976), 23–24.

4. I think this is not true of D. H. Lawrence as novelist.

CHAPTER 4. MEN AND SOCIETY: DECEPTION,
FORMALITY, PATRIARCHY, MOBILITY, AND WORK

1. Tony Tanner, *Jane Austen* (Cambridge: Harvard Univ. Press, 1986), 89, 84.

2. Ibid., 88, 89, 79–80.

3. Johnson, *Jane Austen,* 69, 49–50, 56.

4. Ibid., 58.

5. Ibid., 67.

6. Ibid.

7. Ibid., 57.

8. Johnson grounds her antipatriarchal reading of *Sense and Sensibility* partly on the fact that "the most striking thing about the tales of the two Elizas is their insistent redundancy. One Eliza would have sufficed . . . to discredit Willoughby. . . . But the presence of two . . . points to crimes beyond Willoughby's doing, and their common name opens the sinister possibility that plights such as theirs proliferate throughout the kingdom. This . . . invites us to consider how much male behavior in *Sense and Sensibility* redoubles with what is depicted in their tales" (*Jane Austen,* 57). From there, Johnson moves through Willoughby to the full "redoubling" as completed, she claims, in Edward. Her argument derives its persuasive force from its explaining something that needs explaining, the surprising amount of space Austen gives to the awkwardly presented Eliza stories. For me, however, her reasoning founders on its requiring a reading of Edward (and Willoughby) that the text does not support.

9. In *Jane Austen's Sense and Sensibility* (New York: St. Martin's, 1992), 93–103, Gene W. Ruoff also emphasizes what he calls the "heavily gendered" status of travel and movement in the novel. And he has developed this idea in directions I missed. The following is a sample of Ruoff's interesting discussion of this theme: "The world is not all before the Dashwood women because their freedom of choice and movement are restricted. . . . All movement by Elinor and Marianne is governed by invitation, the need for economy and the observation of proper decorum for young ladies. . . . Standing in stark contrast is the pattern of masculine movement in the novel. The unmarried males . . . are all marked by sudden appearances and sudden departures. . . . Men's actions can be observed only partially, and they are mysterious. . . . Male characters have mobility. . . . Their greater independence of movement reflects far greater independence of will. . . . Austen's deployment of motifs of travel and action . . . turns the novel into a . . . critique of traditional fictional emplotment. It uses for its framework a familiar narrative form which normally equates . . . meaningful moral action with exciting incident. . . . Austen uses it to generate a different understanding and valuation of action itself. . . . Her most meaningful scenes are often strictly circumscribed, enclosed and almost devoid of overt action" (96–103).

10. See Sulloway, *Jane Austen and the Province of Womanhood,* 109, 180.

11. In the notes to the Penguin text we are using Tony Tanner cites R. W. Chapman's note in his edition of the novel that credits one A. L. Humphreys with unearthing the 1776 book by Richard Graves in which the protagonist, Columella, apprentices his sons to men of many trades. In Graves's words: "By these several occupations Columella flattered himself that his sons would be secured from that tedium and disgust of life which he experienced, and which he had brought upon himself by a life of indolence and inactivity" (370).

12. Jane Nardin, "Jane Austen and the Problem of Leisure," in *Jane Austen in a Social Context,* ed. David Monaghan (Totowa, N.J.: Barnes and Noble Books, 1981), 122–42.

Chapter 5. Elinor's Character: A Heroine as Public Servant (1)

1. It appears that the editor of the Penguin edition of *Sense and Sensibility,* Tony Tanner, has here silently changed the Chapman edition, which reads, instead, for the second portion of Marianne's sentence: "you, because you communicate, and I, because I conceal nothing." See R. W. Chapman, ed., *The Novels of Jane Austen,* 3d ed., 5 vols. (New York: Oxford Univ. Press, 1933), 1:170.

2. Gene Koppel, *The Religious Dimension of Jane Austen's Novels* (Ann Arbor: U.M.I. Research Press, 1988), 19–20. Tave's religious interpretation of Elinor's character is explicit in pp. 112–14 of *Some Words of Jane Austen,* and by retroactive implication from these pages, also in pp. 106–11.

3. David Cecil, *A Portrait of Jane Austen* (New York: Hill and Wang, 1980), 50.

Chapter 6. Elinor's Character: A Heroine as Public Servant (2)

1. Johnson, *Jane Austen,* 69.

2. Ibid., 70.

3. Ibid., 25–26.

4. Ibid., 70.

5. Ibid., 70–72.

6. Ibid., 71.

7. Ruoff, *Jane Austen's Sense and Sensibility,* 79–81.

8. Johnson, *Jane Austen,* 54.

9. Tave, *Some Words of Jane Austen,* 110.

Chapter 7. Problematic Marianne

1. Tanner, *Jane Austen,* 98.

2. Ibid., 98. The first line quoted here, from Marianne, is not quoted by Tanner.

3. Ruoff, *Jane Austen's Sense and Sensibility,* 62. I have noticed three other scholars who follow Tanner here.

In her 1978 monograph *Jane Austen on Love* (Victoria, B.C.: English Literary Studies Monograph Series 13, 1978), Juliet McMaster provides an example of Tanner's likely influence. She cites several bits of evidence which to her mind "all suggest that

Marianne might yield to seduction" by Willoughby just as Colonel Brandon's ward, Eliza Williams, had done. McMaster summarizes the very remarks of Marianne to which Tanner appeals, and McMaster seems to read them much as Tanner does: "[Marianne's] principle," McMaster writes, "since she asserts that the pleasantness of an occupation is evidence of its propriety . . . would hardly save her from Miss Williams' fate" (69).

Although Tanner's name does not appear in the index of Park Honan's excellent 1987 biography of Jane Austen, Honan also shows what I take to be an influence of Tanner's essay when he offers an English lineage for the idea Tanner treated as Rousseau's. Honan, crediting the English philosopher Shaftsbury, bluntly asserts the Tanner thesis thus: "Marianne is a Shaftsburian who sees no authority higher than the feelings" (*Jane Austen: Her Life* [New York: St. Martin's, 1987], 280).

Margaret Anne Doody speaks of Marianne Dashwood's tour of Allenham as behavior that illustrates "the untruth of her Shaftsburyan supposition that feelings are sufficient moral guide, that 'we always know when we are acting wrong.'" Her use of the quoted Marianne utterance as, taken alone, either supporting or equivalent to the "Shaftsburyan supposition" is to me puzzling in its logic. See her introduction to the World Classics edition of *Sense and Sensibility* (New York: Oxford Univ. Press, 1990), xxxi–xxxii.

4. In *Jane Austen's Sense and Sensibility,* Gene Ruoff has proposed a modified version of Marianne's alleged emotive ethic. I omitted from my quotation of Ruoff in the text these words: "Love is outside the social concerns of life. . . . For all her occasional bridling at social conventions, Marianne is not a natural outlaw. Only in matters of the heart does she allow herself flagrantly to step outside social obligations. . . . For Marianne romantic feeling exists apart from ordinary and continuous social feelings. It presents an utter break in one's existence" (62–63).

Ruoff's view is clear: Marianne's ethical argument, presented to Elinor in defense of her behavior with Willoughby at Mrs. Smith's home, asserts an ethic meant to be restricted in its application to situations of romantic love.

This reading fails on two counts. First, Marianne's argument is not put that way: it is formulated in universal terms, as pertaining to right and wrong in general, with no hint of limits in its application. Yet Austen is quite capable of the precision needed to make clear on Marianne's behalf so extraordinary an ethical exemption; Austen did not do this. Second, not even the narrower argument has the implications Ruoff ascribes to it. The reader can easily see this by simply rephrasing Marianne's argument *as if* it applied only to amatory behavior, thus: I (indeed we) *always know* what is wrong in amatory behavior; once I know an amatory action is wrong, I *cannot* take pleasure in it; therefore, since I *did* take pleasure in this amatory action, it was not wrong.

For exactly the same reasons that apply to the other version of the argument, this version has no Shaftsburian or Rousseauistic implications whatever.

5. Tanner, *Jane Austen,* 77, 99. In *Jane Austen's Novels,* Julia Prewitt Brown quotes

with approval this part of Tanner's essay (from its 1969 form, introducing the novel): "Marianne suffers from neurosis brought on by repression, as Tony Tanner's description of her sickness explains, and his mention of *Civilization and its Discontents* is entirely apt" (58).

6. Tanner, *Jane Austen,* 99.

7. Margaret Anne Doody, introduction to *Sense and Sensibility,* xviii.

8. Ibid., xxx–xxxii.

9. Tave, *Some Words of Jane Austen,* 91.

10. Brown, *Jane Austen's Novels,* 62–63.

11. I take the "more than rational distortion" from Wallace Stevens, "Notes Toward A Supreme Fiction."

12. Quoted in Park Honan, *Jane Austen,* 270.

13. Caroline Austen, *My Aunt Jane Austen: A Memoir* (Jane Austen Society, 1952), 5–6, 10.

14. Ibid., 11.

Index of Names